When Children Don't Learn

WHEN CHILDREN DON'T LEARN

Understanding the Biology
and Psychology
of Learning Disabilities

Diane McGuinness

Basic Books, Inc., Publishers   New York

Excerpt from S. N. Kramer, *History Begins at Sumer* (Philadelphia: University of Pennsylvania Press, 1981). Reprinted with permission.

Excerpt from S. N. Kramer, *The Sumerians* (Chicago: University of Chicago Press, 1963). © 1963 by The University of Chicago. All rights reserved. Reprinted with permission.

Excerpt from R. R. Skemp, *The Psychology of Learning Mathematics* (Harmondsworth, England: Penguin Books, 1971). Copyright © Richard R. Skemp 1971. All rights reserved. Reprinted by permission of Penguin Books Ltd.

Excerpt from R. A. Dykman, P. T. Ackerman, and M. Oglesby, "Selective and Sustained Attention in Hyperactive, Learning-Disabled and Normal Boys," *Journal of Nervous and Mental Diseases* 167 (1979):288–97. Copyright © 1979 The Williams and Wilkins Co., Baltimore.

Library of Congress Cataloging-in-Publication Data

McGuinness, Diane.
    When children don't learn.

    Includes index.
    1. Learning disabilities.   2. Sex differences in
education.   3. Remedial teaching.   I.   Title.
LC4704.M4   1985   371.92   85–47562
ISBN   0–465–09178–4   (cloth)
ISBN   0–465–09179–2   (paper)

Copyright © 1985 by Basic Books, Inc.
Printed in the United States of America
Designed by Vincent Torre
87 88 89 90 MPC 9 8 7 6 5 4 3 2 1

CONTENTS

PART I

An Overview of the Problem

PART II

Unraveling the Evidence

Contents

PART III

Three Ounces of Prevention

PREFACE

I began teaching when I was fifteen years old. My pupil was six. Together we explored the intricacies of John Thompson's "Teaching Little Fingers to Play." I was paid in either cookies, cake, or kindness, because in our neighborhood no one (including me) could afford piano lessons. I have been teaching ever since, at home, in elementary and junior high schools, in churches, in county youth music programs, and in several universities, including England's fledgling Open University in 1972. I have seen schools that work and schools that don't, and watched the impact of local tradition and educational theory on how children learn in both the United States and England. In a rural school in the San Bernardino mountains I saw elementary-school children create, rehearse, stage, and perform a variety show with the assurance and presence of professionals. In stark contrast, at a boys' prep school in England, the teachers posted weekly student ratings on the classroom door for everyone to see. I discovered with dismay and astonishment that my favorite boys—the poets, the dreamers, the humorists—were usually at the bottom of the list. The boys who always set out to trick you or pull a fast one were often at the top!

If there is a lesson to be learned from these experiences, it is that children blossom with individual care and languish or rebel the moment they become less important than the system. If the system is too inflexible, too inhuman, then ultimately even the winners are losers. They have learned to play the wrong game. Furthermore, it has become obvious over the years that no matter what it is that society wants to teach, there will inevitably be a population of "learning-disabled" children, children who can't or won't learn what adults want them to learn.

When Children Don't Learn has been in my bones for many years, but I was galvanized into writing it by three separate experiences, which quite unexpectedly forced me to look closely at the practical implications of research I had been doing on sex differences. In 1978 I began a three-year research program sponsored by the National Science Foundation to explore the perceptual, motor, and cognitive aspects of mathematical ability. The purpose of the project was to discover why girls often failed to shine in higher mathematics. The results showed that girls were more likely to be poorer at the kinds of skills that are essential to performance in higher math, especially the capacity to visualize the position of objects in space. These differences between boys and girls were found in children as young as four years of age. The results from these studies have helped bridge the gap between more biologically based theories and the hypothesis that all learning disabilities are caused by social factors, a hypothesis that had tipped the scales too far toward cultural determinism. These and other studies are presented in detail in chapters 7 and 8.

In 1979 I began working on a second grant proposal to study hyperactivity. My interest in this subject stemmed from a model of attention developed by Karl Pribram and myself, and published in *Psychological Review* in 1975. If hyperactivity is produced largely by a child's inability to maintain attention, as had been suggested by other researchers, then our model could help to explain precisely which aspects of attention were deficient in those children who will be labeled "hyperactive." It was only as I began to read the research and attempt to articulate the findings that I realized I could not, in conscience, go forward with the proposal. The research clearly showed that no reliable behavioral or physiological correlates of "hyperactivity" could be demonstrated. Hyperactivity as defined in the literature simply did not exist. Furthermore, almost the entire population of hyperactive children was male, something that my many years of research into sex differences told me was extremely suspicious. As a result, my review turned into a critique that ultimately found its resting place in a desk drawer. Many months later I learned that Enoch Calloway and Laverne Johnson, both of whom had previously done research on hyperactive children, also felt disquieted for the same reasons. Both were kind enough to read my critique and both strongly encouraged me to publish it. The original manuscript has been extensively reworked and expanded on the basis of new data. While a number of recent experimental projects are more sound methodologically than the ones used in the original review, my conclusion remains. The results of my assessment of the literature are presented in chapters 9 and 10.

The third and vital link in the history of this book came in 1981 as a result of an invitation by the Orton Dyslexia Society to speak at a weekend conference on sex differences in dyslexia. The invitation obliged me to delve into the research on reading and reading failure, and I was struck by the similarity between my research on sex-specific aptitudes and the skills that are considered essential to the reading process. Girls appeared to possess precisely those types of skills (essentially linguistic) that are important in learning to read. If a remedial program is to work, it should therefore focus on these types of aptitudes. How children learn to read, which sex differences are relevant, and the biological basis for their development are topics addressed in chapters 4, 5, and 6.

These strands provide the backbone of the book. I am particularly grateful to the individuals who have contributed directly and indirectly to this superstructure. I could not have hoped for a more enlightened sponsorship at the National Science Foundation. I particularly want to thank Joe Lipson and Andrew Molnar for their unfailing encouragement and interest. Thanks are also due to Enoch Calloway and Laverne Johnson, whose support was critical to my maintaining my position on the subject of hyperactivity. The Orton conference opened my eyes to the world of the dyslexic child and began a fruitful and exciting participation in the society's meetings, which are uniformly outstanding. I would like to express my gratitude to everyone at Orton's national headquarters in Baltimore and to the Northern California branch for their hard work and for their talent in asking the right questions and finding the right people to answer them.

The fine tuning I owe to others. I particularly want to thank Pat Lindamood, head of the Lindamood clinic, for her hospitality, for letting me sit in on training sessions, for answering all my questions, and for being such a creative and dedicated teacher. I am also greatly indebted to Patricia Davidson at the University of Massachusetts, who spent four days of her very precious time with me at her home in Boston. I only hope I have done justice to a fraction of all that she shared with me. Her brilliance, her energy, and her integrity are inspiring.

Thanks too to the Montessori teachers who over the years have let me sit and stare and listen, and who have taken so much time to answer all my questions. And a special thanks to the children who never cease to amaze me with their poise, enthusiasm for learning, and willingness to share this enthusiasm with me.

Preface

Equally important are those people who offered support by being there, by reading chapters, by arguing points and forcing me to be logically consistent. There is Sandra Scarr, whose friendship and confirmation of my unorthodox ideas have been more important than she could possibly know. My editor, Jo Ann Miller, has become a dear friend. I want to thank her for being so supportive and thoughtful, and for her enthusiasm for the book, which means everything.

A very special thanks is due to my daughter, Julie, who painstakingly read every page and, in her inimitable fashion, brought me out of the clouds when necessary, challenged my grammar, and insisted I keep an even tone. Last, my enduring gratitude to Karl Pribram, who read and reread each version, scribbled endless notes in the margins, offered his talented eye for organizational improvements, and who steadfastly believed in my ideas.

But my greatest inspiration for this book has come from the children themselves, especially my own. *When Children Don't Learn* is dedicated to them.

When Children Don't Learn

Introduction

Some children learn easily, some with difficulty, and some, apparently, not at all. There is nothing new in this. Individual differences in learning have been acknowledged since schools began more than four thousand years ago. In the past it was thought that slow learners were stupid, lazy, or simply not motivated to study, and there was no attempt to specify a particular deficiency, such as problems in reading or math. Recently, in an attempt to be more precise, schools have begun to adopt a totally different set of labels. Terms such as "hyperactivity," "dyslexia," and "minimal brain damage" have become part of everyday vocabulary.

Unfortunately, labeling of any kind produces deleterious consequences. The tendency to reduce learning problems to shorthand, quasi-medical jargon causes more damage than the simple statement that "Johnny is having trouble learning to read" or "Joe is a nuisance in class." Most parents who have had the misfortune to be told that their child is "learning disabled," "hyperactive," or "dyslexic" are well aware of the problem. The schools' appropriation of clinical terminology has resulted in an enormous population of parents who believe that their children have some irredeemable congenital or pathological disorder. In fact, based on some follow-up research on learning-disabled children, it appears that this kind of irresponsible labeling can produce symptoms much worse than those that led to the diagnosis in the first place. Labeling of any kind is often undesirable but labeling in the absence of pathology or any formal diagnosis is especially pernicious.

The implications of these terms are very powerful and are rarely spelled out. In most cases I have come across, whether of parents with learning-disabled children or adults who have been labeled dyslexic, there is a belief that something is wrong organically, as if having dyslexia is like having leukemia. Because it is generally acknowledged that brains have something more to do with reading than other organs of the body such as the heart or liver, it is but one step to infer that something is wrong with the brains of dyslexic children or adults. But what does the term dyslexia actually mean?

One of the major dictionary definitions of the prefix *dys* is "poorly" or "with difficulty." However, a second common meaning is "disease," so it is not surprising that laymen commonly interpret the terms "dyslexia" or "disability" in this way. Recently I met a bright young man in his twenties who told me, in tones mixed with pride and distress, that he "had" dyslexia. I explained that dyslexia means "reading with difficulty," or "reading poorly" and that it is not possible to *have* reading poorly. It is not a disease. I asked him if he would say "I have running slowly." But he was not the least bit influenced by my logic, and persisted in making statements such as: "When I discovered I had dyslexia. . . ." Somehow "having" something made him special, mysterious, and expunged the feeling he had all through school that he was just "stupid."

A similar problem arises when children have been labeled "hyperactive": It has become the rule rather than the exception to infer some type of brain damage. The term "minimal brain dysfunction" was adopted by a committee at the National Institute of Health to identify a group of children who had a variety of severe behavioral and learning disorders. In practice it has become popular to equate "minimal brain dysfunction" with "hyperactivity," despite the fact that children diagnosed in classrooms as hyperactive are rarely found to have neurological deficits. "Hyperactive" simply means "more active than most." However, as we will see in chapters 9 and 10, just as there is no evidence for pathology, it has even been difficult to demonstrate that "hyperactive" children are more active than other children their age.

At this point it is time to let the cat out of the bag: 75 percent of dyslexics and nearly 90 percent of hyperactive children are male. The children most often branded with these punitive labels are little boys. Of course, for nearly four thousand years only boys attended school, and when girls were finally admitted, the sexes were segregated. However, with the advent of coeducation, differences in learning and behavior between girls and boys have become too obvious to ignore. Teachers face a preponderance of boys in their remedial reading classes, and child psychologists treating hyperactive children rarely look across their desks at little girls.

But girls do not escape entirely. At about the time when algebra and geometry enter the curriculum, more girls than boys are in difficulty. Furthermore, girls are considerably underrepresented in those branches of the physical sciences that rely heavily on higher mathematics, such as physics and engineering. This brings us to the third "disability" to be discussed in the pages that follow. The most popular view of the problems girls have in advanced mathematics is that it is the result of a "phobia." This phobia, it is alleged, is a direct result of social "conditioning." Here we have another example of how terminology borrowed from the clinic has been misapplied. A phobia—an extreme and irrational fear—usually has as its common targets heights, spiders, snakes, and a fear of the out-of-doors. The word "conditioning" comes from a corruption of the expression "conditional response," coined by Ivan Pavlov to describe the phenomenon of producing an unlikely response to a stimulus, such as salivating to the tone of a bell previously associated with the arrival of a meal.

It is not at all clear what these expressions mean when applied to schoolgirls (or boys) who are poor at mathematics. So prevalent is this practice that college classes are even described as being designed for "math phobics." This implies that a dislike for mathematics is pathologically irrational or more terrifying than a dislike of any other school subject. It is just as likely that young children develop similar anxieties about learning to read. But at six or seven they are too inarticulate to be able to express their distress about how they are affected by the pressure, the intense importance attached to a disliked activity, and the belief that they are different.

These categories of learning problems are commonly grouped together under the heading "learning disabilities," which was intended to be an umbrella term for children who exhibited a variety of *specific* learning problems. However, the problems already inherent in labels like "dyslexia" are compounded when a variety of learning difficulties are subsumed into one category. In addition, it will never be possible to arrive at a useful definition of "learning disabilities" because of a fundamental categorical error. We can categorize objects like chairs, tables, and footstools and occasionally these can then be subsumed into a superordinate category, in this case, furniture. Furniture, like most superordinate categories, is very difficult to define. Basically it constitutes everything found in and around the home or workplace that makes it possible to avoid having to conduct one's daily affairs on the floor.

However, many things that superficially share a common property cannot rationally be subsumed under one heading. For example, paper towels, newspapers, books, magazines, notepads, stationery, photographs, and so on cannot be grouped together in a category, even though they are all made of paper. Similarly, to subsume every type of learning problem under one convenient heading leads to a definition that has no explanatory power. The true definition of "learning disabilities" is: The failure to learn anything at a normal rate, for whatever reason.

This definition immediately reveals a number of thorny conceptual issues: What is a "normal rate"? Is someone who can't learn how to play baseball "learning disabled"? And if not, why not? Finally, what causes the person to fail to learn at the normal rate? Is this due to external events such as parental upbringing, a poor teacher, a death in the family, or to internal events, such as low intelligence or poor perceptual skills? Or is the learning problem the result of some *interaction* between these factors, such as poorly developed skills promoting impatience in the teacher, which leads to a fear of school, which in turn prevents learning?

Categories such as perceptual dysfunctions, reading problems, conduct disorders, lack of motivation, distractibility, and low I.Q., do not constitute a sufficiently coherent subset to fit into a general framework. In her book *Learning Disabilities*,[1] Sylvia Farnham-Diggory has provided an exhaustive and amusing account of the arguments among educators, clinicians, and politicians as to what "learning disabilities" really means. But despite the warning flags she raises, she does not see beneath the problem and concludes that learning disabilities constitute a mystery that science must unravel.

On closer inspection, it turns out that the concept of learning disabilities rests upon a more primary set of assumptions. First, students are called learning disabled only in those skills that society designates as important to the culture: reading, writing, and mathematics. As already noted, we do not call people learning disabled because they have poor athletic ability. In other words, learning disabilities are created by social sanctions for certain types of activity in preference to others. This means that whenever a particular skill or aptitude is demanded or required by a particular culture, it comes to constitute a value. Social values then determine what is deviant. When values are strong they act as proscriptions for the entire population. Social values exert pressure on all citizens to conform, to be the same, and therefore come to reflect a set of universal principles. Property and ownership are such intense values of our society that any violation of these "rights" by a citizen leads to punishment and even imprisonment. Although a failure to acquire literacy and numeracy may not invoke such extreme responses, allegations of deviancy may be equally punitive.

Also underlying the universalizing of a particular skilled behavior as a value is the inference that this skill is biologically given. Most children learn to walk. Most children learn to talk. Pediatricians have norms for the ages that these activities are most likely to begin. If a child fails to walk by the age of two, then medical advice is sought. But the same reasoning cannot be applied to the acquisition of a skill that is not an innate part of the human repertoire. Writing and mathematics are inventions and do not develop spontaneously from the biological propensities of the human species. It took over one thousand years to develop the first phonetic writing system and another one thousand years to refine it. Just because some children find it easy to master a phonetic alphabet or manipulate algebraic equations does not mean that those who find it difficult are deviant or phobic.

Another way of stating the same problem is to imagine a situation in which a different type of skill came to be valued in the same way as reading. Suppose that our society believed that all young children should be trained to build and repair machines. For six hours each day, five days a week, children went to school and took machines apart and put them back together again. Obviously not every child would be good at this, and even if a few showed some aptitude, it is unlikely that they would choose or prefer this activity over others. In no time at all there would be a group of children who began to complain. There would be another group who, no matter how hard they tried, always put their machines together incorrectly. Nothing they ever built would work. Now suppose that we called these children learning disabled and put them in a class called "Remedial Mechanics."

Does this seem nonsensical? It is no different from expecting all children to show an aptitude for reading. And from all the evidence we have today, if schools taught mechanics rather than reading, the remedial classes would have a higher proportion of girls instead of boys.

I have attempted to point out a few of the critical errors in our thinking about learning. In the remainder of this book I will explore in more detail all the implications of the current philosophy and the ways in which the differences between the sexes can be employed to shed light on the problem of why and how children fail to learn what society wants to teach. As we will see, when the data from research on sex differences and the body of evidence on academic achievement are brought together, there are some surprising results.

This book is both an overview of the learning disabilities field and a detailed review of a large body of evidence. Parts I and III are more for the general reader. Part II is more for those professionals who have a particular interest in problems in reading, math, and behavioral control, or in sex differences, and for parents with a "dyslexic," "hyperactive," or "math phobic" child.

Part I examines all the ramifications behind our current educational philosophy and reveals how and why children become classified as learning disabled. Chapter 1 covers the evolution of the age-graded classroom and how sex-specific learning problems have come to light. Chapter 2 reveals the implications and consequences of an unquestioning acceptance of current diagnoses, and Chapter 3 analyzes the true significance behind the various theories put forward to explain learning disabilities.

Part II is a detailed analysis of the experimental evidence to support the arguments presented in part I. Chapters 4, 5, and 6 explore the evidence on which skills are essential in learning to read, how females are favored or "buffered" for these same skills, and provide some interesting new data on the organization of the male and female brain that could account for these effects.

Chapters 7 and 8 discuss the nature of mathematics, and how the different aptitudes and interests of males and females either enhance or block the development of mathematical expertise. Chapter 9 is an account of all the methodological (and logical) reasons why a diagnosis of "hyperactivity" cannot be maintained. Chapter 10 provides the evidence for this conclusion.

Part III deals with practical issues. Given all we know about the psychology of learning, which methods hold the most promise for teaching our children the skills they need to develop in the classroom? In chapter 11, I have focused on three especially outstanding programs. Chapter 12 is a personal aside to parents, telling them what I would do if my child were labeled "learning disabled."

PART I

An Overview of the Problem

1

Learning What Society Wants to Teach

A Tale of Two Cultures

Tashay held his bow tightly in his left hand and slowly, carefully, drew the arrow back. There was a crack and then a shout as the arrow split the Mongongo sapling in two.

"Ha! I did it, Kumsa. Look, look. Now it's your turn. Try my arrow, it will bring you luck."

Tashay's father was the best hunter in the village. He had taught Tashay well, but he had always said that Tashay had a natural talent for hunting. "It is in the bones of my family," he was fond of saying.

Kumsa looked at Tashay sheepishly. "You know well that I cannot aim my arrows. If I used your arrow it would be lost forever."

"Come on, Kumsa, it is only an arrow. I can make another. You must learn to use your bow, otherwise your family will starve. You may never even get a wife. You must try. I will be your teacher."

The two boys practiced until the sun began to set, just as they had done for many years. They were firm friends, friends of the blood. They would do anything for one another, but Tashay was unable to teach Kumsa his skill. It was just not in Kumsa's bones.

For the !Kung San peoples of the Kalahari Desert, life presents relatively little choice. From the age of about twelve years, girls are trained to forage for food, cook, and care for children, and

13

boys are trained to hunt. Richard Lee, who studied the !Kung for over fifteen years, never observed women hunting anything larger than lizards and snakes, whereas hunting became the men's sole occupation from the age of fifteen years. Although we in the West are only just breaking out of a similar pattern of dividing labor according to sex-linked roles, the lack of choice seems excessively constraining. Suppose a !Kung man doesn't like hunting or isn't any good at it?

Such questions haunt the !Kung as well, because they have evolved a number of social sanctions to ensure that men will learn to hunt and keep hunting. One of the most powerful early inducements is that manhood can only be attained with the first successful large kill. Until a young man kills his first buck he is not considered eligible for marriage. With this kind of incentive it might be imagined that ultimately all !Kung men become outstanding hunters. Not so. In a survey of 127 men Lee reports that hunters did not hit their prime until they were around forty years old. The average number of kills per man doubles with each decade of his life until he reaches forty. Furthermore, the number of years of practice does not necessarily guarantee that a man will make a good hunter. Half of the men in the group with the most success (in the age range thirty-nine to forty-eight years) account for 70 percent of the kills. Talent for hunting is clearly a factor in performance, as illustrated by the fact that the skills in the poorest half rise from zero kills at ages fifteen to twenty-eight years, to only 30 percent during a lifetime of hunting.

Because it takes such a long time to become a successful hunter and because there are such great individual differences in skill, the !Kung do everything to help. Good hunters are strongly encouraged to share meat and "lucky" arrows. Boasting and arrogance about success in the hunt are considered extremely bad form. Prayers and incantations are delivered on behalf of an unlucky hunter, and relatives will provide food as long as he makes some effort. Nevertheless, a poor hunter often goes through life without either a mate or true respect, a powerful example of natural selection for genes that ensure survival.[1]

Our society is so complex, the tasks to be done so numerous, that we cannot imagine such a poverty of choice. Yet in one respect we are the same. Instead of focusing exclusively on hunting, gathering, and cooking, our children go to school. And although there are many rewards for many kinds of talents, these talents rarely count inside the four walls of a classroom. Take as an example the story of Donny and Paul.

> Donny and Paul are hard at work in a third-grade classroom. Paul is seven, a quiet boy who used to worry his parents because he was so fearful of strangers and new situations. He is not very athletic, and it took him months to learn to ride his bike. He has always been overly sensitive to criticism and often bursts into tears when challenged to keep trying. Paul was very reluctant to go to school until Donny, his devoted friend, was moved into his class. The two boys couldn't be more dissimilar. Donny is an athletic nine-year-old whose expert pitching carried his little league team to victory. He is engaging, articulate, and extremely popular with his classmates. But in the classroom these are not the differences that matter: Paul is totally absorbed with a Grimm's fairy tale, while Donny is "dyslexic" and is struggling through a primer.

If the two boys had been brought up with the !Kung, or the aborigines, or in the New Guinea Highlands, Donny would undoubtedly be a far greater success than Paul. These stories illustrate the way in which society determines who will succeed and who will fail. For !Kung men survival means learning to hunt; for men and women in our culture, survival means literacy and numeracy.

Set Up to Fail

In Western cultures the term "learning disabilities" is reserved for those children who fall behind in reading, spelling, or math, and/ or fail to achieve the success in school that would be predicted by their ability. We do not call Paul learning disabled because he is unathletic and has poor social skills. While we feel quite comfortable with the fact that there are enormous individual differences in athletic, mechanical, artistic, and social abilities, we find it difficult to accept that individual differences might exist, *for completely natural reasons*, within a classroom. We accept the term "dyslexia," while similar derogatory labels for deficiencies in sports (dyscoordia), music (dysmusica), mechanical ability (dysmechanica), and sociability (dyssocia) strike us as ridiculous. We talk about a talented athlete, a talented mechanic, a talented pianist, but rarely speak of children as "talented" readers or spellers.

There are some important unstated assumptions behind this practice. The first is that talents such as musical or mechanical aptitude are considered to be inherent traits of the individual. By contrast, literacy and numeracy are thought to be routine skills readily accessible to everyone at a similar level of competence, rather like learning to use a knife and fork. Second, we don't allow for enough variation among individuals and we impose a deadline on when these skills are to be acquired. Unlike the !Kung, we are too impatient and tend to have less tolerance of individual differences. Under pressure from employers, colleges, and parents, educators have come to intensify their focus on the "losers." Losers are an indication to everyone that there might be something wrong with the educational system; rather than fix the system, it is easier to blame the child.

How did this state of affairs come about? Although it is never possible to document fully the precursors of prevailing social attitudes, two historical events are highly pertinent to the issues of how and when children can be expected to master certain skills. The following account shows that history inevitably provides us with more than one solution to the problem of individual differences in the classroom. In this case the solutions are almost diametrically opposite.

Teaching versus Classifying

During the late nineteenth century two great figures emerged in the field of education. One was Maria Montessori, an Italian doctor, and the other Alfred Binet, a psychologist working in Paris. When Montessori finished her medical training in Rome, she became interested in the problem of mentally retarded children.

Her studies led her to the work of two French researchers, Jean Itard and his pupil Edouard Seguin, who had developed techniques for teaching deaf and subnormal children. Adapting their approach, she developed a method to teach mentally retarded children to read, a feat that had been deemed impossible. Exalted with the success of her new method, Montessori was eager to try these techniques on normal children. When she heard of an experimental rehousing project in San Lorenzo, near Rome, she jumped at the opportunity to head the new school. There the Casa dei Bambini was born and Montessori faced her first class, a scruffy group of street urchins who authorities believed were unteachable. Her success is now legend, and the Casa dei Bambini drew visitors from around the world.[2]

Montessori's methods will be taken up in some detail later in this volume, but the essence of her approach is that it is centered on the child and is oriented to long-range goals. The progress toward these goals is invariant, one skill building on another, and the fact that children advance at different rates is little cause for concern. As every child is working at his or her own pace, the progress of any one child is completely independent of that of the other children. This, plus the wide age range in Montessori classes, guarantees that each child can spend as much or as little time in each stage as is necessary and that each can move ahead in some areas while taking more time in others. The overall purpose of a Montessori school is to develop the greatest potential in all children, whatever their age, whatever their talent, and no matter how slowly they learn. One of Montessori's major insights is that learning will become exciting to children in direct proportion to the extent that they can discover solutions for themselves. To this end the teaching methods and learning materials are carefully crafted to ensure that discovery is the primary mode of learning.

Alfred Binet was set a radically different objective by the Paris school district. He and his colleague Theodore Simon were provided funds to devise a test to classify children according to ability. The aim was to identify the retarded and select out the duller children for remediation. The reasoning was identical to the reasoning given today: If the slower learners are removed from the classroom, they can receive more individual attention, while the rest of the students can progress with their studies.[3]

Binet was selected for this project because of his outstanding research on the nature of intelligence and on the feebleminded. He based his early method, discussed in his classic monograph on intelligence in 1903, entirely on verbal reports.[4] By the time his intelligence test appeared in 1905 and the revised version in 1908, nonverbal tests (drawing and line estimation) were included, but verbal tasks (word associations, naming pictures, following instructions, rhyming, verbal memory, and reasoning) still predominated. Binet was a brilliant psychologist. He viewed intelligence as judgment, insight, and reason, independent of acquired knowledge. Nevertheless, his test items still require a good deal of knowledge about the world described in words. This approach fit the popular philosophy that the most obvious distinction between us and all other animals is language.

Binet and Simon's second approach was to make an assumption about the relationship between age and ability. It seemed obvious to them, as it does to us now, that children become more skilled and more knowledgeable as they grow older. A measure of intelligence, therefore, had to be related somehow to what each child understood and could report at a particular age. Testing large numbers of children would result in an average value for the number of items passed or failed for the age group as a whole. Binet and Simon insisted that intelligence scores were only approximate and preferred to use the term "mental level," never "mental age." Despite these warnings, in 1911, the year of Binet's death, Wilhelm Stern in Germany proposed a unitary score based on mental age; thus the intelligence quotient was born. It was soon adopted throughout Europe and the United States. Stern's solution was to take an individual child's score (called mental age) and divide this by the average score for the group (called chronological age). Taking this ratio, MA/CA, provides an estimate of the child's IQ.

What is not widely known about the initial results from pilot studies was that boys predominated among the children who received low scores.[5] If it had been reported, this result could have led to several important realizations, the major one being that a methodology based on "chronological age" is invalid if the sexes are combined. Boys and girls develop different skills at different ages. Rather than reporting this result, Binet and Simon changed the test so that the sex difference disappeared, a solution that has been characteristic of all subsequent IQ test construction. All items that strongly favored girls were discarded and more items that favored boys were incorporated.

Later, when David Wechsler began to devise a test of intelligence that did not rely so heavily on language or acquired knowledge, the same problem of balancing the sexes arose. (Wechsler's initial test results revealed a female superiority on almost every subtest.)[6] For this reason the Wechsler test contains items that seem on face value to be totally unrelated to intelligence, such as tests of coding speed and block design that require children to translate numbers into letters as rapidly as possible or to arrange blocks in a pattern illustrated by a picture. Since some items were chosen to balance the sex effects in the total score, it is not surprising that only recently has any relationship between these tasks and any definable intellectual ability been discovered. The evolution of the sex-unbiased IQ is often believed to be the result of an attempt to ensure that the sexes are equally regarded in intellect, that is, that the test is *fair*. However, if in the early tests more girls had received low scores than boys, it is likely that the test would not have been revised, as it would have confirmed what everyone believed.

These examples illustrate the point raised earlier about how social attitudes evolve. Montessori provided the almost perfect means for ensuring that no one need to fail. She never specified anything about chronological age and, moreover, her techniques were outstandingly successful. Yet the educational establishment has chosen to ignore her contribution and her work has been kept alive largely by the intellectual community. Her influence has been felt most strongly in preschools, especially in educational materials, the lack of emphasis on age-graded performance, and the physical appearance of the classroom. While Montessori did not have the answer to every problem that arose in the classroom, she most certainly did have one answer—an excellent method for teaching reading.

Binet and Simon's brilliant work was misguidedly taken as an indication that children advance in a fixed progression for all skills from one age to the next. Binet always stated that different children have different talents developing at different rates. Through his practical experience with testing children, he was powerfully struck by the range of variation both between and within individuals. It is interesting that, in addition, Binet's data show quite clearly that a five-year age spread at *each* upper elementary grade was common in the Paris schools. However, currently, American schools are organized according to chronological age with a variation of only two years in a classroom. This kind of rigidity is exaggerated by the fact that every child is expected to learn the same thing at the same time and at the same rate. Because some children will always be slower than others, the age-graded classroom will inevitably create a population of "learning-disabled" children. Similarly, children with learning problems are made painfully aware of the fact that they are often "too old" for their grade level. Instead of employing Montessori's philosophy, which was to establish learning goals irrespective of age, we expect a specific level of ability to emerge at a specific age. If it does not appear, the most common solution is to give up and pass children into the next class because they are "getting too old."

Sex Differences—They Won't Go Away

Despite the myriad attempts to eliminate their effect in test performance, sex differences still pop up in the classroom. With universal coeducation these differences are too overwhelming to ignore. But we should not disguise our tests or rearrange our schools so that the sex differences go away; rather, we should rearrange our *thinking* about education in general. Sex differences are an important reminder that individuals have different talents, different abilities, and different ways of acquiring knowledge.

In addition, the patterns of sex differences allow us to gain a greater insight into how cognitive skills or cognitive styles emerge during development. We now know that there are three major differences between males and females that are important to the educational process. The first is that females rely more heavily than males on acquiring knowledge through language. They typically prefer verbal solutions to problems, a tendency that can get them into trouble later in classes in advanced mathematics. While females are busy learning about the world through talk, males are busy exploring the environment firsthand, literally *with their hands,* which makes them appear more hyperactive.[7] Finally, it seems that boys' hands-on exploration subsequently becomes combined with visual information and later emerges as an aptitude for visualizing the movement of static objects in space, an ability that is important in geometry. In other words, the major areas in which "learning disabilities" occur are largely the cognitive domains in which the sexes are most at odds; dyslexia, more common in boys, is a result of poorly developed auditory and language skills; hyperactivity, again seen more frequently in boys, is characteristic of children who put their hands into the world at inappropriate moments; and math phobia, more common in girls, is in part due to a lack of interest in inanimate objects and the consequent inability to visualize spatial relationships between them.

To set the stage for a full understanding of the significance of these sex differences in learning, we will begin with the most common learning problem, reading. There are now firm data on the distribution of sexes in remedial reading populations, and these data apply in most countries around the world. In general, given a normal environment and normal classroom setting, the male/female ratio in special reading classes is, at the most conservative estimate, three to one; in other words, over 75 percent of the reading-disabled group are males.[8] In clinical populations, where children have been referred for behavior disorders, these ratios become more extreme, and the male/female ratio for reading difficulties rises to six to one, or 85 percent males. Furthermore, a correlation is found between behavior disorders and reading difficulties in *boys,* while no such correlation is found for girls. The high incidence of reading difficulties in emotionally disturbed boys and the strong relationship between reading scores and the severity of the disturbance provide a clue that reading failure may be at the root of some of the behavior problems. However, a correlation cannot provide any information about causes.

In accord with the theory that chronological age is an important factor in education, "achievement test batteries," which measure progress in various skills such as reading and early math, have been standardized for every age as well as for each racial and socioeconomic group. This allows the teacher to determine whether a particular child is normal (average) for his or her specific age, race, and socioeconomic class. However, these norms have never been independently standardized by sex. This ommission reflects educators' beliefs that while social factors, such as cultural practices or impoverished environments, might be relevant to reading scores, sex differences are not. This is assumed despite the fact that the most striking differences found between any specific groups (race, social class, or sex) in remedial populations are *sex* differences. Because of the way norms are established, it is impossible to determine how these sex differences are distributed across various types of populations. For example, are the same sex effects found in black or Asian students, or are they peculiar to white races? Are the sex differences similar in low- and high-ability groups? One can make assumptions only from the evidence that has been collected during research on reading and math carried out with large populations. From these data, it appears that the sex effect in verbal skills is maximal in the mid- to lower-ability range, but disappears in high-ability groups. For instance, no sex differences are found in verbal scores among the top-scoring students in over a decade of annual talent searches for junior high school students sponsored by Johns Hopkins University. In contrast, however, the Johns Hopkins team has discovered a very different result in the mathematics section of their program. There, while boys and girls enter the competition with very similar scores, only *boys* have exceptionally high scores during a competition when they are tested on the mathematics part of the Scholastic Aptitude Test (SAT). In one group that scored in the top 20 percent, all were boys.[9] As sex differences are never found in tests of basic arithmetic, this result suggests that the distribution of boys' and girls' scores on tests of higher mathematics is the opposite, or the mirror image, of the sex distributions for verbal ability. That is, sex differences are minimal in the *low*-ability groups but maximal in the *high*-ability groups.

Last, as noted earlier, there is the hyperactive child, who is almost exclusively male, with male/female ratios reported as high as nine to one, or 90 percent boys.[10] Despite the belief that hyperactivity has a recognized medical etiology, in practice the diagnosis is carried out with a pen-and-paper test. The test items focus largely on such things as distractibility, inappropriate behavior, immunity to adult control, and so forth. The tests are filled out by parents or teachers, and it is their "tolerance for annoying behavior" or their inability to diminish it that ultimately becomes the defining criterion.

Not only are hyperactivity scales invalid on constructional grounds, but there are no established norms for "activity," hyper or otherwise, for children of any age. In fact, when activity levels are measured in small populations, boys are found to be more active than girls, while hyperactive boys are more active only in certain settings, such as in formal classrooms. What is significant is that these hyperactive boys appear more active because they are not engaging in the appropriate classroom activities. These boys call attention to themselves because they frequently do what they are not supposed to do. As will be seen in a later chapter in tracing the history of this so-called disorder, the current diagnosis of "hyperactivity" turns out to be as much a tale of a medication seeking a patient population as a genuine clinical problem.

What does it mean to be normal? The answer to this question always depends on what you are measuring and whom you measure. One major problem is classifying people into groups. Are seven-year-olds the same as eight-year-olds? Are boys the same as girls? In the next chapter it will be seen that ignoring sex differences in establishing "norms" can have profound consequences.

2

Normality and the Nature–Nurture Controversy

In the early school years, males are considerably overrepresented in the remedial reading populations. For every girl classified as learning disabled, there are three boys. This raises a problem. If there are an equal number of boys and girls in school, how can any special group, whether learning disabled or gifted, contain more of one sex than the other? A three-to-one ratio of males to females should be statistically impossible. The problem lies in how the scores on reading achievement tests are standardized. Although—to the dismay of many educators—the method for selecting children for remedial help is quite arbitrary from one school district to the next, the rule of thumb is usually that the child is delayed in reading and/or writing and spelling for his or her age. In most school systems the cutoff is when children are two years or more behind achievement test norms.

Who Is Normal?

A test norm simply reflects the average score for the average child at a given age. However, because achievement test norms have not been established for each sex separately, a discrepancy is produced in sex ratios for children diagnosed as learning disabled. If girls were selected for remediation who were two years behind average reading scores for girls, and boys selected who were two years behind other boys, the sex ratio would be one to one. Instead, remedial populations consist of those children who are two years behind the combined average achievement test scores of both sexes. As girls are advanced compared to boys in a number of verbal abilities, this procedure unduly penalizes boys. The failure to standardize achievement tests for each sex means that boys are being compared to girls who are from one to two years advanced in verbal development. The result is that the current techniques select about 20 to 25 percent of the boys from the classroom for remediation and only 5 to 8 percent of the girls.

One major issue is that of defining "normality" and the notion that chronological age provides a valid measure of ability. To be normal only means that you are more or less average with respect to some similar group on a particular dimension. For example, the normal height for women is about five feet four inches and for men, about five feet nine inches. If we used the same approach as the one adopted for reading test scores, these values would be combined to five feet six and one-half inches. That would mean that a woman who was five four would now be considered shorter than normal and a man of five nine would be considered taller than normal. The physical differences between the sexes in appearance, height, and weight are too obvious to ignore. But most people are uncomfortable with the idea that the sexes may differ in behavior or in certain learning skills. This resistance places us in a moral dilemma. Should we pretend that boys and girls are identical, or should we acknowledge the facts and establish two sets of norms for achievement test scores, one for boys and one for girls? Two sets of norms would be *fair* and accurate, and at least a step in the right direction until we can abolish the age-graded classroom. Overnight about 10 percent of all boys—

millions of them—would suddenly be normal readers for their age and sex. We also need to reconsider the entire problem of age norms as well as how to teach reading, so that these problems in learning to read are minimized at the outset.

Another difficulty lies in our thinking about how children learn. It is currently popular to hold the opinion that intellectual abilities are entirely a product of the culture. In a democratic society we believe that everyone is equal, but more often than not, equal has been incorrectly defined as "no difference." As noted earlier, there are well-defined social reasons why different social classes and different races have different opportunities for intellectual development, but there are no such social reasons for boys to be penalized at the expense of girls.

The question of "normality" becomes even more problematic when the issue of hyperactivity is considered. Reading scores reflect the ability to read through lists of words. A child can have a score ranging from zero to 100 percent correct. The scores are quantitative, but they also reflect a qualitative dimension of poor to good. It is better to score somewhere near the top of the scale than near the bottom. Hyperactivity questionnaires, on the other hand, tap a range of undesirable behaviors. The picture that emerges from studying the test items is that of an uncontrollable renegade. Unlike reading test scores, a high score on a hyperactivity questionnaire is bad.

In addition, the designation "hyper" is the polar opposite of "hypo." Both are deviant dimensions representing extreme degrees of unbalance. *Hyper* means to have too much of something, *hypo,* too little. The terms are familiar in connection with physiological disorders, such as hyperventilation, where breathing too rapidly and too deeply can produce dizziness or fainting. *Hypo*ventilation, breathing that is too slow and shallow, causes lung congestion. The ideal is a normal breathing pattern that causes no dysfunction.

When a scale is designed to measure extremes of behavior such as hyperactivity, it implies that there is a standard, an acceptable or normal level of activity. But a bipolar scale must be constructed to tap the full range of activity, from too little to too much. A hypoactive child would be unresponsive and passive. As these children are rarely a problem in the classroom, no items in the questionnaires tap these abnormally low levels of activity. Thus hyperactivity questionnaires are invalid on constructional grounds

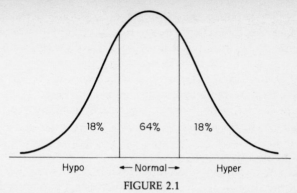

18%   64%   18%

Hypo   ← Normal →   Hyper

FIGURE 2.1

Distribution of male scores on a measure of hyperactivity. The cutoff values indicate the proportion of boys who would be "normal" if 10 percent of all schoolchildren were classified as hyperactive, and if hyperactivity scales included both ends of the continuum of hypo- to hyperactive.

alone, quite apart from violating statistical concepts.

If children are diagnosed "hyperactive" on the basis of a questionnaire measuring an extreme range of activity levels at one pole, then children must also be diagnosed *hypo*active by questions designed to tap the opposite pole. This is the only valid procedure. If this were done then the following situation would arise: Males outnumber females in the hyperactive populations by six to one to nine to one, or 86 to 90 percent. The incidence of hyperactivity varies from school to school but generally ranges from 5 to 15 percent (see chapter 9). If for every group of 100 children, 10 are classified as hyperactive, of those 10, 9 will be boys. What this means is that 18 percent (2 × 9) of all *boys* are hyperactive. In order to comply with the logic implicit in the scale and the rules of statistics, if 18 percent is adopted as a cutoff for one end of a bipolar measure of deviancy, it must be balanced by an equal cutoff at the other end of the scale. But two times 18 percent equals 36 percent, and to classify 36 percent of all boys as "abnormal" or "deviant" makes a nonsense of the meaning of the word normal. This effect is diagrammed in figure 2.1.

Contrast this with the explanations given for female difficulties in algebra and geometry. During the early school years, no sex differences are ever found in tests of addition, subtraction, multiplication, and long division. Nor are there observable differences in the ability to grasp the concepts of fractions, decimals, and percentages. Sex differences emerge when, and only when, algebra and geometry are introduced into the curriculum (see chapter 7). As this occurs at different ages in different countries, and for different ability groups, there should be little disagreement that sex differences are more specifically linked to subject matter than to social or environmental factors. Yet the argument most commonly advanced to explain female deficiencies is a sex-role socialization explanation.

Many of these problems could be resolved and much suffering avoided if we admitted that some learning skills are sex-related and that any attempt at remediation should begin by understanding the nature of certain sex-specific aptitudes. In other words, rather than hindering progress, acknowledging sex differences will enhance it. Such an admission will take the pressure off young boys, who are slower to acquire verbal skills than girls. In addition, instead of focusing all our resources and energies on studies of the impact of social conditioning on learning, we can spend more time discovering efficient learning strategies. By the same token we will learn what strategies are *inefficient* and can begin to work on more effective forms of intervention. Linda Brody and Lynn Fox have begun such investigations in their exploratory work on teaching algebra to girls in an all-female classroom, using more verbal explanations and more problems that reflect girls' interests.[1]

Escaping the Nature-Nurture Bind

Finally, it is important to break away from the mentality that everything can be explained by culture along with the corollary view that biological predispositions are immutable. Otherwise we will be caught in the same bind involving the impact of genetics versus the environment that has strangled research on intelligence for the past hundred years. Recently, Sandra Scarr, a psychologist who has studied intellectual development for many years, has proposed a solution to the bind.[2] Since we have gone nowhere with the nature-nurture issue, Scarr questions why we do not ask instead: What is *easy* and *difficult* for a species member to learn? If we want to assign greater weight to biology than to culture, we look at those behaviors that are easy to acquire. A bipedal gait and speech are good examples of biological predispositions in the human. On the other hand, reading, mathematics, architecture, and so forth are cultural inventions and require a greater boost from the environment. However, both easy and difficult tasks have ingredients of biology *plus* culture. No element of human behavior is totally independent of biology, and no biological function is independent of the environment.

For most females, reading is easy and appears to be less influenced by the environment, as will be seen in chapter 5. For males, reading is more difficult and hence is profoundly affected by a number of situational factors. By contrast, boys tend to have less difficulty in algebra and geometry than most girls. If higher mathematics is easier for boys, then girls need a greater boost from the environment to succeed in mathematics.

All of the research points to the fact that performance in complex tasks, such as reading, writing, and mathematics, is dependent on the adequate development of specific sensory and motor capacities. When these capacities are not developed, the student will fall back on inappropriate strategies that subsequently lead to failure. Thus a task is difficult in proportion to the number and efficiency of these initial sensorimotor skills. For example, as we will see in chapter 4, reading is dependent on auditory discrimination of speech sounds. When this discrimination is not finely tuned, the child will resort to other methods, such as attempting to memorize the visual appearance of each word. This strategy will ultimately break down, because the essence of a phonetic alphabet is that it dramatically reduces the load on memory. Instead of learning a manageable number of sound-letter correspondences, children who rely exclusively on vision must learn tens of thousands of different patterns. Students who learn in the appropriate manner will rapidly outdistance those who do not.

When children employ inefficient learning strategies, expectations begin to outdistance performance. If this happens, children start to feel they are losing control, and they may redouble their efforts. Children who are losing ground often rush through their work, which only makes things worse. If the task is to finish twenty problems in half an hour, and it takes children the same time to do five, then the inevitable result is to trade quantity for accuracy. As things go from bad to worse, even the teacher's instructions will be drowned in a sea of panic. Any further learning is blocked because the surge of adrenaline that accompanies panic makes it impossible to process new information. When any task becomes too difficult and failure is imminent, there is only one ultimate solution, and that is to quit. There are two general reactions to failure. One is to withdraw and become depressed; the other is to initiate displacement behavior that serves to fill the time. The most innocuous displacement behavior is daydreaming. Less innocuous is making noises. More irritating still are overt attempts to attract attention, such as wandering around the room and annoying other children, or calling out for information at inappropriate moments. In extreme cases some children will resort to highly aggressive behaviors that are caused largely by an overwhelming sense of frustration. All of these behaviors, from daydreaming to physical violence in the classroom, are behaviors that have been attributed to the "hyperactive child."

Correlations Are Not Causes

At this point it is important to introduce a statistical concept that will be referred to throughout this volume. When two or more events are "correlated," it only means that they co-occur, that is, they tend to go together. It does not mean that one event causes another. Researchers have found that behaviors such as daydreaming, inattention, and inappropriate actions such as calling out and wandering around the room tend to *co-occur*. (When more than two behaviors or events co-occur, this is called a "factor," after "factor analysis," a statistical test that calculates the relationship between a number of different behaviors or events.) A statistical relationship between events (a correlation or factor) cannot provide any information on causality. Daydreaming does not *cause* making weird noises. Wandering around the room does not *cause* daydreaming. Furthermore, this constellation of events could be caused by unseen factors stemming from failure to learn and the ensuing panic and frustration it provokes. In other words, these behaviors may cluster together because they are the outcome of something hidden, something that may not have been measured. Nevertheless, people who do not fully understand the implications of statistical tests often make inferences about causality.

A second mistake is to assume that behaviors that cluster together constitute an entity, in this case a "syndrome." When "factors" are derived from a set of measurements, it is common to name them. Names are created by the capacity of the researcher to deduce from a constellation of behaviors the common theme of the relationship. "Hyperactivity," a term borrowed from neurology, is a recent creation of psychiatrists and psychologists who discovered that specific drugs such as Ritalin inhibit behaviors like wandering around the room, making weird noises, and fidgeting. Since these behaviors tend to go together and are inhibited by a drug, it is assumed that they reflect some disease or disorder, just as, for example, blurred vision, vomiting, and headache are symptomatic of a brain tumor. The application of the medical model to studies of behavior problems leads to two critical errors of attribution. First is the inference of *causality* and second is an assumption that the cause is *organic*. If a drug reduces the behavior problem, then this is taken as an indication of pathology.

Because of these misconceptions, it is common to find that clinicians or psychiatrists dealing with these problem children frequently attribute learning failure to the *symptoms* it produces. That is, depression or "hyperactivity" is seen to *cause* the learning problems. However, all evidence from experiments (the only technique we have to infer causality) has shown that the truth is just the reverse. Attempts to change behavior in classrooms either by giving drugs or by behavioral techniques focused only on behavior do not improve learning (and in the latter case, often not even behavior); however, attempts that focus on improving academic skills by means of remediation and behavioral management dramatically improve behavior. This means that depression and "hyperactivity" are much more likely to be the *result* (not a cause) of external events and the child's perception of how to deal with them. Even in the case of highly antisocial behavior such as fighting or cruelty, we know that aggression is *triggered* by outside events.[3] Each individual has a different threshold for how much threat or frustration he or she will tolerate. A child who exhibits aggressive behaviors has a low threshold for tolerance of frustration, but the aggression is also *produced* by external stressors. It is just as important to remove the external triggers or stressors as to attempt to modify the reactivity.

Of course, there are children who suffer from depression for other reasons and who exhibit "hyperactivity" as a symptom of some neurological or biochemical disorder. But these children are extremely rare. It is quite another matter to suggest that *all* children who are hyperactive or have trouble learning to read have brain damage, especially when this population constitutes about 20 to 30 percent of all schoolboys.

Many researchers studying learning disabilities voice alarm that too great an emphasis on sex differences will have strong political implications. Factions wielding greater power may indeed use knowledge about sex differences for political ends. Knowledge can always be used for good or for evil. It is my contention that hiding the knowledge concerning sex-specific aptitudes in learning has done far more harm than good. In particular, it has caused a great deal of suffering in many boys who *normally* are slower to acquire reading skills when compared to girls. Even more pernicious is the spectacle of young boys on medication for a "disease" that has no valid diagnosis. In the light of these abuses, there seems little justification in hiding these facts from the public in the mistaken belief that only scientists have the prerogative to know the truth.

3

Theories: Promising and Unpromising

It is important to examine in some detail the kinds of theories that have evolved to explain learning problems and their origins, because it is theory that guides research and comes to have an impact on popular opinion. In this sense theories are more powerful than experimental results. A theoretical perspective influences not only the way data are perceived by the experimenter, but the way his or her proposal is interpreted by the agencies that fund research. If a research project has a theoretical framework too far removed from current dogma, the research will never get funded. In addition, theories are more easily communicated than data. It is the theories about learning that influence popular opinion and not the data, which are often too complex or too fragmented to describe easily. Only when the evidence points consistently and overwhelmingly in a particular direction can a theoretical position be modified.

A variety of theories have been generated to explain learning problems in otherwise normal children and the sex differences that relate to them. These theories are applied to children who are completely normal in every way except for a particular problem in a particular setting. None of the theories presented here is intended to apply to children who have uniform learning deficits such as those found in the mentally retarded, or in autistic, schizophrenic, and Down's syndrome children, where abnormalities in brain function have either been discovered or seem likely on the basis of research.

Let us begin with the most popular and hence the most familiar theories, because they are the most important to my thesis. Their importance lies not in whether they are accurate but rather in their seductiveness. They are easiest to grasp, hardest to dispel, and ultimately the most dangerous because they tend to stymie innovative research and thus progress in achieving a better understanding of the problem. Also, because they are so imbedded in the popular mind and are sustained by federal funding to research institutions, discerning parents and teachers find it nearly impossible to take a stand against them.

All theories are only approximations to the truth. The truth is always elusive and changeable, but some theories are more true than others.

Unpromising Theories of Learning Disabilities

BRAIN DAMAGE

The brain damage theory, or minimal brain dysfunction (MBD) hypothesis, has been developed from the following rationale: If a child has difficulty learning to read, shows confusion in the visual orientation of symbols, and/or fails to grasp the phonetic structure of the alphabet (which leads to bizarre spelling mistakes), or, in the case of the hyperactive child, consistently fails to behave properly in the classroom, something must be wrong with the child's brain. This conclusion follows from two unstated inferences: (1) that learning to read and write are biological givens for the human race; and (2) that children must at all times sit still in the classroom and pay undivided attention to the teacher.[1]

Because the deficit is so situation-specific, the brain damage theory adds the corollary that as nothing appears to be amiss with the child's spoken language or general intelligence, then the brain damage must be "minimal." When any term such as "minimal" ("ideopathic," "essential," and "primary" are a few others) is used in medicine, it not only means that there is no valid diagnosis, but it also means that clinicians haven't the vaguest notion of where or what such tissue damage might be. When attempts are made to discover differences between normal children and those with specific learning problems by various types of neurological tests, nothing can be found (as shown in chapter 10). Yet the theory still persists despite the lack of hard evidence. There are two major reasons for this. First, extreme cases of reading failure cannot be just the product of a developmental delay. Reading failure can persist into adult life despite exhaustive attempts to teach reading skills and high motivation to learn. Such people have statistically "abnormal" brains. Their brains are indeed unusual or *different*. However, as will be seen in chapter 11, reading techniques that are 100 percent successful are available. Therefore, people with severe reading problems cannot have truly defective brains, or else the training wouldn't work.

A second reason why the brain damage diagnosis persists is that clinicians can always point to a failure to find brain damage in other extreme populations whose behavior might warrant such a diagnosis, such as in schizophrenics or autistics. But it is imperative that scientists be more stringent, especially in those cases where a child's behavior in other respects is totally normal. It is not just sloppy thinking, but it is dangerous as well, to believe that even though something cannot be proven, it still constitutes a fact; otherwise the whole of science can be turned on its head.

And there are no facts pointing to brain damage. There is no evidence that *most* children diagnosed as "dyslexic" or "hyperactive" have gross neurological abnormalities, or exhibit what neurologists call "soft signs," such as absent reflexes, abnormal pupil dilatation, abnormal visual tracking patterns, hearing loss, or motor problems. Yet despite the fact that researchers have been unable to demonstrate any brain damage, soft or otherwise, in these children for over two decades of research, the search still goes on.

Meanwhile, some researchers have attempted to look for indirect signs of brain damage by measuring various peripheral physiological indicators such as heart rate or the electrical activity of the skin or the scalp. These indices have long been known from other research to accompany behavioral changes in attention and learning. The procedure is to select a learning-disabled population, subsequently called the "patient group," and match them to a control population in age and sex, but who have normal learning skills on the measure in question. Any differences in physiological responsivity exhibited by the learning-disabled group in comparison to the controls are considered "abnormal" and are taken to be symptomatic of brain dysfunction. That the results of these studies are totally inconsistent from one study to the next does not seem to matter to these workers, as will be seen in chapters 9 and 10. But more important, the entire rationale behind the experimental design is incorrect. If learning behavior is abnormal and these physiological indicators correlate with *behavior*, then no further inference can be made about neural processing, abnormal or otherwise. In fact, the underlying neural generators of the physiological indicators reflecting higher mental states, whether heart rate, electrical activity of the skin, or electroencephalogram (EEG), *have never been discovered.*[2] So should any consistent result be found, it still would not provide any strong evidence of brain damage.

What these experiments are really demonstrating is that there is a relationship between the efficiency with which certain tasks are accomplished and specific physiological responses. If you are inefficient at the task, for whatever reason, then your physiological responses will be different from those of someone who is efficient. The thinking behind most of these studies is identical to a situation in which a doctor compared heart rate changes in an inactive overweight person and an athlete and diagnosed brain damage instead of prescribing some exercise.

The major difficulty with the brain damage model as an explanation of learning problems is the unstated inference that there is basically no difference between human brains. In actuality, brains are different not only initially, but can become organized differently by virtue of the way a child learns about his or her world. People can have completely normal brains but still have difficulty in learning to read or fail to concentrate on classroom pursuits. Returning to the example of the hypothetical school where children learned mechanics, suppose that the primary goal of the school system was to educate children to become the inventors and manufacturers of *tools*. We would hardly suggest that every student who showed little aptitude for mechanical ability, who was unable to read a circuit diagram or repair a washing machine, was "brain damaged." There is no reason other than a cultural one why these abilities should not be valued equally with literacy and be trained from an early age.

SEX-ROLE STEREOTYPING

Brain damage theories are intended to apply to male and female populations equally. However, because more boys are in difficulty in the early school years, the "brain damage" label, in practice, applies largely to boys. For this reason, other theories have emerged that deal more directly with the issue of sex differences in children with learning problems. The most popular is the sex-role stereotype theory. Whereas the brain damage theories represent the extreme version of a biological rationale for learning disabilities, the sex-role theory is the extreme version of a cultural rationale. Yet both positions are based on the same unstated assumption— that everyone is, or should be, essentially the same. According to a cultural model, individuals are socialized into the roles that society requires. We have abundant evidence that this is so from the study of remote cultures, such as the !Kung.

However, it is a completely different issue to apply the evidence on socialization for roles in a culture to a model purporting to explain how people come to have different talents and aptitudes. If learning was entirely a product of the environment and innate ability played no part, then all !Kung men would be great hunters and we would all be like Albert Einstein or Marie Curie.

It requires some extraordinary twists of logic to apply the socialization argument to sex differences in cognitive development. One begins with this general scheme: Boys are socialized to be inattentive, assertive, and independent; hence they will never conform in the classroom and fail to learn. Furthermore, it is not masculine to read. Girls are, by contrast, trained to be docile, passive, conscientious, and do everything the teacher asks. Thus their reading skills are more advanced. However, in junior high school, this reasoning begins to break down. If it did not, boys would be found to have trouble in all school subjects, including mathematics, and girls would not. Therefore, the scenario is changed. It is now *precisely* the boy's independence of mind and ambitiousness that fosters mathematical aptitude (although this correlation has never been demonstrated), and the female's passivity—precisely the quality that earned her earlier success—that suddenly predisposes her to fail. Furthermore, society expects males to be good at math (reasons unstated) and girls to be bad (again, reasons unstated), but conveys the opposite dictum about reading.

It would be far more parsimonious and practical just to accept the fact that more girls are better at reading, more boys at higher mathematics, and then to begin to find out *why*. A sex-role stereotype hypothesis contains no basic corrective principles other than to ask society to rearrange its stereotypes—something that, as history attests, is very difficult to accomplish.

But there are more convincing arguments against this view than the general outline just presented. Take, for example, the issue of sex-role content in reading primers. Everyone agrees that the sexes should not be portrayed in any stereotyped fashion in classroom material, for what is at issue here is self-esteem and self-confidence. However, when one examines the content of reading primers in the light of sex differences in reading skills, one must confront the fact that despite years of attempts to change the primers, they still represent boys in exciting and interesting pursuits and girls as passive onlookers. From everything we know about learning to read, interest in the reading material itself is a critical factor. Therefore, *most reading primers* are biased toward male success and against females. Yet it is the boys and not the girls who are in difficulty. And boys have been educated in schools for four thousand years, girls for only one hundred. Thus boys' skills are boosted by the social environment, exactly the opposite of what is being claimed. A further problem for the theory is that the remedial reading classes are filled with boys, scarcely a procedure that can be said to discourage or neglect male literacy.

Again, focusing on the early school years, the problem arises concerning how stereotyping can explain hyperactivity in young boys. In fact, male behavior is a very convincing example of the *failure* of socialization. The actual characteristics of the hyperactive pattern are (1) behavior that is totally inappropriate to context (the classroom) and (2) an apparent inability to maintain attention to classroom pursuits. In order to produce this combination of behaviors by socialization, one would have to insist, first, that the child be patently aware of every social context and learn to do the opposite of what was required. Second, the child must also be taught never to pay any attention to an adult.

In reality, as parents of a "hyperactive" child will attest, this is exactly opposite to what they have been trying to do. The fact that boys are consistently punished more than girls for these very behaviors suggests that socialization is not working. Meanwhile, little in the way of instruction for context-appropriate behavior seems necessary for girls. They are neither cajoled nor beaten into conformity. The distinction between the reaction of girls and boys to parental discipline is highlighted in a fascinating study by Robert Hess and Teresa McDevitt at Stanford University.[3] They analyzed the mother's styles of discipline in early childhood through questionnaires and extensive observations. Forty-seven children were followed for nine years. Academic ability was measured by standardized tests on reading readiness, reading, vocabulary, and math given at ages four, five, and twelve years.

Two disciplinary styles had a profound affect on *girls'* performance. Their test scores were strongly and negatively affected by the use of appeals to authority, such as "Do this because I tell you to." On the other hand, their performance was positively affected by a style that required the child to provide verbal explanations, such as "Can you think of the reasons why Mommy wants you to do this?" These influences were as robust at twelve years as they were at four years. In contrast, none of the four major disciplinary styles that mothers typically used, including those based on direct commands or appeals to the consequence of actions, had *any* impact on the boys' test scores. From this finding it appears that boys' school performance is totally immune to female discipline or attempts to "socialize" them. This is not to say that the mother's behavior has no influence on her son's progress in school. There is a strong relationship between the efforts made to teach boys *skills* and their subsequent ability, as will be seen in chapter 5.

If sex-role stereotyping seems a cumbersome theory for the early school years, it becomes totally unwieldy as a hypothesis to explain sex differences that arise later, when children confront higher math. The first problem the theory faces is to explain how girls are "socialized" to be good at addition, subtraction, multiplication, fractions, decimals, and mental arithmetic, but suddenly—overnight, as it were—are poor at algebra and geometry. Additionally, the socialization must be highly specific to algebra, geometry, and all the physical sciences that require higher mathematics, or the theory collapses. Meanwhile, boys who score identically to girls in tests of arithmetic are encouraged to outshine them in higher math. (These are often the very boys who couldn't learn to read or spell.)

Sex-role theorists offer a counterargument that the problem girls have with math has something to do with puberty. According to this view, the phobia arises when girls begin to realize that it is unfeminine to compete with boys, and thus they cease to do so. This point of view falters, however, when one considers how well the girls are doing in all the other subjects where they compete with boys, such as biology, botany, zoology, foreign languages, English composition, drama, art, music, and so forth.

The problem with the sex-role stereotype hypothesis is that it itself is a kind of stereotyping—that is, you must form an idea of how sex roles are stereotyped before you can adhere to the theory. When this approach is applied to learning difficulties it has the additional problem of being guilty of mixing apples and oranges.

Stereotyping, in any extreme version, is unfortunate and dangerous, and carries enormous political implications, not only for men and women, but for races, tribes, and nations. Stereotyping diminishes sensitivity to both commonalities between peoples and to their differences and is a sign of intolerance and bigotry. A powerful stereotype affecting girls states that they should have few academic or occupational ambitions. But social pressures that influence the choice of a career should not be confused with a belief that those social pressures also create differences in ability. Career choice and ability are not the same thing.

THE GLOBAL DEVELOPMENTAL LAG

A more moderate, or middle-of-the-road, biological theory is the developmental lag hypothesis, which states that there is a general maturational lag between males and females, with males retarded by up to as much as two years.[4] This theory is derived from data obtained on *physical* development between the sexes, where males show slower rate of bone growth, a considerably later onset of puberty, and ultimately reach full maturity at a later age. The major problem with the theory is that no one has established any relationship between physical growth and mental growth. In fact, all the evidence we have to date shows that there is *no* relationship. There is no way you can predict from the size of an infant or young child, or even from accelerations in developmental milestones like walking or talking, what his or her subsequent intellectual development will be. The theory also carries an implicit assumption that if you are small for your age or late to mature, you will be delayed intellectually compared to children of the same chronological age, something that everyday classroom experience demonstrates is nonsense.

As it is set up, the theory is vulnerable to disproof; if males can demonstrate only one example of an acceleration in a cognitive skill, it will collapse. This is not to say that there may be developmental differences in *different* abilities between males and females, something for which we now have considerable evidence. Both the points of male precocity and differential intellectual development will be taken up later.

VISUAL PERCEPTUAL DEFICITS

The theory of visual perceptual deficits has been generated specifically to explain reading problems and is not related to broad issues of general learning problems or to sex differences. Though it is a popular theory and seems a plausible explanation for some forms of learning disabilities, in fact there is little evidence to support it. However, since I will argue later that one of the primary difficulties in learning to read is due to auditory and not visual processing deficiencies, I will discuss this theory briefly.

First, one of the more general findings to emerge from studies on primary visual functions and reading problems is that there is no relationship between them. There is also an interesting sex-related effect in vision. Females are found to exhibit significantly more minor visual problems, specifically hyperopia (farsightedness) and myopia (nearsightedness) than males from quite early ages.[5] Optometrists who test students referred because of reading problems report a tendency for myopic children to be better readers and also note that frequently males who are poor readers have excellent eyesight, or visual acuity.[6]

The more common assumption of a visual hypothesis is that some higher-order perceptual deficit retards reading, as young children frequently suffer from letter confusions and also letter reversals in writing. A longitudinal study to examine this issue was carried out by Robert Calfee and his colleagues at Stanford University.[7] They found no relationship between the amount of letter confusions shown by children at five to six years when they were learning to read and their subsequent ability on reading tests. In a comprehensive series of experiments on the relationship between reading and visual perception, Mildred Mason discovered that poor readers, two years behind the norm for their chronological age, are *identical* to good readers in the speed with which they locate letter targets in strings of letters, such as "glkmp." The two groups were also equal in their speed in locating a symbol in a string of unfamiliar symbols, such as "#^@?}+." However, the performance of good readers improved dramatically when they were asked to find a target letter in ordinary English *words*. By contrast, the poor readers' performance was identical in all the conditions, indicating that they processed words and nonwords in exactly the same fashion.[8] What is clear from this research is the fact that the poor readers have no difficulty with visual processing of patterns or symbols.[9]

Finally, one does not need to be able to *see* to have reading problems. One of my students, Phyllis Lindamood, carried out a study on blind subjects using a test of phonetic analysis, developed by her parents, called the Lindamood Auditory Conceptualization test (LAC).[10] The LAC test measures the capacity to discriminate and combine phonemes (the smallest segments of speech). Performance on this test is highly correlated to performance on reading tests in students with normal vision. Lindamood found an identical relationship between the LAC and performance on a Braille reading test in a population of thirty blind adults. The blind subjects who were most impaired in learning Braille showed the greatest difficulties in phonetic analysis. Figure 3.1 illustrates the range of scores on the Wide Range Reading Test for the blind subjects divided into two groups scoring above or below the 95 percent level of accuracy on the LAC test. It is remarkable that there is no overlap between these two groups.

In conclusion, there is no evidence that learning problems in otherwise normal children stem from brain damage or from visual problems. Similarly, the sex differences that emerge in these

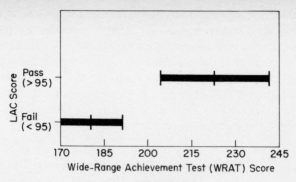

FIGURE 3.1

Blind subjects were divided into pass and fail groups on the Lindamood Auditory Conceptualization test (LAC). The bars indicate the range of scores for these groups on the Wide-Range Achievement Test (WRAT) in reading for Braille. A high score is superior.

populations cannot be explained by either a sex-role stereotype hypothesis or a model based on a global developmental lag. In fact, in the remainder of this volume I review the evidence to show that not only have these theories failed to find support, but they have been contradicted over and over again by the data.

Next we turn to the more promising theories. These theories have been derived inductively, following an analysis of a large body of experimental results. As such they are in sharp contrast to the deductive theories just presented, which were formulated *prior* to research and continue to guide research in spite of the fact that they are continually disconfirmed. Promising theories in the field of learning disabilities appear much less dramatic and significantly more benign, and hence are less likely to capture the popular imagination.

Promising Theories of Learning Disabilities

The following account of promising theories explaining individual differences in learning focuses largely on sex-differences research for two main reasons. First, the categories of learning disabilities are sex-related. Second, and more important, the literature on sex differences clearly indicates that individual variation in brain organization, cognitive development, sensorimotor skills, and talent or interest is perfectly *normal*. One doesn't have to be brain-damaged or a victim of socialization to be different.

SEX DIFFERENCES IN THE ORGANIZATION OF THE BRAIN

While brain damage theories of learning disabilities fail to be supported by any evidence, this does not mean that different individuals may not have differences in *brain organization*. One of the strongest proponents of this view was Samuel Orton, a neurologist, who carried out pioneering studies on people with severe reading disabilities.[11] Whereas Orton and his followers have not been successful in determining any clearcut differences in characteristics between the brains of normal and delayed readers, current evidence has pointed to structural and hormonal differences in male and female brains. In view of the large sex differences in reading and higher mathematics, such evidence is undoubtedly pertinent.

Since the turn of the century, anatomists have attempted to describe gross structural differences between male and female brains. Apart from a few global effects, such as slight differences in the ratios between certain portions of the brain, these attempts have largely failed.[12] More recent studies have looked in detail at the size of the various cortical areas (the gray matter that forms the brain's outer layer) by measuring the distance between the folds on the surface of the brain. Anatomists have also measured the absolute size (weight and volume) of portions of the hemi-spheres. In all human brains studied, in *both* male and female, the posterior, or rear portion of the left hemisphere, is larger than the right.[13] This combination of a larger posterior left hemisphere coupled with a larger right frontal region is a feature of human brains, and is presumed to represent greater development of language-related and planning skills. Ape brains show no such asymmetries.[14] Once again, studies on gross anatomical divisions revealed no sex-specific effects.

A more likely source of sex differences in the brain are the sex hormones, which are known to regulate brain function. Evidence on mammals ranging from rats to nonhuman primates indicates that several brain regions are particularly influenced by sex hormones. Structures in the brain that regulate complex perceptual and cognitive behavior are known to take up the hormones in great quantities. One such structure, the amygdala of the forebrain, is an area highly sensitive to sex hormones. The amygdala is involved in the regulation of attention and the control of distraction and appears to be critical to the learning process. Sex hormones have also been found in most of the cells along the pathways that relay messages from the sensory organs to the central portions of the brain.[15]

Clinical data on humans with brain lesions suggest that the two hemispheres are organized differently in males and females. The general finding has been that while damage to the left hemisphere in both men and women produces deficits in a variety of language tasks, these deficits are far greater in males than females. This has led some researchers to argue that in the female, language has a greater right-hemisphere involvement than in the male, who reserves his right hemisphere for spatial tasks.[16]

In addition to the common suggestion that females have a greater representation of language in the right hemisphere, a more recent set of studies indicates that males and females appear to possess a different type of neural organization *within* the left hemisphere. Doreen Kimura has reviewed 216 cases of men and women with brain damage and has found that aphasias, or disturbances of language functions, are caused by a wider area of tissue damage in males than in females.[17] Similar findings are reported by Catharine Mateer, working with George Ojemann, who discovered that during stimulation of parts of the brain prior to surgery, it was possible to disrupt language over a wider region of tissue in men than in women.[18]

These studies will be presented in more detail in chapter 6, but taken together, the evidence of the past five years is highly supportive of a model that indicates that females are "buffered," or favored, for language development. It is far more difficult to disrupt language functions in females both because some verbal functions are represented in the right hemisphere of the brain, but also because they have a more efficient organization of neural connections underpinning language on the left side. So far it is not known which brain systems relate to the superior capacity in males for abstract spatial and mathematical reasoning.

SEX DIFFERENCES IN LEARNING

Despite decades of research on intellectual development, the definitive account of each particular aptitude–across the entire age range has yet to emerge. One of the problems has been the failure to consider sex differences, leading to considerable confusion concerning the time course for each emerging skill. Deborah Waber has pointed out that we have failed not only to consider the sex of the subjects as an important variable, but also to chart the maturation of each particular type of ability well into adulthood.[19] Thus we know very little about if, or when, these abilities begin to plateau. This is particularly important as it is not at all clear, with the current set of data, whether males are "lagging" in language skills or whether they simply never catch up.

The global lag theory formulated to explain the slower development of language skills in males in early school years cannot be maintained. The crucial evidence against this theory comes from a number of studies, including my own, that have demonstrated young males' superiority for three-dimensional problem solving. These studies will be reviewed in chapter 8. In order to maintain a global lag model, one would have to infer that, since males score approximately one year in advance of females from the age of four years, their ability is even *more* remarkable. That is, if they were lagging by two years to begin with, then their acceleration in spatial problem solving would put them three years ahead of girls.

It seems more productive, given the current data and the imprecision in defining criteria for many learning skills, to assume that different skills develop at different rates for boys and for girls. Some of these developmental progressions have been reasonably well charted—in particular, sex differences in early language development. In the following chapters, the details of the developmental aspects of sex differences in learning will be presented whenever possible.

SENSORIMOTOR INTEGRATION

One theory that has had support from research in psychology is that higher intellectual functions develop from more primitive sensory and motor functions, which combine to create new modes of thinking. Jean Piaget was one of the earliest proponents of this type of model.[20] This theory seems particularly pertinent to the study of sex differences and differences in what has come to be called "cognitive style."

As children develop and begin to be able to predict events in the world, they learn to integrate their sensory perception of patterns in the environment with their own behavior. And they discover, for example, that certain behavior can alter the environment, including even sensory input. A smashed toy is changed not only in function but in how it looks. Babbling is a product of the motor systems used in speech that also creates audible noise.

Smashing toys, running, falling, throwing, jumping, and many exploratory behaviors are produced by the extrapyramidal motor system, or the gross-motor system, which regulates action by means of large muscle units. Generating speech sounds, singing, playing the piano, drawing, and writing are the outcomes of action mediated by the pyramidal, or fine-motor, system. In the course of early development boys are more biased to use gross-motor action and girls toward using the fine-motor systems.[21]

As it is known that cerebral development depends on sensori-motor development, one possible explanation for a sex difference in cortical organization is that in males large muscles account for approximately 40 percent of total body weight, and the brain is either organized initially to program these large muscle units or becomes programmed to do so over time. Recent evidence from Robert Martin's laboratory at University College, London, indicates that the absolute brain-weight difference between the sexes is established by age five (130 grams heavier in males), even though body weight is identical at this age. It is as if the brain "knows" that boys' bodies will grow at another stage.[22]

In females, large muscle represents only 23 percent of total body weight. Thus females' brains would be expected to have more of the cells in the brain devoted to the fine-muscle system. A further distinction is that males frequently engage in a type of robust gross-motor play called "rough-and-tumble play" that is less common in females. In fact, this form of mock combat among males is nearly universal in all higher mammals. Rough-and-tumble play is thought to be a rehearsal for combat in real-life situations and later plays a role in establishing male dominance systems.[23]

Whatever conclusions are reached concerning the brain organization subserving these different types of motor behaviors, it is generally true that males have greater control over whole-body movement in strength, accuracy, and speed, even in early childhood. It also appears that gross-motor control becomes primarily integrated with the sensory input to the *visual* system and from the sense organs relaying the position of the limbs in space, leading to a remarkable efficiency in visuomotor integration. In the male this is developed to a high degree, as demonstrated by particular aptitude for accurate judgment of objects in motion and the timing of muscular reactions. This gives males an edge in all sports where not only strength but *speed* is of the essence. (It may also explain why more males than females have become fascinated by video games.)

The function of fine-motor control as it is revealed in action is the regulation of midline and distal muscles and appears to involve fluency between successive movements. (At least that is the characteristic of all fine-motor behaviors such as speech, singing, and digital coordination.) Because the fine-motor system is intimately connected with the midline speech structures such as vocal cords, tongue, and palate, the feedback from these systems arrive at the ear and not the eye. This means that a primary integration takes place between the auditory channels and the pyramidal motor system. Thus one possible explanation for female excellence in linguistic abilities stems from the precision that develops in this integrative process. So far all data on sex differences in either auditory sequencing ability, such as speech production and perception, or fine-motor fluency, show females accelerated throughout childhood and superior even into old age.

For a visuomotor learner, knowledge about the world is acquired most rapidly by coming to grips with it at firsthand, by manipulating objects and watching the outcome. For many males the hands become extensions of the eye. With experience, this sensorimotor process becomes integrated into a complex three-dimensional schema, in which problems can be solved by imagining object properties in the mind, without the need to explore. It is important to remember that in many males learning proceeds in this hands-on exploratory fashion for quite an extended period, well into the time when they are expected to sit still and *listen* to the teacher.

People with highly developed auditory fine-motor skills will be more inclined to learn about the world at "secondhand," that is, through linguistic channels, to ask more questions and accept more answers without having to discover them directly through overt action. Because they have good language comprehension, such people are much more amenable to being taught, especially if the learning situation is geared to explanation rather than exploration.[24]

A QUESTION OF INTEREST

There is no generally accepted psychological theory to explain why people become interested in one thing rather than another. Why are you reading this book, for example? Neuropsychologist Karl Pribram has suggested that interest derives from the rewards (reinforcement) produced by one's actions, and goes on to point out that not just *any* action can be reinforced in this manner.[25] A young child is praised for taking his or her first steps, uttering the first intelligible babble, and various behaviors that rapidly become automatic, but praising a normal adult for these same behaviors would be absurd.

Therefore, another concept besides reinforcement needs to be invoked, and this Pribram calls "competence." Behavior can be rewarding when, in and of itself, it exceeds a *known* level of competence. When this occurs we are *interested*; that is, interest arises when one's actions (or thoughts) exceed one's expected competence. Conversely, one is bored at any task where competency is not challenged, or frustrated by any task for which one's competency is inadequate.

When you take children who are predisposed to learn about the world of objects (more often male) and ask them to listen to people talk, they will disappoint you, because they are not *interested* (competent) in gathering much information from this activity. On the other hand, children who are predisposed to learn about the world through talk (more often female) become *interested* in

49

people, because people have something to impart. Furthermore, there is a biological relevance to being interested in the behavior, verbal or otherwise, of other people if you are the sex that gives birth to offspring.

Interest in objects can lead to interest in the descriptions of object relations in time and space (higher mathematics). Interest in people rather than objects makes these exercises appear to be meaningless. The primary question many girls would like to ask when they are introduced to algebra and geometry is: What does it *mean*? This is the question most difficult to ask and most difficult to answer.

I have not included a more moderate theory of socialization to account for the sex effects in learning difficulties, not because I believe that cultural or social factors play no part in the learning process, but rather because I believe this type of theory cannot explain the consistency of the sex differences in ability throughout many cultures of the world, as revealed by psychological tests.

The greatest influence of society is on values, rather than on specific individual behavioral differences. Our culture, like many others, values males more than females, but it also places an extremely high premium on literacy. It is fortunate that females excel in this realm, or else there would be more prejudice against female intellectual aptitude than currently exists. Despite all the machinery set in motion to improve male ability, girls are still ahead. Would this machinery have been introduced if the males were accelerated in reading?

To date, there are few remedial classes in higher mathematics. Furthermore, the bulk of research on female "math phobia" has focused most often on socialization and attitudes and rarely on remediation. Equally, we have ignored the possibility of *biologically* rooted predispositions in students who show exceptional talent in higher math and the physical sciences. These innate abilities would be expected to promote superior strategies in math problem solving, yet there are few studies on these strategies and virtually no research on the influence of early training on subsequent aptitude in higher mathematics. There are few elementary-school programs for developing skills that might become useful in algebra and geometry.

In the following chapters I take up each type of learning problem in more detail and compare the evidence from studies on learning to the evidence from research on sex differences. There is a striking relationship between the two sets of data. These chapters present a detailed assessment of a large body of research. The same points could be made without such an intensive analysis. However, the fact that the evidence goes *against* popular opinion and supports less popular theories makes this approach essential.

PART II

Unraveling
the Evidence

4

Reading: The Ear Determines What the Eye Sees

During the past twenty years our understanding of the reading process has expanded enormously. In part this is due to what has been called a "cognitive revolution" in psychology that began in the late 1950s. The revolution was produced by innovations in methodology involving new statistical tools and more sophisticated research strategies, many borrowed from research on the rapidly developing "information processing" technology. In tandem with these new developments was a growing dissatisfaction not only with behaviorism, but also with the body of research on the nature of human intelligence. For nearly a century, psychologists had generated batteries of tests such as intelligence scales, achievement tests, and personality inventories, but only a few had questioned the assumptions behind them. Did they really measure what everyone believed they measured? Although the best of these tests could provide a rough guidepost to future academic performance, no one knew why. And, when they were employed as predictors for any specific learning skill such as early reading success, the tests were largely useless. It became obvious that though these tests were measuring *something* important, they were too coarse-grained. The test items confounded too many perceptual, motor, and cognitive elements for anyone to be able to discover which were critical and which were irrelevant.

The new approach began by questioning old assumptions and led to the development of considerable refinement in research methods. Psychologists were now able to break down complex tasks such as reading, into their component parts. From these efforts it has been possible to discover the primary units required for analysis of human performance. There were often surprises, such as the discovery that the basic unit of speech perception and production is *not* the finest discriminable sound (the phoneme) but the syllable. However, when these same techniques were applied to reading, they revealed that not only was phonemic analysis crucial but that additional and independent skills were equally important.

Before these discoveries, most people believed that reading was a straightforward process in which a student merely had to learn to associate a set of sounds with a set of visual symbols. Failure to do so indicated that the child was stupid, or couldn't memorize, or was just plain lazy. The solution to reading failure was simply more and more drill ("more of the same only slower"). This is not to say that many educators needed psychologists to point out what is involved in learning to read. There has never been a shortage of voices crying in the wilderness, especially the voices of classroom teachers. Maria Montessori was one such person, and other great teachers who have been involved in remediation include Anna Gillingham, Bessie Stillman, Margaret Rawson, Pat and Charles Lindamood, and many more.[1] Yet over the years only a select few have heeded these voices. Often their work did not appeal to the general educational community because what they claimed was counterintuitive, as, for example, their unanimous insistence that reading is more related to hearing than to seeing. Similarly, all these talented teachers discovered that effective remediation techniques require the integration of multiple sensory and motor tasks. It is only in the past two years that research on the brain has revealed the neural basis for this insight.

One of the reasons why these methods have not been generally adopted is that teachers rarely, if ever, carry out controlled experiments. This means that the success of a particular reading program can always be attributed to some idiosyncracy such as the special talent of a particular teacher. And quite apart from this, how can one evaluate the different claims? If method A is just as successful as method B, or appears to fail in the hands of teacher X, who is to be the judge? It is precisely in resolving this type of dilemma that the scientific method is so powerful, and at last, after decades of research on reading, the answers are beginning to come in.

Following is a survey of the more recent research on reading failure, including a detailed account of the critical skills involved in reading. In the next chapter, the sex differences in these same abilities are reviewed. There is a striking similarity between the two sets of data—in almost every case, the particular skills involved in learning to read are the same skills in which females have the edge.

What Is Reading?

Reading is more than just learning to match twenty-six letters to their corresponding sounds. It is a complex set of operations involving the visual and auditory senses, knowledge of a spoken language, memory, and motor skills. At each level, from sensory to linguistic to motor, there are a series of transformations, or recodings carried out by the brain, ranging from the simple to the complex. At the most basic level, a child has to remember the visual appearance of each letter. Some of these letters are difficult to tell apart, such as *d* and *b*, *m* and *w*, and *p* and *q*. Once the symbols are mastered, the next task is to memorize each letter name and its corresponding sound or phoneme. But in order for this to be possible a child must be able to discriminate phonemically, that is, to be able to *hear* the difference between "g" and "k" or "t" and "d," as well as to be able to produce these sounds in speech. When phonemes are combined into syllables, short-term memory comes into play. Short-term memory allows us to remember a series of items in the correct temporal sequence, such as distinguishing "fa-mi-ly" from "fa-ly-mi." A familiar example is the word "nuclear," which often is mispronounced: "nucular."

Short-term memory deteriorates rapidly over time and is particularly disrupted by interference from any distracting stimulation. This means that the *speed* at which each individual item can be decoded is extremely important.

So far we have only reached the level of the word. When words can be decoded fluently, the reader needs to call upon his or her knowledge of the language. A child must be able to anticipate the structure of sentences on the basis of grammatical rules and to determine the meaning from the context of the story. The capacity to be able to utter grammatically correct sentences and to comprehend the meaning of spoken language is essential to this process. Therefore it is not surprising that in learning to read, difficulties can arise anywhere along the route. What is surprising is that it has taken researchers over eighty years since Montessori's pioneering efforts at the turn of the century to be able to specify the reading process in all its complexity and to devise tests to pinpoint adequately each child's particular deficiencies.

It is now generally acknowledged that the two earliest stages involved in the reading process, visual discrimination and learning letter names, seldom cause problems in learning to read. There are few children with either of these problems, and they rapidly outgrow difficulties with these tasks. The evidence on this issue was discussed in chapter 3. While for a few children problems begin when learning sound/letter correspondences, for the majority, the major stumbling block occurs at the stage where syllables are decoded into phonemes or where phonemes must be combined into syllables.

Phonemic decoding and encoding is the central problem in the mastery of any phonetic writing system. For a long time it was believed that students of English had a far worse time than students of languages with fewer complex vowel sounds, such as Italian, Spanish, and German. In addition, English spelling, or orthography, contains a large number of irregularities, and problems in learning to read were often attributed to these idiosyncracies. This led some educators to believe that it might be easier to learn whole words (the "look-say" approach). After many years of using this technique, more problems were created than were solved. Although students of English might need to learn a slightly larger set of rules than is necessary in other languages, adopting a system based on phonetic and orthographic rules is far more efficient than memorizing each word separately.[2] But even more important, for the past ten years evidence has been accumulating that reading problems are less related to orthography than to auditory perception, specifically the ability to decode *speech* sounds.

In brief, current studies comparing children with and without reading disorders have demonstrated that there are at least two major principles involved: success in learning to read and write is highly dependent on linguistic competence, especially analysis of speech sounds, fluent production, and verbal comprehension, and second, on short-term memory for temporal sequences. These two major dimensions are comprised of six categories of skills: (1) phoneme/syllable decoding, (2) phonological coding, (3) naming fluency, (4) short-term memory, (5) fine-motor fluency, and (6) language comprehension.

PHONEME/SYLLABLE DECODING

In a study investigating the relationship of phonemic decoding to reading aptitude, Charles and Pat Lindamood and Robert Calfee at Stanford University tested 660 children aged five to eleven years with the Auditory Conceptualization Test, which was devised by the Lindamoods.[3] In this test the child is asked to assign letter sounds to colored blocks and to arrange the blocks in various sequences. Part 1 of the test involves simple one-to-one matches between each sound and a different colored block. (This identifies those people who have severe auditory or language problems, and almost everyone does well on this part.) However, part 2, which requires the subject to combine sounds using the blocks, is particularly discerning in identifying reading-delayed children (and adults). For example, a child may be asked to assign the phonemes "a," "s," and "p," to three blocks of different colors ("a" = red, "s" = green, "p" = blue) and arrange them in the order just given. Next the child will be asked to rearrange the blocks in a different order: "If that is 'asp,' show me, 'sap.' " Poor readers of all ages generally fail this part of the test. As this test only requires the child to remember phonemes assigned to colored blocks, there can be no doubt that the deficit is specific to *auditory decoding* and not to problems with the English alphabet.[4] The Lindamoods' techniques will be taken up in considerable detail in chapter 11.

II / Unraveling the Evidence

Research from the Haskins Laboratory at the University of Connecticut has also been directed to the question of how speech is perceived by the listener. As part of this project, Isobel Liberman has been studying the development of children's capacity to decode speech sounds. She has found a strong developmental progression first in the ability to segment words into syllables, followed somewhat later by the ability to segment syllables into phonemes. She studied this progression in four- to six-year-olds. Only 50 percent of the four- and five-year-olds could segment words by syllable, whereas 90 percent of the six-year-olds could do so. Phonemic segmenting was much more difficult and was impossible for the four-year-olds. Only 17 percent of the five-year-olds, as opposed to 70 percent of the six-year-olds, could segment by phoneme. Liberman attributed this dramatic increase in efficiency to development and to learning. What is important about these results is the knowledge that the ability to segment by phoneme is not automatic; it must be taught. In two separate follow-up studies, it was found that children's ability to segment speech sounds at four and five years of age was highly related to their subsequent success in learning to read.[5]

The results of these and other studies show that one of the major distinctions between good and poor readers is a general facility in the production and perception of speech. Often it has been found that children who have delays in language development are also slow to learn to read. Paula Tallal and her associates at the University of California in San Diego have studied children who had been referred because of poor speech.[6] They discovered that one of the most discerning tests to pinpoint the origin of the language problem is one involving speech discrimination. When two syllables, such as "be" and "bi" (ba-by), were presented in rapid succession (less than 500 milliseconds apart), the language-delayed children often reported the sequence in the reverse order. When the rate was slowed down to 500 milliseconds or greater, the same children had no difficulty with this task. (Normal children had no problems at either speed.) These results indicate that the reason for the language delay is perceptual and that speech problems are related to an inability to perceive the temporal order of speech sounds. The problem is similar to trying to follow a conversation in a foreign language when the person is speaking too quickly. In this situation we become acutely aware of the time and effort it takes to decode speech, especially unfamiliar sounds. When the scores on the speech perception test were compared to performance on a standard reading achievement test, there was a high positive relationship between them. In another set of studies, Paula Tallal and Rachael Stark separated children who had difficulties in learning to read into two groups, those with and without language problems.[7] They found that the poor readers with normal language development still had difficulties in discriminating between certain vowels, such as "dab" and "daeb," and in categorizing consonants.

Tallal believes that the language system of the brain is specialized to process what she describes as "the rate of change" of acoustic material and not phonemes per se. This means that the left hemisphere is specialized to handle very rapid transitions in sounds. Adults with brain damage who fail to comprehend speech sounds can understand speech perfectly well when it has been grossly slowed down.

PHONOLOGICAL CODING

Phonological coding is related to phonemic and syllable segmenting but refers more generally to a sensitivity to the tonal aspects of language. This sensitivity involves a special type of memory, called "echoic memory," in which sounds are held temporarily for processing. When children play with words, they are using the immediate "echo" of the sound they just produced. Wordplay in children involves alliteration or rhyme, whereby either the sound of the initial consonant or the carrier vowel is matched by a similar sound, a homophone. Children who are well versed in this type of play learn to translate letters or words to sounds almost automatically. In turn, they acquire reading skills more rapidly than poor readers who concentrate on the visual appearance of the letters.

Sensitivity to linguistic sounds, whether spoken or written, produces confusion if people are asked to remember lists of words that sound alike. For example, R. Conrad and A. J. Hull, two English psychologists, demonstrated years ago that items that sound highly similar are more difficult to remember than ones that sound distinct.[8] For example, read this sequence of letters:

BTGVPD. Now close your eyes and say the letters out loud. Next, try this: KYQFXR.

Isobel Liberman reasoned that if good readers automatically decoded letters and words into sounds (in addition to meaning), they should be more confused than poor readers by letters or words that were similar phonologically. In other words, good readers would be more disrupted when they had to remember items that rhymed.[9] Liberman and her coworkers conducted a series of experiments in which five- to seven-year-old children had to remember lists of items such as letters, words, or sentences. She tested good, average, and poor readers. The good readers were better than the other groups on all lists where the items *did not rhyme*. However, when the performance of the three groups on rhyming items was scored, the good readers had declined noticeably in their performance in comparison to the other two groups. It did not matter whether the items were letters, words, or sentences, presented to the ear or to the eye, the interference produced by rhyming was considerably greater for the good readers. What is especially interesting about these results is that poor readers had nearly identical scores for the lists of rhyming and nonrhyming words or sentences, showing that they were almost totally unaffected by phonological similarity. These findings are illustrated in figure 4.1, where good and poor readers are compared.

English psychologist Alan Baddeley has suggested that there are two phonological codes, one that is purely sensory and engages echoic memory, and a second "articulatory loop" that has motor involvement and is essential to verbal short-term memory.[10] When learning to read, a student has to sound out a series of phonemes using the fine-motor muscles involved in speech. These patterns of articulation must then be held in sequence until the word is finally retrieved or recognized. This is true even in experienced readers who no longer have to vocalize out loud when they read. Baddeley's research has shown that when you prevent silent articulation even in college students, the ability to detect errors in passages of prose declines. Liberman's results suggest that both codes are operating in the good reader, first by entering items into a phonological (echoic) store and second by rehearsal in short-term memory via an articulatory loop.

In an extensive longitudinal project based upon Liberman's

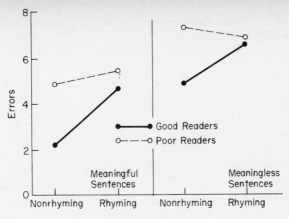

FIGURE 4.1

A comparison of good and poor readers on memory for sentences containing words that did or did not rhyme. The results for remembering meaningful sentences are shown in the left panel. Memory for meaningless sentences is shown on the right.

SOURCE: From V. A. Mann; I. Y. Liberman; D. Shankweiler, "Children's Memory for Sentences and Word Strings in Relation to Reading Ability," *Memory and Cognition* 8 (1980):329–35. Reprinted with permission of the authors and the Psychonomic Society.

approach, two British psychologists, L. Bradley and Peter Bryant, tested 118 four-year-old and 285 five-year-old children, none of whom could read.[11] They asked the children to listen to lists of three or four words. In each group of words, all but one word had a sound in common in the first, middle, or last position, such as pig, pin, hill; bun, bus, rug; or doll, hop, top. The task was to pick out the odd man out. Memory and IQ were also measured. Three years later the same children were tested on the Schonell reading and spelling tests and the Neale reading test. There was a strong relationship between the performance on the sound categorization test and reading and spelling scores, even with memory and IQ controlled. In addition, the authors set up a training program for one group of children to foster skills in categorizing sounds on the basis of phonological similarity. After two years in this program the children were four months ahead of children in ordinary classrooms. A second group of children was trained in the same way but was also trained to relate the sounds to the shapes of plastic letters. After two years these children were over twelve months advanced in reading, while their spelling scores were an astonishing twenty-three months ahead!

NAMING FLUENCY

Naming is the ability to translate the visual image of an object into its verbal label. Reading skill depends on the speed, or fluency, with which this translation takes place. This is determined both by the time it takes to search through memory for the appropriate sound match to the letters and to the fluency of the motor output, or articulation. A number of experiments have shown that poor readers are slower in tasks requiring the rapid naming of items. It does not appear to make much difference whether the items are pictures, colors, or letters. For example, Martha Denckla and Rita Rudel tested good and poor readers on the time it took to name lists of pictures of objects, colors, letters, or digits.[12] On the color-naming test alone, it was possible to identify 70 percent of the poor readers. These results confirm earlier work suggesting that performance on letter and picture-naming tasks were the best predictors for reading failure. In a test of children of different ages, Carl Spring and Carolyn Capps found that naming speed for digits, colors, and pictures improved with age, but that even the youngest good readers (aged seven to ten years) were superior (faster) to the *oldest* poor readers (aged twelve to thirteen years).[13] This is a dramatic demonstration of the importance of fluent naming skills for success in reading.

SHORT-TERM MEMORY

We have already touched on one of the short-term memory tasks involved in learning to read, articulatory rehearsal. A fundamental question is whether or not short-term memory is independent of the type of items that are held in memory. This question has been answered in a series of tests carried out by Tallal and Stark.[14] They studied good and poor readers aged seven to nine years who had completely equal language development. Both groups of children had identical scores in verbal IQ as well as in tests of expressive and receptive language, showing they could produce and comprehend speech equally well. Despite their normal ability in language, the poor readers were approximately three years behind in reading grade level.

The children were tested on a very large battery of items. The major difference between the two groups was in the short-term serial memory tests. Poor readers were significantly worse in tests of visual-verbal memory (remembering a sequence of letters), nonverbal auditory memory (remembering a series of tones in the correct sequence), and nonverbal cross-modal memory (remembering a sequence of items presented visually and matching that to an auditory sequence). As the last two of these tests are unrelated to verbal skills or articulation, it can be concluded that some poor readers have particular difficulty with temporal organization in auditory memory as well as in translating between auditory and visual sensory information.

Despite the fact that the poor readers had a very large deficit in these memory tasks, their performance on the *visual* short-term memory task, in which they had to remember a series of patterns in the correct order, was completely within the normal range. The fact that no differences were found between the two groups in nonverbal visual memory adds further support to the conclusion that poor readers have no difficulty in processing or remembering visual information (see chapter 3).

When short-term memory is tested over time on a series of highly similar items, performance begins to decline. This effect has been called proactive interference, which means that after hearing or seeing the same type of material over and over again, it becomes increasingly difficult to remember it. Psychologists have discovered that if there is a sudden change in either the category of the items (changing from remembering lists of furniture to lists of plants), or the modality, such as changing from a visual to an auditory presentation, performance will instantly return to near the original level. This effect is called release from proactive inhibition.

Sylvia Farnham-Diggory and Lee Gregg studied this effect in good and poor readers using forty lists of four-letter sequences presented either to the eye or the ear.[15] At the end of each series, the modality was switched. At the beginning of the test, the results were similar for the two groups. Both began with accurate performances, which declined over trials to about 65 percent accuracy. However, when the modality was switched, the good readers rebounded to their initial levels of performance, whereas the poor readers either scarcely improved or actually got worse. These differences between the groups are illustrated in figure 4.2. What this suggests is that poor readers find it difficult to shift from one sensory mode to another, an ability essential in reading. It appears

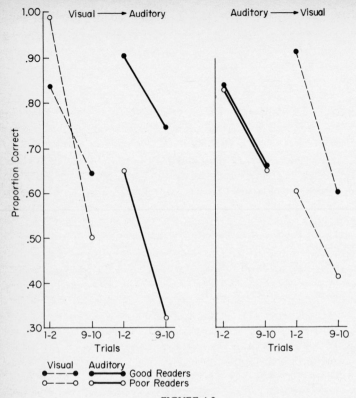

FIGURE 4.2

A comparison of good and poor readers on their ability to remember strings of four letters. Memory scores for the first and last two trials of the visual or auditory presentations are shown on the left side of each panel. Memory scores after the modality was switched are shown on the right side of each panel.

SOURCE: From S. Farnham-Diggory and Lee Gregg, "Short-term Memory Function in Young Readers," *Journal of Experimental Child Psychology* 19 (1975):279–98. Reprinted with permission of the author and of Academic Press.

that once engaged in either a visual or an auditory mode, poor readers seem locked into that particular mode.

An equally interesting finding from the same experiment was that poor readers scored 100 percent for the first two trial blocks when they began with material presented in the *visual* mode. This score was well above that of the good readers, who scored an average of 84 percent. This not only indicates that there is nothing wrong with visual processing of poor readers, but that their highly efficient visual skills may produce a bias that may be a handicap in learning to read.

FINE-MOTOR FLUENCY

Fine-motor fluency is the capacity to perform rapid sequences of movements, especially with the parts of the body controlled by the fine-motor nerves—fingers, toes, vocal cords, and tongue. We have already seen that rapid naming is important to reading skills. What has only recently been discovered is that control over the fingers and hands is also related to reading. For example, Nathlie Badian discovered that drawing ability was highly related to reading performance,[16] and Shelley Smith reported that one of the key predictors of reading failure was poor performance on a pegboard task in which pegs have to be shifted to different holes as rapidly as possible.[17] These results suggest that part of the naming fluency effect may be due to the ability to perform a series of rapid movements in sequence, specifically those involving the fine-motor system.

LANGUAGE COMPREHENSION

Last, other studies have reported that language comprehension, the ability to determine meaning from speech, is a critical factor in reading fluency. E. O. Jarvis tested 183 seven-year-olds on various tests, such as digit span (a short-term memory test), auditory discrimination, and verbal comprehension. The strongest predictor of scores on three reading achievement tests was verbal comprehension.[18] This same effect was reported by Mark Jackson and James McClelland in a study on college students. They report that apart from naming speed, the most critical factor in the student's reading skills was comprehension of spoken language.[19]

How the Skills Combine

At this time we do not know how these six categories are related. It is possible that each of the highly discriminating tests just described is but one cog in a complex of aptitudes involved in "language." There have been only a few attempts to relate these tests in any systematic fashion, and some of these will be described. The methodology relies on the use of various forms of correlational statistics. Correlational analyses help to determine whether apparently different types of tests carried out on the same subjects are related. Well-known examples of strong correlations are those between the amount of food consumed and a person's weight, or between the speed of a vehicle and the time it takes for it to arrive at a destination. If naming speed was found to be correlated to phoneme discrimination, then the two measures may share some common neurological mechanism.

Using the data that had been collected by Isobel Liberman, as well as new data on approximately one hundred more children, Benita Blachman studied the relationship between the ability to segment words into syllables and phonemes, the ability to produce rhymes, and performance on rapid naming tests.[20] She found that segmenting and rhyming were moderately related to one another, but that naming speed was unrelated to either of these abilities. This was true for both kindergartners and first-grade children. The best predictors of reading success for the kindergartners was their combined score on the rhyming test and a test on the rapid naming of colors. By age six the best predictors were phoneme segmenting and rapid naming of colors and letters. In fact, phoneme segmenting and rapid naming together could predict the rank order of the first-grade pupils in reading achievement with 68 percent accuracy. When short-term memory tests were added, the prediction rate rose to 74 percent. This fact indicates that short-term memory is an additional and independent, or unrelated, component to the other factors.

Shelley Smith has been studying families who have a history of reading disorders. Using a complex battery of tests, she discovered that four tests were particularly discriminating in sorting the reading-delayed groups from their normal controls. Each of these four tests—auditory discrimination of phonemes, auditory short-term memory (digit span), naming speed, and speed on the pegboard task (fine-motor fluency)—was relatively independent or unrelated. Although performance on these four tasks could separate nearly all of the good and poor readers, the accuracy of classification improved when tests of visuoperceptual organization and visual memory were added. But the relationship here was reversed, with the severity of the reading problem correlating with *superiority* on tests of visuospatial tasks.[21] This is further indication that some poor readers are strongly biased toward the visual mode. The evidence is now very strong that a tendency to favor the visual mode at the expense of the auditory-linguistic mode can interfere with learning to read.

In one of the most comprehensive programs to date, Badian tested 180 children aged four years nine months on the Holbrook Screening Battery, which consists of fifteen different tasks.[22] Several of the items in the battery are borrowed from the Wechsler Preschool and Primary Scale of Intelligence, or WPPSI. Badian followed these children through to the end of the third grade, testing them each year on the Stanford Reading Achievement test. The best predictors of reading ability in order of importance were, for the first grade: letter naming, name writing, WPPSI information (verbal report and verbal expression), and WPPSI sentences (auditory comprehension). In the second grade the best initial predictors were: WPPSI information and counting (verbal report and rote memory). By the third grade, exactly four years from the initial testing, the following group of tests could predict the good and poor readers with 92 percent accuracy: WPPSI information, counting, draw-a-person, WPPSI sentences, and naming letters. When Badian analyzed her data further to uncover the major relationships among all of the tests, she found that they clustered on two major factors. One, primarily a verbal factor, included the WPPSI tests as well as auditory association and verbal expression, and the second was a fine-motor fluency factor and included the drawing and naming tasks.

In conclusion, although these comparisons have been made using different types of test materials in different laboratories in different parts of the country, the results point in the same direction. It is clear that visual processing has little to do with reading, and in fact a strong reliance on the visual mode is often antagonistic to progress in learning to read. Of primary importance, as shown in almost every study, is the ability to discriminate speech sounds at a very fine level of detail and to produce speech accurately and fluently. Serial short-term memory appears to be independent of the purely linguistic tasks, as some poor readers show deficits in serial memory for tones and lights. Naming fluency seems more related to a general motor fluency than to decoding or retrieval skills. The fact that naming fluency is related to drawing is interesting. While one might also predict a similar relationship between the performance on the pegboard task and naming speed, Shelley Smith found that these two tasks were unrelated. Until there are more comparisons of the type outlined here, the six major categories of skills important in reading discussed in this chapter will have to stand as independent or unrelated abilities.

Badian's tests were successful in screening out those children who had trouble learning to read. Eighty-three percent were boys. All of the dyslexics in Smith's family study were male. Even when female family members had below-normal reading scores, those of the males were considerably worse.

So far the research provides no way of determining which test results are specific to children with reading problems as opposed to those specific to males. If it is *normal* for many boys to have problems in learning to read, then we are quite in error in labeling these boys "retarded" or "disabled." Because most of the research just outlined has not been designed to examine sex differences, these findings must be compared to a data base where sex differences have been the focus of interest.

5

Sex Differences in Reading–Related Skills

Sex and Cognition

The cognitive revolution in psychology has made it possible to unravel the mystery of how children learn to read. The cognitive approach is equally powerful in helping us understand how and why males and females develop different types of cognitive abilities. However, because cognition is often confused with intelligence, these sex differences in cognitive ability have often been taken as an indication that the sexes differ in basic intelligence. This confusion is understandable because the terms "cognition" and "intelligence" are related in meaning. In fact, "cognition" is defined as an "intellectual process by which knowledge is gained." The word "process" provides the clue to the critical distinction between the two terms. Intelligence is a faculty, something that individuals possess to a greater or lesser degree; cognition is something that one does. An example will highlight this distinction. We can say that George is more intelligent than Harold because he has a greater mental capacity to reason and tends to employ more efficient strategies to solve problems. On the other hand, we cannot say that George is more *cognitive* than Harold. The adjective "intelligence" can be applied to a person, but the adjective "cognitive" only to a process. This process can involve a number of different aptitudes.

For instance, chimpanzees are very adept at fishing for termites. Termite fishing, like most cognitive acts, requires a combination of several skills. First, the chimpanzee must be able to distinguish termite nests from other similar-looking objects (discrimination). Second, the chimpanzee must have knowledge about termite behavior; it must know, for example, that termites will cling to sticks of wood (inference). Third, the chimp must devise a means of using the natural behavior of termites to reach the desired goal (insight), and last, the chimp must achieve the goal by creating a tool (invention). Chimpanzee mothers transmit this learned behavior to their offspring by intentionally modeling the correct behavior (communication).[1] The success of this operation is a measure of intelligence, and if we wanted to establish an intelligence test for chimpanzees in the wild, termite fishing would be a good candidate for one of the subtests. But on the basis of a single score we would never know whether the chimps who did badly did so because they couldn't tell termites nests from other nests, or whether they were too clumsy to construct their "fishing rod," or whether they were just too "stupid" to even begin to tackle the problem in the first place.

All intelligence tests suffer from precisely this kind of problem. As we saw in chapter 1, intelligence tests for humans were designed to eliminate sex differences in the total score. This was accomplished by balancing the various subtests so that each sex performs similarly when the scores are added together. Yet quite minor changes in test construction would produce dramatic differences between the apparent intelligence of males and females. If block design and object assembly subtests (measures of visuospatial skills) were removed, girls would instantly become more "intelligent." They would appear quite remarkably brilliant if, in addition, tests of verbal memory were added. On the other hand, if tests of coding speed (the digit symbol substitution test) were removed, boys would appear more "intelligent." These examples highlight the reason why the definition of "intelligence" has long defied psychologists, and why the study of cognitive abilities, with its emphasis on complexity and process, has become more popular and productive.

It will never be possible to determine whether one sex is more intelligent than the other. In fact, this is the wrong question to ask, because the answer will always depend on how intelligence is measured. This leads us to a first principle of the nature of sex differences: The sexes do not differ in intelligence but only in the choice of "tools" they employ to solve problems and in the type of problems they choose to solve.

By and large, the evidence suggests that the most characteristic differences between the sexes are in perceptual and motor abilities. These will determine how attention is paid to the environment and the types of actions that are successful. In general, I believe that biases exist inherently from birth; while both the environment and social factors shape a person's development, the element of choice still plays a role. Individuals will have a preferred mode of processing information or a preferred strategy for solving problems. However, it is important to recognize that biological biases are not immutable. The brain, initially plastic, organizes with experience. The impact of the environment plays a crucial role in brain organization. Nevertheless, we cannot process all of the input available to our senses. One of the functions of the brain is to sift out those signals and events that are most meaningful and useful. Therefore, if males and females have different inherent tendencies or predispositions, they will pay attention to different signals and events.

The distinction between cognitive ability and intelligence has some additional consequences. It means that human language is not necessarily the hallmark of human intelligence, as some have suggested. Language is one of many tools that can be used more or less intelligently. One of the more sophisticated of these linguistic tools is a writing system. As discussed in the last chapter, a number of cognitive operations make reading and writing possible. Many people fail to learn to read not because they lack intelligence, but because they have not developed certain sensori-motor skills. This chapter considers the evidence that the female advantage in reading is due to an innate bias toward developing the types of skills essential to the reading process. Females do not learn to read and write with greater ease because they are more intelligent. People of both sexes are equally well aware of the intellectual logic behind a writing system, especially by the time they reach adolescence, but this is no guarantee that they will all be able to read.

I'd like to provide some words of caution before I review the evidence on sex differences in the skills related to reading. I want to set out a few of the assumptions and the pitfalls in attempting to make sense of sex difference research. First, because it is impossible to impose the kinds of constraints used in the physical and biological sciences on human or even animal behavior, the social sciences must rely heavily on statistical analyses. A statistical test provides a means to reach an approximation of a totally controlled experiment and also compensates for small populations. Statistics are extremely important because without them we would have only opinion and no means of approaching fact. But it must be remembered that each study is only an approximation of the truth.

For this reason, I want to emphasize the importance of a data set, or the body of experimental results taken as a whole. It is important that the data set have a common frame of reference, or address the same type of performance. The problem is one of setting an appropriate level for making comparisons. As this decision is largely subjective, any statement about human behavior can never be absolute. It will always depend on reason and what appears to be logically consistent, a process that can often seem more like philosophy or aesthetics than science.

A second and related problem is the statistical process itself. It has often been inferred that it is possible to "lie" with statistics. This is not the case. Statistics only provides a set of numbers, entirely based on the information obtained. Of course that information can be trivial, obtained inaccurately, and misinterpreted. It is the human who is prone to error, and not the statistical tests. In all psychology experiments there are two difficulties in establishing the meaning of a statistically significant result. One is the problem of statistical power, which relates directly to how many subjects participated in the experiments. Obviously, the more subjects the better, because the distribution of the scores will begin to approximate the normal bell-shaped curve upon which most of the mathematics of statistics is based. Behavioral scientists have established arbitrary levels of probability values based on small sample sizes. Most psychologists, for example, work with groups of twenty to fifty individuals, and the cutoff point to establish a result that is significantly different to chance has been set at 5 percent. This simply means that if the experiment had been carried out 100 times, the same result would occur purely by chance only five times out of that 100.

When this 5 percent cutoff is applied to large samples, such as an entire school district, a "statistically significant" result can emerge that might be quite meaningless in terms of the practical importance of the effect. For instance, in a longitudinal study in Great Britain carried out on every child born during one week in 1946, "highly significant" sex differences were reported on a number of cognitive tests.[2] However, the average scores for the boys and girls in this sample of over four thousand children differed by only a few points out of a possible 100 points. Such findings could be trivial *or* highly important if they impact on the real world.

The second difficulty with interpreting statistics relates to the *distribution* of the various scores. In sex differences research the distribution of scores for males and females is often dissimilar; they exhibit what statisticians call "skew," in which a greater number of one sex is found at either the lower or higher ends of the distribution. Verbal skills research has indicated that the major sex effect is found only in the lower range of scores, where there are many more males than females. Unfortunately, psychologists rarely publish information about these distributions, so it is difficult to pinpoint the sex effect precisely. Because of these problems, it is much better to think in terms of whether the sex differences truly make a difference in the real world. If, as is indicated by the evidence, boys outnumber girls in remedial reading populations by three to one, then this difference does make a difference.

Sex differences research indicates that females have a greater disposition to develop the kinds of auditory and motor skills important in learning to read. The data in this chapter are of particular interest, because there are few cases in which a model based on sex-role socialization would have any explanatory power. This is particularly true of auditory sensory processing.

The Auditory System

The study of human and animal sensitivity to precise changes in sensory input is called "psychophysics." Psychophysics is perhaps one of the oldest experimental disciplines in psychology, with a history going back well over one hundred years. Research in psychophysics has made it possible to understand how our sense organs provide us with a subjective experience of the world around us. In addition, it has revealed to us just how different we are from other animals. The sex differences I will be reporting here are not nearly so dramatic as those between humans and other creatures, such as bats that navigate by sonar or dogs and porpoises that can hear extremely high sounds. They are, nevertheless, surprising, because most males and females are exposed to identical environments.

Cells in the brain respond to patterns of energy in the environment that are transmitted through the senses. Research on animals has shown that the brain's response is limited to three parameters of the incoming signals: their frequency (how fast the signals oscillate), their amplitude (how much power is in each oscillation), and the relationship between two or more incoming signals (phase). Research on human performance mirrors this result, indicating that for each sense modality, the richness of our experience is largely constructed from these three dimensions.

In the auditory system, changes in frequency are experienced as changes in pitch. Variations in amplitude are perceived as changes in volume or loudness. In addition to these very straightforward sensations, combinations of different types of signals can give rise to quite complex perceptual skills. For example, minor changes in loudness, frequency, and phase help us to localize sounds in space. In speech perception, the complex ratios of frequencies of differing amplitudes produced by the voice create each individual's characteristic voice quality, allowing us to recognize friends immediately just by hearing them speak.

Over the years several attempts have been made to enhance or alter the human's sensitivity to sound. It has been shown quite conclusively that pitch sensitivity can be trained, at least within certain limits. Musical training considerably enhances the perception of pitch. On the other hand, attempts to train subjects to hear very faint sounds, those with extremely low amplitudes, have been completely unsuccessful. These results are important because they contribute to our understanding of the impact of the environment on biological function. They are also highly relevant in the study of sex differences. I will begin with the studies that measure sensitivity to variations in amplitude or loudness.

AMPLITUDE

There are three major types of study where sensitivity to loudness has been measured in males and females. The first is called a test of auditory threshold, which is familiar to most of us who have had our hearing tested in school or at the audiologists. In this type of test, subjects are asked to tell whether or not they can hear sounds that decrease in volume until they become inaudible. In the second type of test, subjects are asked to set loudness levels to their own particular level of tolerance or comfort. Last, there are tests that have been designed to determine how sensitive the ear is to very fine differences in loudness.

The response of the human ear at auditory threshold has a maximum sensitivity of about 1,000 cycles per second (cps). This is approximately "high C" in the musical scale. Hearing becomes less and less efficient both above and below this frequency, until all sounds become completely inaudible below 20 cps and above 20,000 cps, which is the limit of human hearing. When we get older or expose our ears to very loud sounds, such as factory noise or rock music, the upper range of hearing deteriorates.

When the sexes are compared, females show a greater sensitivity at threshold for sounds above 3,000 cycles, and their sensitivity relative to males improves at higher frequencies. The sex differences become more pronounced with age, and women suffer much less hearing loss than men. These results have been demonstrated to be independent of environmental factors. John Corso, an expert in auditory psychophysics, studied five hundred men and women aged eighteen to forty-nine years, who were screened for a history of proximity to noisy environments and for auditory problems. Females were found to have greater sensitivity above 3,000 cps. I have found very similar results on a population of fifty college

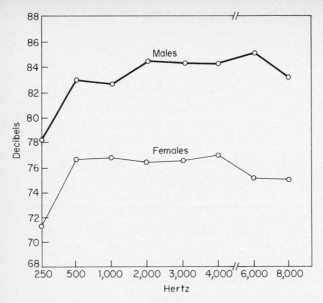

FIGURE 5.1

Comfortable levels of loudness for twenty-five male and twenty-five female college students across the frequency range of 250 to 8,000 Hertz (cycles per second). The criterion for loudness was "the point at which the sound becomes just too loud."

SOURCE: From D. McGuinness, "Hearing: Individual Differences in Perceiving," *Perception* 1 (1972):465–73. Reprinted with permission of Pion Ltd.

students.[3] These results help us to understand part of the females' advantage in the development of language, because high-frequency sensitivity is particularly important in the accurate perception of certain speech sounds, especially the consonants c, s, t, x, and z.

In tests of comfortable loudness the sex differences are perhaps the greatest. I asked fifty British college students to increase the volume of sound until it became "just too loud." The women set considerably lower levels of volume than the men across a broad range of frequencies. The ·difference between the sexes was a constant 7 to 8 decibels across the entire frequency range (see figure 5.1).[4] A decibel, or 10 "bels," is a measure of loudness or power. Previous research has shown that when subjects are asked to set the volume of sound to levels that are "twice as loud," or "half as loud," loudness appears to double at about 9 decibels. Therefore, my results indicate that at levels of maximum comfort, women will hear the same physical amplitude of sound as subjectively *twice* as loud as men.

Some have suggested that this sex effect is due to social factors in which males are permitted to make loud noises and females are not. If this were the case, loudness tolerance would be expected to increase in males and diminish in females during the socialization process, for example, with age. However, in his experiment with English schoolchildren aged five to six years and ten to eleven years, Colin Elliott reported the identical sex difference in comfortable loudness levels as those in my experiment.[5] In a recent experiment on comfortable loudness levels using three types of rock music, American college males preferred to set the volume at an average of 84 decibels, whereas females set the volume at 73 decibels.[6] These values were nearly the same as the values obtained in my own study on British college students. Because this effect is so pronounced and consistent across age and culture, it provides a more plausible case for a biological predisposition in males and females to show differential sensitivity to the volume of sound.

In the third category of loudness measure, subjects are tested on their ability to judge fine differences in volume between one sound and another. The studies just cited would predict a greater sensitivity in females, and this is exactly what has been found. Three separate experiments indicate that the females' judgment of changes in loudness is considerably greater across all ages. A. R. Zaner and his colleagues tested fifty schoolchildren aged four to eight years. The children were asked to listen to a series of sounds and tell the experimenter whether or not they noticed a change in what they heard. The tones varied in duration (short or long), loudness (loud or soft), and pitch (high or low). The girs were found to be much more accurate at detecting changes in loudness. The boys were better in judging changes in pitch.[7]

In a study on adults, Vladimir Pishkin and Robert Blanchard at the University of Oklahoma medical school used a similar approach, but also asked subjects to judge whether a change had occurred at the left or the right ear. No sex differences were found on measures of duration (a 1-second versus a 3-second tone), or frequency (1,000 cps versus 3,000 cps), but the women were consistently more accurate both in detecting changes in loudness and in detecting in which ear the various changes had occurred. The men's performance showed that they were only guessing, with error scores at 50 percent.[8] Pishkin and Blanchard's results are presented in figure 5.2.

In a follow-up study Pishkin and Jay Shurley tested 120 adults aged twenty-five to fifty years of age on a more complex version of the same type of task. Here the dimensions (duration, frequency, and laterality) were presented simultaneously, and the tasks varied in difficulty from one dimension to three. The results are presented in figure 5.3, where it can be seen that females are particularly adept at discriminating between complex auditory signals.[9]

Sensitivity to changes in loudness is important in producing emotional reactions to both speech and music. Rosamund Shuter, an English psychologist, tested two hundred students at London music colleges on the Wing battery of musical aptitude, which includes a variety of tests of musical discrimination and of memory.[10] She found that men and women were similar in the number and type of their musical abilities, but that women had an additional aptitude (a distinct factor). This was a sensitivity to musical "dynamics," or the ability to judge fine differences in the changes in loudness in musical passages.

We know from a variety of studies in psychophysics that attention is directed to signals with high amplitude. That is, if something appears brighter or louder or has a stronger smell, it will capture our attention. The fact that females are so singularly sensitive to the volume of sound means that they will pay *attention* to sound more than to visual stimuli, where their sensitivity is less than that of males. Furthermore, sensitivity to dynamic contrasts in sound will give females an extra advantage in the ability to determine meaning from the prosodics of speech, those aspects of verbal communication that are additional to word meaning. This provides an explanation of why females are so sensitive to someone's "tone of voice."

FREQUENCY

Only one experiment—Zaner's—has shown boys to be slightly better judges of differences in pitch. Pishkin and his colleagues found no sex difference in the ability to judge sounds varying in pitch. In my own experiment, the same fifty subjects were asked to make extremely difficult pitch judgments between tones that

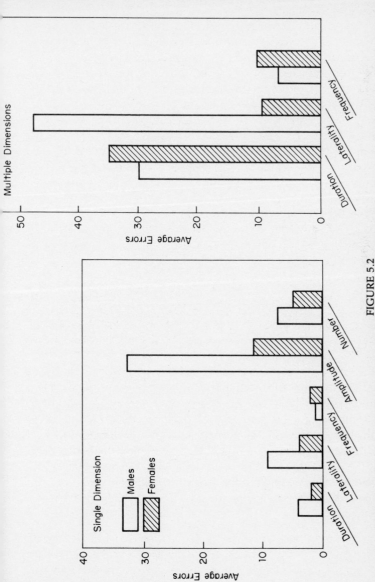

FIGURE 5.2

Errors made by men and women when judging differences between various dimensions of sound. The dimensions varied either one at a time (left) or simultaneously (right).

SOURCE: From V. Pishkin and R. Blanchard, "Auditory Concept Identification," *Psychonomic Science* 1 (1964):177–78. Reprinted with permission of the authors and the Psychonomic Society.

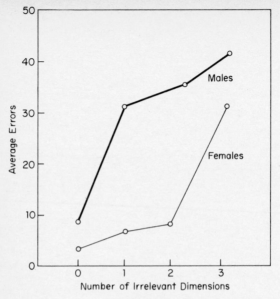

FIGURE 5.3

Combined error scores of men and women judging changes in sounds varying in duration, frequency, and laterality as the number of irrelevant dimensions increases from zero to three.

SOURCE: Reprinted with permission of authors and publisher from V. Pishkin and Jay T. Shurley, "Auditory Dimensions and Irrelevant Information in Concept Identification of Males and Females," *Perceptual and Motor Skills* 20 (1965):673–83, figure 1.

varied from one-eighth to a whole tone of the musical scale. (The smallest increment on the piano keyboard is a half tone.) The number of years each subject had spent in studying a musical instrument was included in the analysis. The results showed that the amount of musical training had a marked effect on the student's performance, but that there were no sex differences whatsoever. This result contrasts with the threshold and loudness tests described earlier, where musical training had no effect on performance.

SPEECH PERCEPTION

The perception of speech is a complex process. It involves discriminating between speech sounds and comprehending the meaning of words, as well as monitoring nonlinguistic information such as inflection, voice quality, and rhythmic and dynamic stress. Unfortunately, very little research has been done on sex differences in speech perception.

About fifteen years ago, Peter Mittler and J. Ward reported on a study of British children assessed on the Illinois Test of Psycholinguistic Abilities.[11] One hundred four-year-old children were tested on a number of different tasks. All tests were given orally and were largely concerned with how well the children processed speech. Girls were found to be accelerated on tests measuring the comprehension of meaning, auditory-vocal memory, and in applying the correct linguistic categories to objects. In a much more difficult test, Paul Mirabile asked 150 children aged seven to fifteen years to listen to pairs of consonant-vowel-consonant syllables. They were recorded and played through earphones, with a different syllable to each ear. The presentation to each ear was simultaneous or varied from 10 milliseconds to 90 milliseconds apart. When the pairs were presented simultaneously, both boys and girls performed extremely poorly. However, the moment there was a delay between each ear, the girls were more accurate in identifying the syllables. Their superiority increased noticeably with increasing delays. This effect was strongly age dependent, with older children being more accurate than younger ones, a fact that indicates that girls are accelerated in their development of speech perception.[12]

An interesting experiment on elderly subjects by Carolyn McCoy illustrates that females' facility for speech perception is not merely the result of a developmental acceleration. McCoy tested sixty subjects over the age of fifty, none of whom had any known hearing deficit. Men were found to be much worse on a test of speech discrimination and also in a listening task in which the subject had to attend to one of two messages presented simultaneously to each ear. Women were superior in this task with both the left and the right ear.[13]

Though there have been only a few experiments on the perception of speech, the results point in the same direction—a female superiority in the perception and discrimination of speech sounds. These findings indicate the importance of speech discrimination in reading performance and provide a partial explanation of why girls are accelerated in reading.

As we saw earlier, the sexes do not differ in tests of pitch discrimination, or in most tests of musical aptitude, nor have I found any sex difference in high school and college students in the perception of rhythm. These results suggest that males are attentive to aspects of the world of sound other than speech. In a series of tests on eighty children, aged five to eight years, Carol Knox and Doreen Kimura studied children's ability to identify environmental noises and animal sounds. Surprisingly, boys were consistently better at both the environmental and animal noises, and their superiority increased with age for the tests using environmental noises, revealing a greater developmental acceleration than that of the girls. Both the boys and the girls did better when the noises were presented to the left ear, indicating a *right*-hemisphere advantage in these tasks.[14]

This is a very important result because it tells us that there is nothing wrong with boys' ability to discriminate among complex sounds and provides yet another example of the fact that a global developmental lag model cannot be maintained. But perhaps more interesting than either of these conclusions are the implications for the nature-nurture question. We now have considerable evidence that boys are more interested in objects than people, and girls are exactly the opposite. Is this because boys have poorer language (left-hemisphere) skills and choose not to attend to people, *or* because their attention is captured by environmental noises (right-hemisphere), or both? Or do the sensory differences arise as a *result* of sensitivity to objects or persons? Would this predisposition regulate attention to the environment? Whichever of these factors is primary, it is clear that a sex-role socialization hypothesis cannot explain the data. Nothing in modern society reinforces success in mastering environmental noises, yet this skill is accelerated in little boys. In schools, where the focus is primarily on language, the girls' advantage will be noticed and encouraged, while the boys' advantage will not.

The Motor Systems

One of the most striking sex differences is the proportion of body weight devoted to muscle. In males muscles have been estimated to be about 40 percent of their total body weight, whereas in females muscles account for approximately 23 percent. (These figures are for the young adult and do not apply to children.) Nevertheless, despite the belief that girls and boys do not differ noticeably in muscle development before the age of puberty, tests of performance would indicate otherwise. The Youth Sports Institute of Michigan State University has followed 550 boys and girls from the age of two to eighteen years. The director of this research, Vern Seefeldt, reports that boys outdistance girls in running by the age of two and one-half. In five out of eight tests of strength, speed, and agility, boys were superior by age seven and one-half, and their superiority increased with age. Girls were superior on only one test—that of muscle flexibility.[15]

The motor system involved in whole body movement, especially that requiring speed and force, is referred to as the gross-motor system. This system is part of a central neural mechanism called the extrapyramidal motor system. The second major motor system, responsible for fine-motor control, is called the pyramidal motor system. These two motor systems regulate very different forms of motor activity; the gross-motor system is largely responsible for total organization of the limbs and torso, whereas the fine-motor system regulates the distal muscles, specifically fingers, toes, and tongue, and is primarily engaged in the *fluency* of action, or sequential motion. The fine-motor system of the brain is a late phylogenetic development, being totally absent in all lower vertebrates. As might be anticipated from the discussion so far, males and females exhibit differential capacities in these two motor systems. Specifically, females have an advantage in fine-motor skills and males in gross-motor skills.[16]

More will be said about the gross-motor system and its possible relationship to visuospatial ability in a later chapter. Here I focus on the fine-motor system because of the relationship between fine-motor skill and language. Although the fine-motor system typically deals with the action of the fine muscles, especially the fingers and tongue, evidence from animal research shows that this system influences fluent coordinated motion in whole body action. This would be particularly evident in human skills requiring internally generated movement such as gymnastics and the dance.

THE FINE-MOTOR SYSTEM

In the research on sex differences in speech perception, females were found to have a more accurate memory for sequences of speech sounds. I will soon take up the evidence for a female advantage in speech production. But let me first call attention to the studies on fine-motor skills independent of speech, which also demonstrate a female superiority. These results are more surprising because they are far less predictable by a socialization hypothesis. Marian Annett asked 220 British children, aged three to fifteen years, to shift pegs rapidly along the holes in a pegboard task. The girls were significantly faster overall, especially with the right hand, which was better than their left. The boys were better with their left hand. The pegboard task was one of the tests that was found to be highly discriminating in differentiating between good and poor readers.[17]

Martha Denckla tested several hundred children between the ages of five and ten. She found that girls were consistently faster, with either hand, at a task that required a rapid sequence of finger-thumb oppositions. Girls showed a constant improvement over the age range, whereas boys appeared to reach a plateau at age eight, and their scores remained largely unchanged over the next two years. When boys and girls were compared on *single* repetitions of thumb or fingers, speed of repetitive hand pats, speed to rotate the arm, and speed of foot tapping, no sex differences emerged. However, when heel and toe *sequences* were measured, females were faster at every age. The youngest girls, aged five and six, showed a marked difference between the feet, with the right foot considerably faster. This effect largely disappeared with age, but indicates that young girls are considerably more biased toward left-hemisphere activation than boys, since we know that each hemisphere controls the opposite side of the body. Overall, the results indicate that girls' advantage is specific to rapid sequential action, or fine-motor fluency.[18]

The suggestion that fine-motor fluency might be involved with fluency of whole-body action has received support from a student project carried out by two of my undergraduate students. Eight men and eight women, none of whom had ever taken dance classes, were asked to watch an instructor perform a series of very simple dance steps and to carry them out in sequence. No verbal instructions were allowed. All the women learned the sequence in one to three trials, but many of the men found it impossible to retain the sequence once they began to move. They had no difficulty with each individual movement but could not put them together as a routine. Several men stayed for over an hour, showing high motivation to learn, but were still unable to execute the sequence correctly.[19]

Timing of fluent sequential action appears to be strongly related to aptitude for language. This relationship is highlighted by the fact that deaf people communicate through manual gestures or "signs." If there is an overall relationship between signing and language systems, we might expect the same sex difference to appear in schools for the deaf. This is exactly what has been found in a study by D. W. Gaffney, who tested children aged five to seven years on their aptitude for sign language. Girls were found to be superior on tests that required accurate decoding of grammar, word order, inflection, and interrogation. Their superiority was independent of IQ, severity of the hearing impairment, and months of schooling.[20]

SPEECH PRODUCTION

Speech is a species-specific characteristic of all human populations. Though the great apes appear to be able to understand some speech, they are not able to produce it, and even when taught sign language they show a greatly reduced vocabulary and impoverished syntax, although they communicate simple desires and feelings quite well. The research on human-ape communication has provided us with an enormous amount of information, but has demonstrated that the apes are not prototype humans locked into a silent world. They appear to have no need to employ a signaling system as complex as human language, even when they are given the opportunity to do so.[21]

What has proved surprising about human language is that it develops regardless of the circumstances, providing that at least two people are interacting. Only in conditions of extreme deprivation where a child is isolated from human discourse does language development fail to occur. The most recent case comes from a U.C.L.A. study of "Genie," a twelve-year-old girl rescued from confinement in a Los Angeles bedroom. Genie had never heard speech, and it was found that despite several years of training, her language skills were no better than those of the great apes: a severely restricted vocabulary, no syntax, and telegraphic utterances of only two to three words in length.[22] Taken in conjunction with other reports of similar cases, these findings strongly suggest that language development has a "critical period" and that some human interaction is required before the ages of five to seven years for normal language to develop. Nevertheless, for 99.99 percent of the human race, including most mentally retarded, speech will develop between any two individuals whether they use an existing language system or not. Many accounts have been given of twins who establish a completely new language that is totally unintelligible to everyone but themselves.

Reviews of the various studies on speech development report that females are advanced relative to males at most ages throughout childhood. They appear to have a greater facility in producing accurate speech sounds and employ more words in phrases or sentences, a measure referred to as the "mean length of utterance" (MLU). In most studies across a wide age range and across various cultures, no sex differences are found in tests of vocabulary.

Despite the assumption that female superiority is merely a product of greater precocity, a more detailed analysis of the data reveals that the sex difference is much more complex. First, it is difficult to demonstrate any consistent sex effect before about eighteen to twenty-four months. Up to this time, both sexes are extremely variable in speech development. Second, after the age of about twenty-four months, the sex difference seems to become *more* noticeable with age, to about middle childhood. It was assumed that sex differences disappear during the early school years. In fact, this is largely because only fine-grained analysis of speech samples reveals any sex differences after early childhood. Since only recently have we discovered the connection between speech and reading, these sex effects have not been related to performance on reading tasks.

Females' overall advantage in speech development has been reported in two longitudinal studies, one in the United States and one in England, which combined data from a variety of tests of verbal behaviors.[23] A reliable sex effect appeared by about twelve to eighteen months, and both investigators also report a strong correlation between early language development in girls and later verbal and intellectual ability. No such relationship was found for boys in either study. In a somewhat more detailed study of language development, Earlene Paynter and Nancy Petty investigated the accuracy with which ninety young children produced consonants and the number of consonants in the child's repertoire from age twenty-four to thirty months. The sexes were noticeably different only at thirty months, with the girls having seven consonants (measured as being accurately produced by 90 percent of the forty-five girls) whereas the boys had five.[24]

Speech surveys are generally carried out on children and adults beginning at four to five years of age, for it is expected that by this age most children have an adequate ability to produce all of the speech sounds of a native language with a reasonable degree of accuracy and in general to speak fluently. In all of the surveys I have examined, it has been found that males produce more dysfluencies, such as hesitations and perseverations, more inaccurate articulation, and show considerably more pronounced speech defects, such as stuttering.[25] Verbal fluency, as measured by the absence of hesitations, and mean length of utterance have been found to be greater in females not only in English-speaking countries but in places with dramatically different languages, such as Nepal and Czechoslovakia.[26]

More recently, studies on the uses of language by men and women, specifically with reference to sex roles, have revealed that women in various countries around the world speak more accurately than men, as for instance in using appropriate word endings such as "ing" instead of "in." This has been explained as due to males being "socialized" to speak badly (!), but it seems just as likely to be the result of the females' greater skill in speech production.[27]

The superiority of females in language development appears to reflect a number of innate aptitudes, among them sensitivity to people and motor fluency, rather than special environmental circumstances. Two sets of findings bear on this statement. First, studies have demonstrated that mothers do not speak differently to their sons and daughters, either in terms of their clarity of speech or difficulty of vocabulary.[28] A Czechoslovakian study confirmed the same female advantage among five-year-olds reared on a collective where there were multiple caretakers. Despite the fact that girls do not receive any special attention, a greater vocal interchange is often observed between mothers and daughters than between mothers and sons, and this difference appears to reflect the interest of the female child in her mother's speech.[29]

Michael Lewis, an American psychologist, discovered that when infants are at the initial babbling stage, females babble more often in response to their mother's speech than males.[30] One possible reason why the mother's speech seems to act as a stronger stimulation to girls relates to the females' greater sensitivity to the changing volume of sound. This means that they would be capable of comprehending the meaning in their mother's vocal inflections long before they understood her words. Even so, it appears that females are oriented toward social stimuli independently of whether they are speaking or silent. In one study females only twenty-four to fifty hours old spent much longer than males (74 versus 49 seconds on average) in maintaining eye contact to a silent adult, which suggests that they are predisposed very early on toward social behavior. In addition, females looked longer when the person was speaking than when they were not, whereas males' behavior in either case did not differ.[31]

In addition to this relationship between social behavior and speech development, females also show a greater facility for nonverbal vocalizations, suggesting that their skill is not restricted to language per se but is due to a general aptitude for sequential fluency. Research in England on monotonism (the inability to carry a tune) has revealed an extremely robust sex difference, with male monotones outnumbering females by at least six to one. Furthermore, there are almost no female monotones past the age of eight to nine years, whereas male monotones are common well into the teenage period.[32]

Finally, it appears that the function of vocalization is a relevant factor. Peter Smith and Kevin Connolly, two English psychologists, categorized the utterances of preschool children into "play noises"

TABLE 5.1

The Percent of the Total Vocalizations of Two Age Groups of Preschool Children Spent Either Talking or Making Play Noises. (The Means are Based on Sampling Every 10 Seconds.)

	Proportion of Time Spent Vocalizing					
	Talk to Child		Play Noise		Total Vocalizations	
Age	Boys	Girls	Boys	Girls	Boys	Girls
2:9–3:9 years	24.3	36.7	19.8	8.2	44.1	44.9
3:9–4:9 years	47.0	65.6	27.7	7.6	74.7	73.2
Percent Change	93	79	40	−7	69	63

SOURCE: From P. Smith and K. Connolly, "Patterns of Play and Social Interaction in Pre-school Children," in N. Blurton-Jones, ed., *Ethological Studies of Child Behavior* (Cambridge: Cambridge University Press, 1972). Reprinted with permission of the authors and Cambridge University Press.

and "conversations." Boys were overwhelmingly more likely to make play noises and girls to talk to other children and adults, as shown in table 5.1. This result occurred despite the fact that the boys' and girls' total vocal output was identical.[33] Not only are boys better at recognizing environmental and animal noises, as Knox and Kimura reported, but often they are hard at work making these noises! In summary, boys spend more time imitating objects and animals and girls spend more time communicating with people.

Taking these results on speech production into consideration, it can be seen that the essential differences between males and females relate more to motor skills and the function of language than to intelligence. However, as will be seen later, sensorimotor skills as well as the differences in reactions to objects or social stimuli are important in biasing the type of cognitive skill that will be favored over others. These factors predict "cognitive style" rather than overall cognitive ability.

Integrating the Senses and Actions

One of the brain's higher functions is to combine information among the various sensory modes and to integrate sensory input with motor programs. Examples of sensorimotor integration would be aiming a baseball bat at a moving ball, or mimicking the voice quality of another person. Combining information between two or more senses not only provides a richer experience of events and objects in the world, but is essential to many cognitive skills. It might even be said that the building blocks of cognitive ability are cross-modal combinations of sensory and motor skills. In some cases these skills are intimately related, such as in speech perception and speech production. In other cases, more unlikely combinations are required in tasks invented by humans, such as writing, reading, and mathematics. The next section considers those cross-modal skills that are relevant to the development of language-related cognitive abilities.

SENSORIMOTOR INTEGRATION

When the speed and fluency of motor sequencing is combined with a verbal or visual task, females' ability is pronounced. Raymond Majeres tested 204 college students on the time to look at items from one list and to tap the matching item in an adjacent list. Majeres used various types of stimuli such as words, colors, and shapes, as well as combinations such as drawings matched to names. The sexes were equal on speed of matching shapes to shapes, but the females were superior on all other tests. Reasoning that the females may have memorized the response-card sequence, Majeres decided to scramble the items on the response card on every trial. This manipulation actually *improved* females' performance, which accelerated by one to two seconds; females were now an astonishing five to seven seconds faster than the males in every trial block.[34] Similar results were found in a population of over 1,000 subjects by Sadie Decker and J. C. DeFries, where females across a wide age range were found to be overwhelmingly superior in a test of coding speed.[35]

Majeres concluded that the female advantage was due to their ability to make a rapid translation from a visual to a verbal code, in other words that their superiority was in cross-modal sensori-motor coding. This conclusion is debatable, however, because many of the tasks, such as the color-color matching task at which the females were particularly outstanding, did not require any verbalization. His conclusion is based on the view that naming colors and symbols would occur automatically, whereas labeling abstract shapes would be less likely.

Evidence from my own laboratory does not support a straight-forward theory based on the notion that females automatically translate all visual input into verbal codes. In a series of studies on nearly 400 students aged eight to seventeen years, we investigated memory for a series of words and pictures. The children were asked to rate each word or picture as "more like a boy" or "more like a girl." Without warning, the students were next asked to write down as many of the items as they could remember. The girls recalled many more items than the boys when they wrote their answers, but the sex difference disappeared when the children were asked to *draw* the list of pictures from memory.[36] This indicates that part of the sex difference in *memory* tasks is due to the females' greater advantage in translating input into writing.

The critical factor in all of the studies that show a sensorimotor facility in females appears to be sequencing speed, but especially speed in generating sequential motor programs that are independent of changes in the visual environment. Kimura has called this type of motor performance "movement without objects," or internally programmed motor acts.[37] In contrast to females, males appear to excel in *externally* programmed motor acts, responding rapidly and efficiently to sudden changes in the visual environment. Reading, writing, and spelling are all examples of sensorimotor performances (without objects) that require complex integration between the visual, verbal, and fine-motor systems, a facility that is particularly well-developed in females.

SENSORY–SENSORY INTEGRATION

The capacity for complex sensory-sensory integration is partic-ularly human and appears very early. Two American psychologists, Patricia Kuhl and Andrew Meltzoff, studied thirty-two four-month-old infants while they watched two faces that were producing different vowel sounds. The faces were filmed and were displayed side by side, with the vowel sound produced between them over a loudspeaker. One face was miming "ah" and the other "ee." The experimenters measured how much time each infant spent looking at each face. Twenty-four of the thirty-two infants looked significantly longer at the face that was miming the vowel they heard.[38] The experimenters do not report on the sex of these twenty-four infants, but the study does illustrate very young infants' amazing auditory-visual cross-sensory integration.

To date the evidence from studies on cross-modal sensory integration shows that there is a sex difference in favor of females only on verbal-visual or visual-verbal tasks. Other cross-modal tasks involving touch and vision appear to be performed equally well by both sexes, as shown by a study of one hundred boys and girls aged six years.[39] Also, it has not been found that the sexes differ in tests of nonverbal auditory-visual integration, such as matching a series of tones to a series of blinking lights.[40]

An example of visual-verbal integration is the Stroop test, which involves naming a series of cards of color words or colors as rapidly as possible. The cards are either nonconfusing or confusing, such as the word "green" printed on a yellow background. The most consistent finding has been that females of all ages are faster in naming the color cards. In an extensive study, Angela Bateson, one of my students, tested sixty college students on four variations of the Stroop test: 1) a color card, 2) a word card (color name in letters), a word of one color printed on a background of a different color, in which the subject had to 3) name either the word *or* 4) the background color. The sexes performed equally in the speed of naming the color words, but females were significantly faster in all other tests.[41]

In an extended series of tests of phonetic-visual cross-modal matching, my student Anne Courtney and I found a striking sex difference on the auditory but not the visual component of a search task.[42] We asked fifty college students to search for target letters or phonemes (A or I) in a visual and an auditory presentation of a series of five-letter words. In the visual part of the experiment, the students saw each word appear on a screen and had to press a key if the word contained a target letter: A or I. Next, they were asked to look for a target *sound:* "a" as in "day," or "i" as in

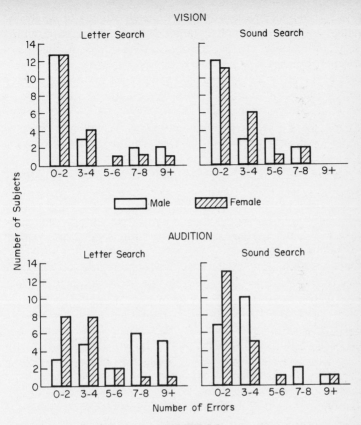

FIGURE 5.4

Distribution of error scores for men and women either looking or listening for a target letter or a target sound in five-letter words. 0–2 is highly accurate; 6 or greater is at chance.

SOURCE: From D. McGuinness and A. Courtney, "Sex Differences in Visual and Phonetic Search," *Journal of Mental Imagery* 7 (1983):95–104.

"night." In the auditory part of the experiment, these same instructions were given when the students listened to the five-letter words over earphones. No sex differences were found in the visual presentation test. However, as can be seen in figure 5.4, when the same subjects were asked to *listen* to the lists of words and make their judgments, strong sex differences appeared. First, the males were much worse in deciding whether a word contained a target sound, such as "*a*" in "slate." But even more astonishing, many of these college men were completely unable to determine whether a word contained a target *letter*, such as determining whether there was an *"i"* in rhyme. Over half of the males performed this task at purely chance levels—they were simply guessing. It was concluded that the males were not only poorer in speech analysis, but that they were particularly disadvantaged in creating a visual image of a word they heard—one reason, perhaps, that males have greater problems in spelling. We were surprised that college men had difficulty on these relatively simple tasks.

These studies provide strong support for the ability of females to translate visual information to a verbal response and to create a visual image of a word they hear, skills that are obviously important in reading and spelling. The next chapter considers the organization and development of the brain that might explain these abilities.

Taken as a whole, the data are overwhelming that females have a definite advantage in all skills related to comprehending and producing language. Therefore, it is not surprising that they would show an advantage in other skills based on language, like reading and spelling. Their proficiency in fine-motor tasks would also boost their writing skills. Most of the evidence reviewed in this chapter suggests that the female advantage in linguistic and fine-motor skills is a product of an *innate* aptitude, and there is no evidence to suggest that their facility is produced by social or environmental factors. If this suggestion is correct, then we would expect to find major differences in brain organization between males and females.

6

The Biological Basis of Sex Differences in Language and Reading

The brain is the absolute frontier between nature and nurture. It is programmed from within by genetic, hormonal, and anatomical constraints, and from without by signals and events in the environment. This Janus-faced aspect of the brain means that it is extremely difficult to discover precisely what connections and actions of brain cells are determined by the genes and which have been modified by input from the environment. This is perhaps the greatest single barrier to our understanding of the relationship between brain and behavior. How then can we arrive at any conclusions about the origin of sex differences in such complex skills as reading, writing, and spelling? The answer is, not easily. But with recent techniques in the brain sciences, both technological and methodological, we are beginning to make progress.

The Brain and Behavior

Information about the human brain has come from a variety of investigative techniques. Early anatomical studies focused on the gross organization of the brain in terms of weight and mass of different types of tissue. The microscope showed nineteenth-century scientists that these masses of tissue consisted of millions of neurons with interconnected fibers. More recently, the electron microscope has revealed the awesome complexity of the neural landscape. The invention of the computer has made it possible to produce images of the intact brain. Computerized axial tomography (CAT scan) scans the brain with X-rays and prepares a series of two-dimensional pictures representing the skull, cerebrospinal fluid, and neural tissue. Positron emission tomography (PET) provides a set of colored brain maps produced by the injection of a radioactive isotope that provides a marker of blood flow changes in the brain.

When it was discovered that the brain spontaneously generates its own electrical activity, techniques were developed to monitor these electrical events. The electroencephalogram (EEG) measures brain activity from the scalp. In other tests, microelectrodes inserted into the brain can monitor activity from a small group of cells or even a single neuron.

These techniques provide descriptions of the brain's appearance, electrical activity, or blood flow, but by themselves they tell us nothing about the relationship between brain activity and behavior. It is only when they are employed in conjunction with behavioral tests that we can begin to understand how the millions of neurons influence our actions, feelings, and thoughts.

The first attempts to discover systematic brain-behavior relationships were studies on animals. By extracting small amounts of tissue in specific areas of the brain and testing these animals in different situations, scientists were able to discover which parts of the brain were essential to certain sensory, motor, and cognitive functions. Animal models have the great advantage of precision. The scientist knows the exact extent of the lesion from brain reconstructions after the animal is sacrificed and its brain analyzed under the microscope. The closer the species to our own, the more these findings can be generalized to human behavior. Nonhuman primates have many behaviors in common with humans, especially emotions, visual sensory processing, and the ability to carry out planned activity. However, animals don't talk, read, play the piano, or do any of those human activities that are so important to our culture.

Therefore, in order to understand the human brain, we have had to rely extensively on research with brain-damaged patients.

The problem with this approach is that brain-behavior relationships are largely based on negative inferences. That is, one must discover what function is *missing* and then attribute that missing function to the site of the damage. This is particularly difficult when the behavioral deficits are subtle or complex. As an example, the frontal lobes of the brain were once believed to control mood, and for a time frontal lobotomies were carried out routinely to improve severe depression. Lobotomized patients generally became more cheerful and their IQ test scores were normal, but their families reported that their behavior was noticeably maladaptive.[1] It was convincingly demonstrated in later experiments, initially through animal research, that the frontal lobes are vital to carrying out planned action and thought.

A further difficulty in studying brain-damaged patients is pinpointing the exact extent of the lesion. Sometimes this is known, as for instance when a surgeon removes a tumor, but more often it is not, as in the case of stroke or head injury. CAT scans have made it possible to be considerably more precise about the location of brain damage, though the technique is still not exact. Apart from the problem of knowing the extent of the brain dysfunction (pressure destroys cells' oxygen supply and is as relevant as loss of tissue), it is enormously difficult to devise tests that reliably measure what they purport to measure. It is only in the past decade or so that modern techniques, more reliable behavioral tests, and sophisticated statistical tools have led to some major breakthroughs in refining our understanding of the human brain. These discoveries have at last provided some clues regarding the organization of the male and female brain. This chapter will explore only one aspect of this brain-behavior relationship—the evidence on language and language-based functions.

Two Major Brain Systems for Language

The major language system regulates and integrates both fluent articulation and fluent decoding of speech sounds. A facility in understanding speech rarely exists independently of a facility in execution, even when this facility in linguistic analysis can be demonstrated only by interpreting and making gestural signs, as shown in the study on deaf children. This is a strong argument for inferring overlapping or related neural systems in the brain for decoding speech input and producing speech output, especially as humans show an uncanny ability to imitate both gesture and speech. Imitation begins with accurate decoding. Some people are such talented mimics that they can reproduce the exact voice quality of another individual. This could not be possible unless there was an intimate connection between specific sensory and motor systems in the brain. This sensorimotor coupling underpinning language appears to depend neurologically on the maturation of the auditory and fine-motor systems, especially those localized to the left hemisphere.

Different and widely distributed systems in the brain store the semantic properties of words and all their attendant associations, providing the basis for vocabulary. The capacity to remember words and their meanings appears to be mediated by processes that involve extensive regions of the brain. It has been demonstrated many times in studies on brain-damaged patients that no amount of brain damage, whether of the right or left hemisphere, ever completely destroys the memory store.[2] What does occur is that the patient loses a particular mode of retrieving memories because the damage interferes with a sensory or motor program. Patients who cannot repeat the word "flower" or name it from a picture are almost always able to demonstrate in some other fashion (pointing or mime) that they understand and remember the *meaning* of the word.

Sex differences in linguistic ability are rarely found in vocabulary skills but are consistently observed in the organization of the first system, the one regulating the decoding and production of speech. Females excel in all tests of verbal fluency as measured by naming speed, the number of words per sentence, and the clarity of articulation, and they are generally superior in using correct grammatical forms and in listening comprehension.

Here we take up several lines of research indicating that verbal fluency in all of its ramifications depends initially on the maturation of auditory pathways and the fine-motor system and subsequently on the neural organization of the left hemisphere.

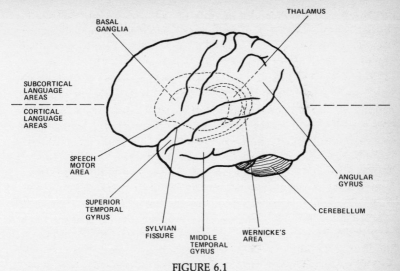

FIGURE 6.1

The left-hemisphere structures involved in language. The subcortical systems lie deep in the brain and are connected to the cortical regions by millions of white fibers.

The Auditory-Motor Systems in Speech

During a child's initial acquisition of speech, from approximately three to twelve months, several neural systems begin to develop simultaneously. This development is signaled by the growth of a fatty sheath, called myelin, around the nerve fibers. Myelination dramatically enhances the capacity of nerve cells to transmit information rapidly from one location in the brain to another. The neural systems that develop are the fine-motor pyramidal system, the basal ganglia, the middle cerebellar peduncle, and the post-thalamic auditory relay. The major structures involved are illustrated in figure 6.1. The fine-motor system is responsible for fast fluent action of the digits and midline systems such as tongue and vocal chords; the basal ganglia and the middle cerebellar peduncle are critically involved in speech motor control; and the post-thalamic auditory relays take the auditory signals that are crudely processed in the thalamus to a finer analysis by the auditory cortex. The cortex is the outer region of the brain, the gray matter, that is so

101

important in the detailed analysis of patterns. In contrast to this delay in the myelination of the auditory speech mechanisms, the visual system is already partly myelinated at birth and is fully myelinated by about three to four months.

According to Ronald Netsell, a developmental psychologist at the Boys Town Institute, these maturational landmarks in the auditory system accompany a noticeable shift from primitive respiratory and nasal noises to the production of a range of vowels, diphthongs, and consonants.[3] The auditory pathways continue to myelinate until the fourth or fifth year, though children can produce words when many of the sensory pathways become myelinated, between twelve and twenty-four months. It is particularly interesting that during this period walking and talking rarely occur simultaneously. This may have an impact on speech development in males, as they tend to be more mobile than females, at least with respect to whole-body movement.

The systems controlling the fine-motor midline structures (vocal tract, pharynx, tongue, and lips) mature by about three to four years. Their precision is on the order of milliseconds. For example, in order to execute the sound "pa," all of these structures have to be coordinated. A few milliseconds before the lips open to make the "p" the pharnyx must be sealed and the vocal cords prepared for generating the "a." This means that all vowel sounds actually modify the consonants that *precede* them. These fine-motor speech systems must then be rapidly adjusted for the next consonant-vowel combination and so forth throughout the length of an utterance.

The delay in the onset of maturation of these systems and their long development help to explain why the sex differences in speech production do not appear reliably until about the second year of life. The early advantage shown by females in articulation and their considerably greater freedom from speech defects strongly suggest that this maturational progression is accelerated in females. A developmental acceleration in any function can act as a bias, inducing females to rely more than males on information from verbal channels.

Netsell has indicated that one of the most critical aspects of the development of clear articulation is the rapid coordination of these various auditory fine-motor pathways. Other research, specifically the work of Pat Lindamood with hundreds of language-delayed children, showed that a primary problem in poor speech production is an inadequate auditory analysis of speech sounds.[4] Thus there are at least two major aspects to speech production: accurate decoding (a cortical function) and the output of this auditory "image" to the speech motor systems. The first is represented in the posterior left cortex, whereas motor production engages the "final common path" at the speech-motor area in the anterior left cortex (see figure 6.1). It is not only important that each image or pattern be sent rapidly to the speech-motor area controlling the articulatory muscles, but the cortex must continually update these patterns during speech production. In chapter 4, I discussed Paula Tallal's theory that the left hemisphere of the brain deals most efficiently with processing input and output that requires a rapid "rate of change," such as a constantly shifting stream of speech. If this is true, then one might expect to find that *any* fluent motor behavior involving a rapid rate of change would be affected by damage to the left hemisphere. In fact, as pianists know, the most complex and rapid passages are written for the right hand, which is controlled by the left hemisphere.

Evidence supporting this hypothesis comes from the laboratory of Doreen Kimura at the University of Western Ontario. She has demonstrated that the fluency of motor performance is a left-hemisphere function. In addition, she has shown that motor fluency relates to the severity of aphasia (loss of speech function) in left-hemisphere–damaged patients.[5] Kimura taught patients with lesions of either the right or left hemisphere a series of simple manual tasks that involved pressing a button, pulling a lever, and pressing a panel. When this series was mastered, she then asked the patients to execute the sequence five times, as rapidly as possible. Her initial hypothesis was that patients with left-hemisphere damage would not remember the sequence, but this is not what occurred. Instead, patients with left-hemisphere damage were noticeably inefficient. They hesitated, made extraneous movements, and perseverated or repeated movements just completed. None of these problems were exhibited by patients with right-hemisphere lesions. Furthermore, the most severely affected left-hemisphere patients—those with the greatest language deficits—showed the most striking abnormalities in this task. Kimura concluded that what was involved in their disability was a loss in *transitional fluency* or, in other words, the inability to execute a rapidly timed series of movements. This theory of left-hemisphere function is nearly identical to the one proposed by Tallal on the basis of her work on children with speech and reading problems, the majority of whom are boys.

These data provide a global picture of the connection between language and fine-motor coordination and the involvement of the left hemisphere. More relevant to my theory are studies that help to determine which of the many brain structures might be the critical locus for major language differences due to sex. The nature of cortical regulation of the language systems has been investigated by William Gordon at Stanford University, using patients with left-hemisphere damage.[6] In order to determine the exact cortical sites involved in a number of different linguistic tasks, he employed a technique developed by Karl Pribram called multiple dissociation. This technique involves combining all areas where lesions produce a deficit, and all areas where lesions have no effect, and then subtracting them from one another. The area that remains is assumed to be critical to the function. The site and extent of brain lesions for each patient are mapped by CAT scan. These patients are then tested on a large battery of linguistic tasks and those with similar deficits are compared.

Gordon's findings were strongly in support of the research reported by Netsell. The auditory structures that myelinate late are precisely the structures that give rise to various language disorders when they are damaged. On the basis of his own and others' findings, Gordon proposed that language reception and production is dependent on cortical control of the basal ganglia systems. The cortex and the basal ganglia are connected by an array of white myelinated fibers running in the brain's internal capsule and corona radiata. Damage to these fibers produces the same deficits as damage to either the basal ganglia or the cortex. This suggests that in order to comprehend and reproduce speech, a rapid exchange of information must take place between these two systems. The basal ganglia seem particularly critical for fluent verbal execution, whereas the posterior region of the left cortex is involved in almost every type of verbal task from grammatical accuracy, to naming pictures or actions, to verbal short-term memory. Figure 6.2 is a map of these functions.

What was particularly interesting about Gordon's results was that the regions of brain cortex controlling the retrieval and

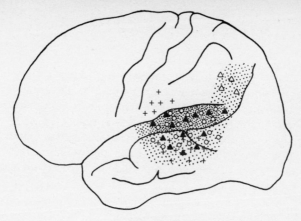

FIGURE 6.2

The cortical regions of the posterior left hemisphere found to be most critical to specific linguistic abilities. The shaded region subserves verbal short-term memory, with the denser shading representing the most crucial area for this function. This area is essentially Wernicke's area. The remaining regions can be identified as follows:

+   *grammatical complexity and accuracy*
○   *naming objects and actions from pictures or verbal descriptions*
▲   *identifying objects and actions that have been named*
△   *identifying letters that have been named*

Statistical analyses indicate that the retrieval of names (naming objects and actions) was considerably more impaired than storage of names (pointing to a picture that is named).

production of names (as for instance to colors and pictures of objects) are adjacent to or overlap the regions involved in pointing to items that were named by someone else. This demonstrates that both expressive and receptive language share neural systems.

Nearly all of Gordon's patients were males. Considering the sex differences that are consistently found in the tasks Gordon employed, one might hypothesize that the cortex of the posterior left hemisphere might be a brain locus of sex differences in linguistic function.

Sex Differences in Cortical Organization

Doreen Kimura mentioned to me several years ago that she had consistently observed that women seemed to suffer far less permanent language deficits with left-hemisphere brain damage than men. Recently she published two research reports on an extensive series of comparisons between the male and female patients, the site of their brain lesions, and their performance on various behavioral tests. In 1983 she reported on 216 left-hemisphere–damaged patients classified by sex and site and type of lesion.[7] Her first major finding was that irrespective of the extent and type of brain damage, men were more likely to suffer from various forms of aphasia than women. The ratio of male/female aphasic patients was two to one (or 66 percent males). Furthermore, the site of damage appeared to be an important factor in determining these sex differences. Males suffered from language-related deficits with lesions in either the front or the back portions of the left hemisphere. Females were far less likely to suffer permanent disability from lesions to the posterior parts of the left hemisphere, the region considered to be the "classical language area" and the one Gordon found to be critical in male language skills.

Kimura divided her sample into those patients with lesions clearly restricted to either the anterior or the posterior part of the left hemisphere. This reduced the sample to 49 males and 32 females. Next she looked at the proportion of patients who were diagnosed as exhibiting aphasia (20 men, 10 women). These proportions are presented in table 6.1, which shows a striking sex difference in the brain regions involved in producing aphasia. The scores on the language tests even for two women who suffered from aphasia due to lesions to the posterior part of the left hemisphere were considerably better than the scores of the other groups. Their receptive language ability was 20 percent higher. This is additional confirmation that posterior left-hemisphere damage in the female brain produces far less serious consequences than in the male brain. In further examinations of the case histories of these patients, Kimura was able to rule out the cause of the lesions (tumor or vascular) and the age of the patient as predictive of this sex difference.

TABLE 6.1

The Percentage of Men and Women Suffering from Aphasia Following Lesions to the Anterior (Front) and Posterior (Rear) Portions of the Left Hemisphere

	Males	Females
Anterior Lesion	40%	41%
Group Size	15	13
Posterior Lesion	62%	11%
Group Size	34	19

SOURCE: Data from D. Kimura, "Sex Differences in Cerebral Organization of Speech and Praxis Functions" (1983).

When Kimura compared the total population with restricted left-hemisphere lesions to the patients with aphasia, the aphasic group was severely affected in their ability to imitate oral-facial movements and to copy manual gestures. This indicates the close relationship between language and gesture, or the fine-motor system. Once again, the two women with aphasia produced by posterior damage showed less effects of the lesions than did the men. The women performed completely normally on these tasks.

In a later report Kimura and Richard Harshman compared the performance of 270 patients with both right- and left-hemisphere damage with a control group of patients who had been hospitalized for cardiovascular disorders.[8] None of the brain-damaged patients had aphasia. Nevertheless, the men with left-hemisphere damage had significantly lower verbal IQ scores on the Wechsler Intelligence Scale than the controls, while scores of the left-hemisphere–damaged women were equal to those of the control group. When the five subtests of the verbal IQ were analyzed separately, an interesting pattern emerged. The major deficit in the left-hemisphere–damaged males was found to be in short-term memory (digit span) and to a lesser extent in a test called "vocabulary," which measures the accuracy and speed of generating definitions of words. The brain-damaged females also had lower than normal vocabulary scores. A surprising result was found in the right-hemisphere–damaged patients. Here the women, but not the men, had lower digit-span and vocabulary scores.

To summarize these results and their implications for both sexes, language is represented largely in the left hemisphere, but females appear to differ from males in the degree of aphasia following posterior damage. Females also have a bilateral representation of specific language-related skills (verbal short-term memory and verbal retrieval of word meaning in the *right* hemisphere). In addition to these results on sex differences, verbal fluency has been found to be intimately connected with the ability to mime gesture and oral-facial movements. Both these fine-motor skills are lost together when the patient is aphasic.

Now the question arises as to how to interpret Kimura's findings. Do the results indicate, as she suggests, that, in females, language is represented more focally in the anterior part of the left hemisphere at the speech motor area and that males have two regions for language? If this is the case, then males ought to suffer less from aphasia, because they have *two* language systems instead of one, the opposite of what Kimura found. A different way of looking at these findings would be to ask whether the sex difference is related to the way that language is represented *within* a particular language region. Men and women seem to be equally affected by damage to the frontal speech output system, a fact that indicates the systems are organized similarly in both sexes. But in females, a far more efficient neural organization may underpin language in the posterior part of the brain; and it is for this reason that posterior lesions do so little harm to their language ability. When any brain function is maximally efficient, it is less influenced by "noise" in the system and can operate with much less tissue. If females have a better-organized language system, it ought to be more resistant to disruption.

Using a different technique, neurosurgeon George Ojemann at the University of Washington has been studying the effect of electrically stimulating the surface of the brain cortex in men and women about to undergo brain surgery.[9] This procedure which disrupts the function of the area that is stimulated, is essential because the surgeon must locate and spare all the tissue that is involved in language. Since the surface of the brain is completely insensitive to pain, patients can report their experience when a mild electrical current is applied to very small portions of the tissue.

Ojemann uses a series of tests that include phonemic decoding, naming, reading, imitation of oral-facial movement, and short-term memory. To date, he has never found stimulation of the right hemisphere to cause any disruption on his tests, but considerable deficits arise with stimulation of the left hemisphere. One of his more amazing observations is that stimulation of one specific location disrupts both phonemic decoding *and* oral-facial movements. In other words, we now have confirmation that an intimate neural connection exists between certain sensory and motor processes, in this case the auditory discrimination of speech sounds and the ability to program the facial muscles that produce those sounds.

Most of these language-related skills are localized in a number of small areas over the brain cortex, forming what looks like a mosaic or patchwork. The phonemic decoding regions, for example, are largely distributed along the Sylvian fissure (see figure 6.1), but can be found in the more frontal regions as well. Every individual has a somewhat different arrangement and location of these patches. Certain functions are completely nonoverlapping, as, for example, short-term memory and naming fluency. It is possible to stimulate the brain surface and completely disrupt a memory task, while naming fluency remains intact.

A third finding that will be important to our discussion comes from data on bilingual patients, where it was found to be more difficult to disrupt the primary language than the secondary language. Stimulation of a much wider region of brain cortex disrupts the *weaker* secondary language. This is direct support for the hypothesis that when any behavioral function becomes efficient and automatic, the amount of cortical tissue needed to produce that activity is reduced. Additional confirmation comes from the relationship of verbal IQ to the surface area affected by stimulation. Patients with low verbal IQs suffered from disruption in language when a considerably wider area was stimulated than patients with high IQs.

These findings are extremely important in helping to interpret the results of a study on sex differences by Ojemann, Catherine Mateer, and Samuel Polen.[10] When the stimulation was applied to the frontal speech motor area of the left hemisphere directly at the region controlling speech, 100 percent of both male and female patients were unable to execute the naming tasks. But when the probes were moved farther forward on the brain, the stimulation

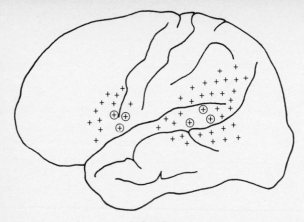

FIGURE 6.3

The regions of the cortical surface of the left hemisphere in which naming was disrupted by electrical stimulation in 50 percent or more of the patients tested. + indicates the areas affected for males only. ⊕ indicates the areas affected for both males and females.

SOURCE: Adapted from C. A. Mateer; S. B. Polen; and G. A. Ojemann, "Sexual Variation in Cortical Localization of Naming as Determined by Stimulation Mapping," *Behavioral and Brain Sciences* 5 (1982): 310–11. Reprinted with permission of the authors and Cambridge University Press.

produced disruption to a much greater extent in men (80 percent) than in women (22 percent). Males suffered from disruption of naming when probes were applied to a number of areas of the posterior region including the parietal lobe and the middle and superior temporal regions. The maximum effect for the females was much more highly localized to a region at the superior temporal zone. Figure 6.3 illustrates the regions involved for over half of the male and female patients. In short, males' naming skills appear to be affected by stimulation almost everywhere on the left hemisphere. For females, the stimulation had to be highly localized for any deficit to appear. Thus females need less available brain cortex to function maximally in language skills. The system is less susceptible to "noise" because females' verbal skills are more efficient.

A densely fibered neural system is less noisy than a sparsely fibered system. Evidence from animal research has taught us that as young brains develop, the fibrous connectors (dendrites) between nerve cells grow rapidly, but the nerve cells themselves do not increase in number. The density of the growth is partly determined by the amount of stimulation in the environment. Not only do dendrites grow, but they do so in an orderly way in the normal brain, forming coherent layers of cells and their connections. Recently, Albert Galaburda of the Harvard medical school has presented evidence on the fine anatomy of brains of two male "dyslexics."[11] He discovered that there were abnormalities or maturational arrest in the migration of cells within layers of the posterior left cortex, whereas the right hemisphere appeared completely normal. These findings are very important and could begin to explain the problem faced by severe dyslexics who fail to learn to read even though they are highly motivated and intelligent. However, these findings should be interpreted with extreme caution. The brain is not biologically programmed to learn to read. In order to learn to read, several sensorimotor operations must be coordinated in the brain. It is these sensorimotor functions that are properties of brains, not reading per se. Thus one cannot speak of the "reading center" of the brain, or even of a "dyslexic brain," which only means a "brain that reads with difficulty." One must discover which of the sensory or motor subroutines were affected by the abnormal cellular migrations, for it is the *subroutines* that go together to make reading possible. We need to know much more about Galaburda's patients, such as whether they had abnormal speech or short-term memory deficits. We also need to consider whether or not there was any seizure activity in this region.

Taken together, all of these findings support the view that sex differences in the brain are due to the organization of the fine structure *within* a hemisphere rather than to any gross differences between the hemispheres. In fact, no studies of gross anatomy have even uncovered any sex differences. In a recent report in *Science* magazine, Christine de LaCoste-Utamsing and Ralph Holloway at Columbia University reported on a difference between men and women in the size of the corpus callosum, a huge bundle of fibers that connects the two hemispheres. Women were found to have a larger posterior portion of this fiber bundle, called the splenium.[12] However, these findings have not been replicated in two independent studies carried out by Sandra Witelson at McMasters University in Canada and by Jerre Levy at the University of Chicago, using much larger populations of subjects.[13] Thus we continue to fail to find evidence to support gross anatomical differences in the brains of males and females. In almost all humans, language functions are localized to the left hemisphere and rapid visual pattern analysis is localized to the right.

One final study indicates that consistency of lateralization of functions carried out on the right or left side of the body does not appear to be involved in sex differences but is related to reading. John Kershner, a Canadian psychologist, has found that strongly lateralized boys—that is, boys who show a high concordance of hand, eye, foot, and ear dominance (whether it be of the right or the left side)—are most often the poorest readers. In Kershner's study 110 six-year-olds were tested for laterality using four sensorimotor tasks. These children were followed up at nine and eleven years. The highly lateralized boys were found to be consistently inferior in reading at all ages than the less lateralized boys. No relationship was found between laterality measures for girls and their reading scores. Furthermore, girls were neither more nor less "lateralized" than the boys.[14]

Kershner's findings relate to studies of handedness, which reveal that left-handers are more prone to reading disorders than right-handers and that girls are consistently more right-handed than boys. Marian Annett, who has been studying this phenomenon for many years on hundreds of British schoolchildren, believes that handedness is a secondary consequence of lateralization for language. The reason the right hand is favored over the left is because the left hemisphere is specialized for the control of fluent motor action.[15]

All evidence points consistently to the fact that girls are favored for language development and that the organization of the left hemisphere in female brains is more precise and less prone to damage and disruption than are male brains. We know that most regions of the brain are influenced by sex hormones and that they operate to regulate or modulate the release of neurotransmitter substances that make electrical activity possible. However, it will be many years before the data on hormone uptake and hormonal regulation have been related to behavior. Meanwhile, hormonal control is in turn regulated by genes and genetic information is organized on chromosomes. We look next at the evidence that sex differences in language are dependent on genetic factors.

Genetic Link to Reading Problems

The neural systems in the brain are both preprogrammed at birth and modifiable by the environment. Because infants are unable to use language systems and, as has been shown, these take some four to five years to develop, one cannot argue from the neurological evidence that sex differences in language and reading are due to biology or to the environment. Additional data must support either claim. It also must be borne in mind that we are dealing with a problem of *degree.* Facility in any behavior is a product of both biology and the environment. The issue is rather: Do females have a greater boost from biology than males? And if so, will they be found to be less at risk from the environment? The answer to both of these questions appears to be yes, and the evidence comes from studies on genetics and the impact of the environment on performance.

There are two major ongoing studies of the genetic determinants of reading disability. One is the Colorado Family Reading Study carried out by J. C. DeFries and his colleagues at the University of Colorado at Boulder, and the second is being conducted at the Boys Town Institute in Omaha. The first study involves over one thousand subjects, half of whom are poor readers, and their immediate families. The other half are a control group of normal readers and their families. The ratio of male to female poor readers is 3.3 to 1 (77 percent male). In a 1980 report, Sadie Decker and DeFries outlined their results on tests of reading achievement, visuospatial ability, and coding speed.[16] Their results showed conclusively that reading problems run in families. The reading ability of the siblings of the poor readers was inferior to that of the siblings of the control group, and the same effect was found for the parents of the two groups. However, this does not *prove* a biological basis for the reading problems, because the effect could just as well be due to environmental factors, such as the number of books in the home, whether or not the parents read to their children, and so forth. Further analyses of their data revealed an interesting effect when the male and female siblings were assessed separately.[17] Brothers of the boys who were poor readers were considerably worse readers than brothers of the good readers, as would be expected. By contrast, there was *no difference* in the reading ability of the sisters of poor readers and those of good readers. As the sisters of the dyslexic girls were brought up in the same environment, DeFries and Decker's study lends strong support to a biological basis for reading problems in the *girls,* indicating that severe reading difficulties are heritable. Furthermore, the parents, especially the fathers, of the reading-retarded girls were in all cases more severely affected than the parents of the boys. DeFries has suggested that reading aptitude in girls has a stronger genetic component (is more biologically based), but that males are genetically more "at risk" to environmental factors. Despite the fact that heritability was clearly involved in reading skill, a simple Mendelian model did not fit their data. When they tested their results with various genetic models, such as the autosomal dominance or recessive models, which make assumptions about the sex-linkage on the X or Y chromosomes, no clear-cut effect was found. They were also unable to rule out a model that specified no genetic relationship, thus leaving the issue unresolved.

Investigations of familial traits may involve analyses of trait distributions in families, as in DeFries and Decker's study, or may involve a biochemical approach, as in the Boys Town study. Eight families of learning-disabled boys were studied, involving seventy people over three generations, all of whom had a history of severe reading problems. This fact indicates that there is a strong genetic influence on the disability. Blood samples were taken from each subject and were tested for a host of genetic markers, including blood groups, chemical makeup, and chromosomal staining patterns, which are known to be heritable.

Reporting on their results in 1982, Shelley Smith indicated that a common pattern in these families was a pronounced staining of chromosome 15.[18] The protein β-2 microglobulin located on this chromosome is known to be influenced by the male sex hormone testosterone and is involved in the lateralization of the brain and in the immune system. It is possible that the β-2 microglobulin is also somehow connected with factors that influence the acquisition of reading skills, but to prove this, much more refined assessments of the correlation between this staining pattern and precise sensorimotor skills will have to be made.

As in the Colorado project, the Boys Town study showed that brothers of dyslexic children were considerably more severely retarded in reading than were the sisters. In addition, the reading skills of the adult males in this population were indistinguishable from those of the male children. As noted earlier, these children and others with reading problems performed poorly on the digit span, auditory discrimination, and the pegboard tests (they did especially poorly in this test with the nondominant hand). The severely dyslexic boys were superior in tests of visual memory and visual-perceptual organization when compared to matched controls.

It is difficult to integrate the findings from these two studies, as one used boys and girls in one-generation families and the other only boys and three generations of their families. Both suggest, however, that there is a heritable component to reading disorders. The data confirm general population studies showing that males are much more at risk to factors that create reading problems. On the other hand, girls with reading handicaps are rare, and their problems appear to be much less influenced by the environment. If the boys are more at risk, then it might be expected that male performance would be more affected by unstable environments than would female performance.

Males at Risk

In chapter 1 we saw that the sex ratios for dyslexia in a normal school environment are approximately three to one, but that in clinical populations or in special schools for the learning disabled, these ratios shift to five or six to one.[19] Furthermore, there is a correlation between behavior disorders and reading difficulties in males, but not in females. These facts in conjunction with the genetic studies suggest that there are two factors at work in reading performance. One is biological and independent of culture, and the other is environmental. Clinical data indicate that males are more vulnerable to environmental factors, and that when the environment is not supportive, male reading ability declines even further with respect to female performance. Females who appear in the clinic with similar emotional difficulties exhibit no deficiencies in reading skills when compared to normal populations.

Teachers have long recognized the importance of the influence of reading material on reading success. If the material is interesting then reading performance improves. However, it turns out that this is true only for males. I already pointed out that the blatant sex-role stereotype of the passive and uninvolved female portrayed in reading primers has no effect on female reading ability. In an attempt to specify the importance of high-interest material on girls' and boys' reading progress, Steven Asher and Richard Markell tested eighty-seven fifth-graders on reading performance using material specifically suited to each child's interest. Over time, it was found that the reading scores of the boys and girls did not differ. However, in the control population, who read material of equal difficulty but selected to be of little interest to 10-year olds, sex differences reappeared, with the girls reading significantly better than the boys.[20]

It appears that males are penalized in classrooms where silent reading is the norm. Elizabeth Rowell tested 240 children in the third and fifth grades in three types of school in Connecticut. In every case in all the schools, boys' reading comprehension was significantly better when they read aloud than when they read silently. It made no difference whether girls read silently or aloud.[21] Males also appear to have more difficulties than females in open classroom environments where large numbers of children are free to interact in adjoining classrooms and work areas. Frederick Gies and his coworkers found that the greatest sex difference on tests of vocabulary, reading, and language arts emerged in an open classroom setting, where females did particularly well. In his sample of 108 sixth-graders, sex differences were less pronounced in the traditional closed classroom setting, where males surpassed females on the vocabulary portion of the test.[22] It is not clear from this analysis whether it is the lack of distraction in closed classrooms that is important to males or whether they are responding to that setting's greater structure. Rowell's and Gies's findings imply that males might do well in a more structured environment where oral reading is emphasized.

Based on a large sample (184) of ten-year-old children in Denmark, researchers report that low socioeconomic class combines with minor birth complications to further depress males' reading scores. A strong relationship between reading problems and these two factors was found for males, but not for females.[23] It was noted in chapter 1 that there was a high correlation between referrals for antisocial behavior in schoolboys and reading difficulties. These data were reported by psychologists William Yule and Michael Rutter, who studied the relation between severity of emotional disturbance and the degree of reading problems in English schoolchildren. No such relationship was reported for girls.[24] A similar result has been reported for an American population by Ivy Lanthier and Thomas Deiker.[25]

Not only does severe environmental stress influence male but not female aptitude, but male performance can also suffer from minor and more immediate environmental stressors. S. Cotler and R. J. Palmer studied 120 children in the fourth to the sixth grades on tests of reading comprehension by asking students to match paragraphs for meaning.[26] The children were put under mild pressure by inducing anxiety through praise or criticism. The girls were consistently superior at matching paragraphs, but the sex effect was enhanced by criticism, which strongly affected male performance.

In their study of 117 adolescent inpatients, Lanthier and Deiker also discovered that there was a strong relationship on a battery of tests in reading, language, and mathematics between the scores of 66 disturbed adolescent males and their *mother's* scores. No relationship was found between the scores of any of the 51 adolescent girls referred for emotional problems on various tests and those of either parent. Additionally, the girls were significantly ahead on the language achievement test and the total test battery. This could suggest a genetic relationship between male ability and their mothers *or* the impact of a more academically gifted mother on her male offspring (an environmental effect). The latter explanation seems more likely in the light of the results of a large investigation by Victor Cicirelli.

Cicirelli studied 600 middle-class white families.[27] In the population as a whole, females were superior to males on the verbal elaboration subtest of the Minnesota Creative Thinking battery and on the California Language Achievement test. In two-, three-, and four-child families, Cicirelli found, in general, that boys' performance increased noticeably (as did IQ scores) if they had at least one female sibling. Male children were particularly at risk in families where all siblings were male, especially in the families with three or four children. In ninety two-child families, firstborn girls had the highest IQ (118) and firstborn boys had the lowest (108), with secondborn boys and girls being more similar (114 and 111). The findings for three-child families show little effect of the sex constitution on IQ or reading for girls, but again, both IQ scores and reading scores increase if boys have at least one sister. The IQ for boys with two brothers is 109.6; with two sisters, 118; and one brother and one sister, 117. Reading scores also reflect this trend, rising from an average of 6.8 to 7.6 and 7.9 for boys with one or two sisters. An identical trend was found in four-child families.

Cicirelli does not report the siblings' ages. It is possible that his results would be even more striking if the boys with older versus younger sisters were compared. The data, however, strongly suggest that in small families, the mother is very important to her son's language development, but as the family size increases, the boy is considerably advantaged if he has a sister, especially, one would suspect, an older sister. It does not seem to matter a great deal to girls' language development whether they are in a large or small family or whether they are surrounded by brothers or sisters.

These results bring us to the crux of the nature-nurture issue. In a constant environment, as shown by the genetic studies, sex differences in language emerge that are independent of the environment: a biological program. These studies provide some clues as to why the brain organization for language is different between the sexes. In extreme environments, the performance of males, but not of females, swings dramatically. Males appear at risk to many environmental situations. One might also ask if the *predisposition* to risk is also biological. The complex relationship between the environment and biology is thrown into high relief, and the meaninglessness of a nature-versus-nurture argument becomes apparent. Sandra Scarr's solution, discussed in chapter 2, is of obvious importance here: What is "easy to learn" is most rooted in biology and least influenced by the environment. What is "difficult to learn" is most upset by environmental stressors and least biologically fixed. There is a continuum between biological and environmental determinants, not a dichotomy. We now have considerable evidence that females have a greater biological boost to develop linguistic competence and all that entails. With this knowledge, how can we organize our schools to promote the best interests of children who have difficulty learning to read and write, especially boys? Some possible solutions are presented in chapter 11.

7

Mathematics: Is Society Picking on Girls?

The Mystery of Math

Research on reading has taught us that learning to read is more complex than we imagined and that what seems obvious from a crude analysis of a skill is not necessarily true. New discoveries were possible because reading research was brought into the mainstream of "information processing" psychology. The essence of this approach is to break down perceptual and cognitive functions into smaller and smaller units and to study how these units relate to performance in more complex abilities.

Currently, most of the effort in mathematics teaching has been driven by theory. This is similar to earlier days in reading research where "look-say" methods or the Initial Teaching Alphabet were introduced in early elementary grades with little or no experimental basis for expecting better and more lasting results. A number of new approaches in mathematics were initiated both in the United States and abroad, such as Nuffield math and science, the Illinois Math Program, and the Madison project. But the fine-grained analysis of mathematics as a discipline and detailed research on the outcome of teaching approaches is a long way off. One of the difficulties is that mathematics is infinitely more complex than reading. There are many branches of mathematics and numerous mathematical skills. Even sophisticated mathematicians describe themselves as "algebraic thinkers" or "geometric thinkers" and avoid areas of their discipline where they are weak. This means that quite apart from identifying which subcategories of mathematics are relatively independent, we must specify each of them in terms of the necessary perceptual, motor, and cognitive skills.

A further and more serious handicap is that mathematicians rarely become teachers or psychologists. Just as it is necessary for anyone studying reading to understand how to read in order to do research, this is even more true in mathematics. But mathematicians who can articulate mathematical concepts in classrooms are rare, those who understand the psychology of learning, rarer still, and those with these abilities *plus* the talent for research are almost nonexistent. For this reason mathematics research is nearly always a team effort. However, progress is still slow because unless a research psychologist has some deeper understanding of mathematical thought, he or she will be unable to frame the appropriate questions.

It is for these reasons that it is impossible to begin this chapter in the same way as I began chapter 4. We have only a rudimentary idea of what skills are important in learning mathematics, and this applies not only to the more complex forms such as algebra and geometry, but also to counting and simple addition. Workers interested in these issues are few in number, and often their analytic skills and aptitude for teaching are in such demand that they have little time for research. Nevertheless, some progress is being made. Much of the effort has been directed to breaking old assumptions and framing new questions. Joyce Steeves at Johns Hopkins University has been working with elementary schoolchildren, and her experience has largely confirmed the pioneering studies carried out by Jean Piaget in Switzerland.[1] He discovered that a series of stages must precede the conceptual understanding of simple addition. First children must be able to have a concept of topological space, to identify and classify objects and object relations. Next they need to comprehend the concept of serial order, ranking items or objects from smallest to largest or shortest to tallest, and so forth. Only when these ideas have been understood can the concept of *number* have any meaning. Learning to count does not guarantee that children will automatically learn what a number system represents.

Not only must children have the capacity to grasp the relationship between numbers and serial order, but they must also learn that numbers do not change; they cannot be transformed. Piaget calls this the "conservation of number." In addition, children must also learn that properties of rigid objects, such as length or area, cannot be transformed. When all of this is known, then it is time to learn to add.

These ideas have also been emphasized by Richard Skemp, a psychologist and mathematician working at Warwick University in England. He devotes an entire chapter in his excellent text, *The Psychology of Mathematics*, to the "naming of numbers."[2] Skemp offers a very penetrating perspective on the current situation in mathematics education. In the opening pages of his book he outlines a first principle that is essential to understanding math: "Concepts of a higher order than those which a person already has cannot be communicated to him by a definition, but only by arranging for him to encounter a suitable collection of examples" (p. 32). However, according to Skemp, almost all textbooks on mathematics consistently break this principle: "Nearly everywhere we see new topics introduced, not by examples but by definitions: of the most admirable brevity and exactitude for the teacher (who already has the concepts to which they refer) but unintelligible to the student" (p. 32).

Skemp's analysis of the mathematical process carefully builds from the simple notion of forming categories, to an examination of the increasing complexity of mathematical concepts and how they relate to and incorporate previous concepts. Yet nowhere in his book—or in any other—is there an account of what students who are gifted in mathematics *do*. In other words, it is easy to understand how most children develop a concept of green, or of a cup and saucer, but what is different about the child who develops the sorts of concepts that are relevant to mathematics? In other words, if, as Skemp points out, mathematics textbooks provide no key to the basic concepts required in the solution to the problems, how do some children seem to know them anyway? To take an obvious example, by the time they arrive in the geometry classroom, all students have a concept of a triangle. But it isn't the concept "triangle has three angles" that is relevant to understanding Pythagoras. Instead, it is the special *topological* properties of triangles, the relationship of the intersecting lines to the space they enclose as well as the unenclosed space surrounding them. How would a child come to know this unaided? How can the study of triangles appear relevant or interesting to some children but totally inscrutible and meaningless to others?

It will be at least another decade or two before we can begin to have any answers to these questions. An important first step toward this goal has been taken by Patricia Davidson at the University of Massachusetts. Davidson began as a teacher of mathematics and, like Skemp, became interested in the psychological factors involved in learning mathematics. She is currently developing a series of test batteries in which children's specific abilities and disabilities can be discovered. Davidson agrees with Steeves and with Skemp that math problem solving should proceed from the concrete to the abstract, and she is particularly aware that a child can perform effectively with abstract material and have no real understanding of the concrete form of the principle involved.[3]

For this reason Davidson studies children's problem solving using one of three modes set out by Piaget: concrete, pictorial, and abstract. A child may understand the problem easily in one mode but not in the other two. Children are also given a choice of solving the problem in all three modes and presenting their answer in one of the three. For example, a child might grasp a problem in its symbolic form, prefer to work it out with concrete objects, and show how it is solved by drawing a picture or a graph. Conversely, a child might grasp a problem in its concrete form and solve it in the abstract mode, with an equation. This means that there may be at least nine types of mathematical approaches. It is too early to determine how children fit into these various problem-solving modes, and we will have to wait until a large group of children have been tested.

Meanwhile, Davidson and her collaborator, Maria Marolda, have been carrying out research on children with learning problems at the Boston Children's Hospital.[4] They have been able to demonstrate that children fall into one of two major categories, which they call Learning Style I and Learning Style II. Learning Style I children are attentive to detail and solve all problems in a serial order, step by step. These children are more adept at problems of addition and multiplication than subtraction and division. They execute problems according to a set of memorized rules and procedures in a cookbook fashion. Because these children move from procedure to procedure, they are particularly poor at estimating, and they rarely recognize if they get an answer that is wide of the mark.

The second type of learner tackles problems much more holistically and relies less on language or rote memory. These children have a clearer grasp of the entire problem, quickly recognizing when an answer is obviously wrong. They have an advantage in subtraction and division over the other type of child, and they are especially good at counting backward. On the other hand, they tend to dislike word problems and become extremely impatient with multistep procedures.

It remains to be seen how these particular types of learners develop. It seems that the first type of learner would suffer in any mathematical discipline where topological factors were more important than systems of rules or logic. This would be especially true in geometry. Whatever the outcome of Davidson and Marolda's studies, it is clear that either strategy is effective in simple computation, provided it is used with skill. (As an aside, I would predict that Learning Style I would be more typical of most females and Learning Style II more typical of most males.)

Davidson's work will be taken up in more detail in chapter 11.

In this chapter I consider the issue of sex differences in mathematics. First it is necessary to review the evidence on the particular aspects of mathematics where sex differences appear. Next I consider in some detail the evidence for the current and most popular theory that sex differences in mathematics is entirely a product of socialization and sex-role stereotypes.

A Sudden Onset

In one week during March 1946, 5,362 boys and girls were born in England. These children became the total sample for the National Survey of Health and Development longitudinal study. By 1971 Jean Ross and H. R. Simpson were able to publish the

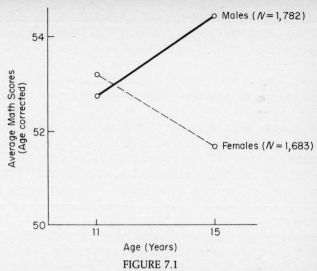

FIGURE 7.1

The shift in the average math scores of British boys and girls from eleven years to fifteen years of age. These scores have been normalized for each age.

NOTE: Based on data from J. M. Ross and H. R. Simpson, "The National Survey of Health and Development: 1. Educational Attainment," *British Journal of Psychology* 41 (1971):49–61.

results on educational attainment.[5] Test scores were reported for the children at eight, eleven, and fifteen years on various tests of verbal, nonverbal, and mathematical achievement. Of particular interest was the finding that there were no differences between the sexes on arithmetic scores at age eleven (the first age at which arithmetic scores were reported). By age fifteen, however, the girls' scores had declined with respect to their *own* previous levels and the boys' scores had increased. These effects are diagrammed in figure 7.1, which illustrates the average scores for 1,782 boys and 1,683 girls at each age. The scores were standardized at each age (with a mean of 50 and a standard deviation of 10) so that they may be directly compared between one age and the next.

Ross and Simpson's results are particularly important because English children are required to continue in the math program until the age of fifteen, and all children study algebra and geometry from the age of twelve. Therefore, the results are not due to differences between the boys and girls in the number of mathematics courses taken. The sex difference in mathematics did not reflect an overall difference in ability between the sexes. The girls were consistently ahead in verbal intelligence: 54.43 to 51.75 at age eleven and 53.68 to 52.23 at age fifteen. Sentence completion scores at age eight also showed the girls to be more advanced (54.00 to 52.30). The girls were ahead on reading achievement tests at age eight and eleven, but these differences disappeared by age fifteen. There were absolutely no sex differences in vocabulary at any age.

Another study, this one carried out in the United States, is relevant to the issue of the relationship between sex differences in mathematics and the age at which these effects emerge. Thomas Hilton and Gosta Berglund report on a similar type of national survey, the Growth Study, involving 632 boys and 688 girls in a high-academic accelerated program and 249 boys and 290 girls in a nonacademic program.[6] The students were tested at grades 5, 7, 9, and 11 on the STEP math achievement battery. In each case the boys and girls had taken the same number of math courses. Figure 7.2 illustrates the sex differences in the two populations and the grades at which these sex differences appear. Statistical analysis indicated that the sex effects in the academic group were marginally significant at grade 7 (age twelve) but highly significant at grades 9 and 11, (ages fourteen and sixteen), and that the difference between the sexes *increased with age.* Sex differences did not appear until grade 11 in the nonacademic group.

The figure indicates that the high-academic boys and girls between the ages of twelve and fourteen achieved the same average STEP math scores as the nonacademic group at age sixteen (270–275). This means that sex differences appear in either group only when the students reach a specific level of mathematics performance. In other words, these results can have nothing to do with onset of puberty, fears at adolescence, or social pressures; otherwise one would have to assume that all of these influences were specific to ability and not to age, something that is not only unlikely but impossible. The more reasonable conclusion is that the sex differences arise as mathematics becomes more abstract.

Further support for this conclusion is revealed by Hilton and Berglund's findings that female interest in mathematics declines markedly in the older academic girls, but not at all in the nonacademic girls. No sex difference in interest in mathematics was found in either population at age twelve. This strongly suggests that the accelerated girls' boredom or disinterest is related

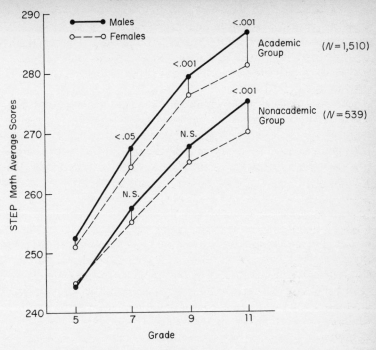

FIGURE 7.2

The performance of American boys and girls on the STEP math achievement test for grades 5 to 11 (ten to sixteen years) in an accelerated high-academic group (N = 1,510) and a nonacademic group (N = 539).

SOURCE: From T. L. Hilton and G. W. Bergland, "Sex Differences in Mathematics Achievement—A Longitudinal Study," *Journal of Education Research* 67 (1974): 231–37, a publication of the Helen Dwight Reid Educational Foundation. Reprinted with permission of Heldres Publications.

to the degree of abstractness of the mathematical problems they encounter rather than an increasing distaste for mathematics produced by social attitudes about math or science. Hilton and Berglund also document a large sex difference in an increasing interest for males in both groups in scientific pursuits, but this interest appears earlier and is considerably more pronounced in the academic males.

Despite their results, which show high-academic girls disadvantaged by age thirteen to fourteen, but low-academic girls not disadvantaged until age sixteen, Hilton and Berglund conclude that, although no direction of causality can be inferred from the relationship between attitude and performance, the sex differences

127

emerge because of sex-role–stereotyped attitudes about academic disciplines or, as they put it, "sex-typed interests." They go further to state that no physiological or psychological factors need be invoked to explain these results, a conclusion that seems completely unwarranted.

As was noted in the opening chapters, the explanation for the sex differences in higher mathematics has consistently focused on social variables to the exclusion of any type of biological or other environmental theory. Hilton and Berglund's conclusions are similar to thousands of others on this issue, and their attitude pervades the research.

In another series of studies on sex differences, the authors came to a conclusion opposite to that of Hilton and Berglund. This research is part of an ongoing project on gifted children carried out at the Johns Hopkins University. The Johns Hopkins talent searches have been in progress since 1972, and thousands of children from the southeastern states have been involved. In a recent article in *Science,* Camilla Benbow and Julian Stanley report on children involved in the project for the years 1980 to 1982.[7] Children were eligible to participate in the project if they scored in the top 3 percent in verbal and math ability, or overall IQ. The children were under thirteen, in the seventh and eighth grades, and had completed an equal number of courses in mathematics. Table 7.1 has been taken from this report.

Male performance on the math subtest of the Scholastic Aptitude Test (SAT) is clearly superior, and the ratio of boys to girls increases with higher scores. As this is a college entrance test, and these are junior high school children, performance at this level of sophistication must be determined by a genuine aptitude for abstract mathematical reasoning, rather than to what has been learned in the classroom. In contrast to these results, no sex differences have ever appeared in tests of verbal ability in the twelve years this project has been ongoing. Of particular interest is the ratio of boys to girls achieving scores of 700 or better on the mathematics portion of the SAT (800 is a perfect score).

All the children had taken an equal number of mathematics courses and all reported a keen interest in the discipline, preferring it to biology, physics, or chemistry. In follow-up studies on these mathematically gifted youngsters, the authors discovered that despite the boys' natural flair for mathematics, the girls consistently

TABLE 7.1

The Number of High-Scoring Students on the Scholastic Aptitude Test in Mathematics (SAT Math) among the Selected Seventh- and Eighth-Graders—19,883 Boys and 19,937 Girls—in the Johns Hopkins Regional Talent Search for 1980, 1981, and 1982. Scores of 700 and Higher are from Students in the Johns Hopkins National Talent Search.

SAT Math Score	Number	% of Total	Ratio of Boys to Girls
Johns Hopkins Regional Search			
420 or more			
Boys	9,119	45.9	1.5:1
Girls	6,220	31.2	
500 or more			
Boys	3,618	18.2	2.1:1
Girls	1,707	8.6	
600 or more			
Boys	648	3.3	4.1:1
Girls	158	0.8	
Johns Hopkins National Search			
700 or more			
Boys	260	†	13:1
Girls	20	†	

Boys average score = 416.
Girls average score = 386.
Highest score = 800.

SOURCE: From C. P. Benbow and J. C. Stanley, "Sex Differences in Mathematical Reasoning Ability: More Facts," *Science* 222 (December 1983):1029–31, table 1. Copyright 1983 by the American Association for the Advancement of Science.
† Total tested is unknown.

received higher math grades. In addition, a larger percentage of the mathematically able girls intended to major in mathematics in college. This finding—that mathematically able girls remain in math classes and outperform the boys—runs completely counter to a socialization prediction. The major sex difference is that there are so few girls in this population.

Benbow and Stanley believe that the socialization hypothesis cannot account for sex differences in mathematical reasoning. They speculate that environmental factors, sex hormones, physiologically induced differences in activity levels, or different brain-hemisphere localizations and genes might be responsible, and conclude: "It seems likely . . . that putting all one's faith in boy-vs-girl socialization processes as the only permissible explanation is premature" (p. 1263).[8] Although Benbow and Stanley caution their readers about generalizing these results to the average population, their results support the finding that the sex difference in mathematics becomes more noticeable with age and with academic aptitude. When Ross and Simpson broke down their data into five academic levels, they found that the girls were trailing in math scores in the nonacademic populations by two percentage points, but by four percentage points in the high academic groups, again suggesting that the problems girls face increase with the abstract reasoning involved in the more advanced mathematical subjects.

Because of the polemical cast to the conflict over nature-nurture issues in the realm of mathematics and sex differences, it is important to restate the Scarr hypothesis. No researchers, including Benbow and Stanley, deny that environmental factors are important in these sex differences. Rather they say that because of other factors, possibly due to direct or indirect biological differences, it is *easier* for males to acquire skills in higher mathematics. Because it is more *difficult* for females, the environment will have a greater impact on female performance. The argument is identical to the one presented in chapter 6 regarding reading ability. In mathematics, females are "at risk" to environmental influences to a much greater degree than males. Therefore, adverse environmental influences—especially, the view that girls are *supposed* to be poor in mathematics—will have a greater impact. If you are "permitted" to be poor, then it is far easier to quit when the going gets tough. (Notice that no such option is permitted for young boys learning to read.) What Benbow and Stanley and others, including myself, object to in the socialization theory is the belief that socialization *causes* differences in intellectual aptitude. This inference about the direction of causality occurs even when researchers deny the possibility of deriving cause-effect relationships from simple correlations, as, for example, in the conclusions of Hilton and Berglund.

But apart from the problem of how one is to interpret the results of these studies, what evidence is there that social, environmental, or biological factors influence the development of these sex differences? Whichever theory turns out to be most valid, it must account for the fact that sex differences are almost never found in tests of computation involving arithmetic principles. For the remainder of this chapter I consider the evidence for the socialization hypothesis. In chapter 8 I take up some of the alternative theories and the evidence to support them.

Attitude or Ability?

I have already touched upon the difficulty of inferring causes from studies that use correlational statistics that were designed to determine what factors or events are related. Correlational procedures cannot adequately demonstrate a causal relationship between any social or environmental factor and a learning handicap, because one can never determine the *direction* of causality from correlations, even when there is a temporal relationship between two events. The classic example of this fallacy was given by the philosopher David Hume, when he likened the theory that antecedent events produce subsequent events to the belief that the rooster's crow causes the sunrise. The problem is even more acute when one attempts to relate attitudes to abilities. For example, suppose that a correlation is demonstrated between the ability of children to draw and their positive or negative attitude to art. Does the attitude produce the ability or the ability the attitude? All studies stressing the socialization model face this problem.

There is only one way to determine whether the environment makes a difference to any particular skill, and that is to alter the environment and look at the subsequent effect on the skill. Many experiments of this type were described in the last chapter, as in the study investigating the effects of closed and open classroom environments or oral versus silent reading techniques on boys and girls learning to read. In these cases the experimenter intervened in the environment, training one group of children with one method and one or more groups using different methods. If the manipulation of a particular environment results in a measurable change in behavior, it can be concluded that this manipulation affected the outcome. Even here one must be cautious about inferring that a manipulation caused an effect until the experiment has been replicated, the results are consistent, and one can determine that the impact of the experimenter's manipulations were *indeed* due to what the experimenter believed he or she was doing.

I am laboring this point because the research on sex differences in mathematics is singularly prone to Hume's fallacy. In fact, I will not discuss most of the "research" on this topic because it fails even to attempt correlational analysis. These studies gather questionnaire data on attitudes about mathematics; experience with parents, teachers, peers, and so forth. When the data are tallied, they generally show that many girls over the age of thirteen to fourteen do not like mathematics and that girls tend to have more difficulty and feel less confident about mathematics than boys do. From these results it is concluded that society is causing girls to have bad attitudes, and that these attitudes cause their dislike of math and their poor performance.

The gravest difficulty with this type of study is that the scores representing the attitudes are never correlated with math performance, so there is no way to determine whether attitudes toward parental or peer pressure and teacher encouragement are even related to the sex difference in mathematical ability. Second, there is never any control condition, such as a questionnaire on whether girls feel or perceive that they are more or less encouraged in *any* academic discipline compared to boys. If fathers do not encourage girls in mathematics, do they then encourage them in biology, where girls do well? I very much doubt it.

Unfortunately in only a few studies has the research team made some attempt to relate the information on social and attitudinal factors to mathematical aptitude. It must be borne in mind that these studies are not experiments. They are entirely correlational, and for this reason one cannot specify the direction of causality. Two major surverys have focused in detail on both social and attitudinal factors and mathematics performance in boys and girls. These are an ongoing project carried out under the supervision of Elizabeth Fennema and Julia Sherman in Madison, Wisconsin, and a study of Palo Alto High School students carried out by Jane Stallings at the Stanford Research Institute.

Although the Johns Hopkins team found little evidence that attitudes affect students' performance in their high ability groups, this could be due to the fact that all of these children were gifted in mathematics and therefore not representative of the general population. Fennema and Sherman chose to study normal children, and they have carried out a detailed survey of over 1,200 students in grades 9 to 12 in four high schools in Madison, Wisconsin.[9] All students had completed the same number of mathematics courses. Several tests were employed, such as the Scannell Mathematics Achievement Test, a vocabulary IQ test (the Quick Word), and the spatial relations component of the Differential Aptitude Test. The students' motivation and attitudes toward math, as well as their perceptions of their parents' and teachers' attitudes, were also measured, and the various scores were correlated. The results for the spatial relations test will be reported in the following chapter.

In three of the four schools, sex differences in math achievement were found in the expected direction. The combined sex effect across all schools was very large, with a probability of over one in a thousand ($p < 0.001$). There was no sex difference in the vocabulary test, which confirms consistent findings of an absence of sex differences in vocabulary. Sex differences were found in a number of the questionnaire items. Boys were overwhelmingly more likely to rate math as a "male domain" than were girls, they reported more confidence in math, and they were more likely to report mathematics as useful and to have more positive perceptions of both their mothers' and their fathers' attitude toward their mathematical ability. Boys also participated in more math and space-related activities outside the classroom. The sexes did not perceive their math teachers differently, nor did they report differences in the degree of motivation or in their attitudes toward succeeding in mathematics. Although these effects were not always consistent across all four schools, the trends were similar.

Fennema and Sherman correlated the scores on the questionnaire items with the scores on the various achievement tests. In order to illustrate the actual power of the raw correlation scores, I have computed the variances by squaring each correlation value. This provides a percentage estimate of how much these relationships share in common. For example, if height and weight were correlated at 0.60, this would mean that one could predict height from weight, or weight from height, with 36 percent accuracy (0.6 × 0.6). These variance estimates are presented in table 7.2. The values represent the percent of the total contribution to mathe-

TABLE 7.2

Percent of Variance Contributed by Ability and Attitudes to Math Achievement in Grades 9 to 11. Variance Scores Have Been Computed from the Correlations in the Original Table.

Variables	Males (%) (N = 574)	Females (%) (N = 555)
Quick Word Test	22	24
Spatial relations subtest	26	21
Confidence in math	17	16
Perception of teacher's attitude	13	14
Motivation	9.5	6.5
Perception of mother's attitude	4	8
Usefulness of math	6	5
Perception of father's attitude	5	5.5
Number of math-related courses taken	4	2
Math is "a male domain"	0.5	4.5
Attitude to success in math	1.5	1
Math-related activities	1	0

SOURCE: Based on data from E. Fennema and J. Sherman, "Sex-Related Differences in Mathematics Achievement, Spatial Visualization, and Affective Factors" (1977).

matical ability by each particular attitude or achievement score. These values are given only for the students in grades 9 to 11 (ages fourteen to sixteen), as there were too few female subjects in grade 12 to make the results reliable. It is important to note that these values are not additive. Each value reflects only the *individual* relationship between a single pair of scores.

The two cognitive measures, vocabulary and spatial ability, are found to be strongly related to mathematics. Of the various attitudes, confidence (which did show a sex difference in the original analysis) accounts for approximately 16 percent of the variance in math performance and is a similar marker for both sexes. The teacher's attitude to the student (where no sex difference was found) is also a reliable relationship. The correlations for both sexes look remarkably similar, and there is no evidence from this analysis that attitudinal factors are more pronounced in the girls' scores than in the boys'. This illustrates that boys are not more or less "independent" of the attitudes of adults than girls.

Yet the key question remains: Are the attitudes *causing* the math deficiencies or are the math deficiencies *causing* the attitudes? Do you feel confident in mathematics because you are good at it, or does confidence *make* you good at it? Does the teacher's positive attitude to you reflect his or her knowledge of your math scores or a sex-role bias? Without appropriate experimentation, these questions cannot be answered except on logical grounds. A clear example of the problem is illustrated in the high correlation found between the Quick Word test and mathematics ability. Should one conclude that vocabulary *causes* mathematical ability or that mathematical ability *causes* vocabulary? The answer is neither, because both the vocabulary test and the mathematics test reflect a higher-order aptitude called General Intelligence.

Despite the problems of interpretation, Fennema and Sherman conclude that these results "lend credence to the belief that sociocultural factors are highly important concomitants of sex-related differences in mathematics achievement and spatial visualization." They suggest that the critical problem is confidence, especially that "the lesser confidence of girls in their ability to perform in mathematics is consistent with their lesser confidence generally, an attitude not necessarily changed when performing at an equal or superior level to males."[10]

Note that Fennema and Sherman accurately state that girls are less confident in general than boys. This is a consistent finding in many studies on sex differences. If it is true, then why do researchers tie only mathematics performance to confidence? Sex differences do not appear in many other school subjects. If confidence were *causing* performance, it ought to affect performance in every academic subject where girls compete with boys, not just mathematics.

In a reanalysis of some data from the tenth- and eleventh-grade students, Sherman and Fennema examined the groups of students who intended to continue in mathematics and compared them to those who did not.[11] Far more boys than girls intended to continue. The only attitude that distinguished between the sexes was the males' considerably more stereotyped view of mathematics as a male domain. Girls continuing in math showed a far *greater* motivation for studying mathematics than boys. High motivation (which is usually accompanied by greater self-discipline) provides an explanation of Benbow and Stanley's results that showed that girls got better math grades despite lower natural aptitude. No other attitude measures showed any sex differences, which indicates that boys and girls perceive their parents' and teachers' encouragement, or lack of it, in much the same way.

In 1980 Sherman reported a study where children were followed over a three-year period.[12] She tested 260 girls and 223 boys in grade 8 and was able to follow up 135 of the girls and 75 of the boys at grade 11. The students were given a mathematics concepts test and a math problem-solving test along with the cognitive measures and attitude scales just described. A sex difference in mathematics ability was not found in grade 8 but was very strong in grade 11, despite the fact that all students had completed an equal number of courses. The only attitude measure that differentiated the sexes at any age was "math as a male domain"; here too males, but not females, displayed highly stereotyped attitudes about mathematics being a male discipline.

Sherman carried out a multiple regression analysis, which provides an indication of the importance or accuracy of each measure in predicting mathematical ability. By this technique she was able to determine the four most important predictors of math performance. Knowledge of math concepts in grade 8 was the best predictor of knowledge of math concepts in grade 11. The number of math courses taken was the next best predictor, followed by confidence in learning math and spatial ability. Confidence was a stronger predictor for males and spatial ability was a stronger predictor for females.

Math problem-solving ability in grade 8 predicted math problem-solving ability in grade 11. The second best predictor was spatial ability; next, math concepts; and next, the number of years of math courses taken. For girls a marginal predictor (2 percent of the variance) was their attitude at grade 8 concerning math as a male domain, and for boys, 4 percent of the variance in grade 11 performance was accounted for by their grade-8 score on attitude to success in mathematics. The findings of this longitudinal study are consistent with all other results presented so far, showing that *ability* rather than attitude is the most reliable predictor of success in mathematics.

Finally, in a report to the American Psychological Association in 1979, Sherman discussed a series of interviews with 87 high school girls with varying math backgrounds, all of whom had equal verbal and spatial ability.[13] One of the most important results of this investigation was the finding that girls with a high level of math ability, who were attempting a four-year math program, were significantly *more* worried about appearing smarter than boys and had a greater fear of success than the girls with less aptitude for mathematics. In other words, the most ambivalent attitudes were found in those girls who were continuing in mathematics, the exact opposite of what would be predicted by a socialization hypothesis. One interpretation of this result is that the high intellectual aptitude of these girls, which allows them to continue in the math program, is *causing* them some discomfort. Highly gifted girls pay a price in terms of their anxieties concerning social success, but it appears that they are willing to pay it.

In all these studies, the students' perceptions of the attitudes of parents and fellow students show little relationship to their math performance; this is the opposite of what would be predicted by a sex-role socialization hypothesis. Teacher's attitude showed a modest relationship for both boys and girls. All in all, the strongest predictors of success in mathematics were math ability, spatial ability, and confidence in learning mathematics. All other factors contribute very little to math performance. When considering the evidence, it seems clear that *ability* in mathematics is the most straightforward predictor of success in mathematics, precisely the conclusions reached by Benbow and Stanley.

Fennema and Sherman did not attempt to study the differences between the sexes in different *types* of mathematics. It is possible that sex differences vary with different course material and that attitudes may be related to these variables. In 1979 Jane Stallings examined sex differences for each subdiscipline separately.[14] She also looked at a number of attitudinal measures. Boys were found to perform significantly better in calculus, analytical geometry, geometry, and algebra I. No sex differences were found in algebra II and trigonometry. Females were superior in arithmetic. The reasons why sex differences appeared in some of the higher mathematics disciplines and not others cannot be explained at this time.

Stallings considered the attitudes of 420 geometry students in eleven schools, all of whom were continuing in mathematics. Boys reported speaking more often to their math teachers than girls but also reported significantly *more* feelings of anxiety than the girls. Males were ahead in spatial ability, and there was a tendency for males to report more positive parental support. Stallings did not correlate this information with performance in tests of geometry, so there is no way to determine whether or not these differences are important.

A number of factors distinguished between groups of girls continuing and girls not continuing in math (189 versus 42). The largest effect was found for math anxiety, with those not continuing showing considerably higher scores. The next largest difference was the report of greater difficulty in mathematics from the noncontinuing group. Third, performance on the spatial relations subtest distinguished the two groups, with the girls who dropped out performing considerably poorer. Support from both fathers and mothers was greater for girls continuing, and girls who were not continuing reported speaking with the teacher much more. In fact, the noncontinuing girls had a greater interaction with the teacher than the continuing boys, showing that girls do not feel inhibited in seeking help.

Although Stallings did not report correlations between performance scales and attitudes, on the basis of the breakdown into the two female groups, one could predict results similar to those of Fennema and Sherman. Again, should a correlation be demonstrated between those factors that were most discriminating—anxiety and reported difficulty in math—there would be no way to determine whether either was *caused* by mathematical ineptitude or vice versa.

Mathematics is important because math skills pave the way to a career in science. What happens to girls who choose science as a career? Are women who go on in science different from other women? And if so, is this due to ability or attitude? A number of surveys have been carried out in the past twenty years to discover what is special about women who do choose science as a career. Reporting on the combined findings of fifty-four research reports comparing female scientists or women training for a career in science to male scientists and to women in careers outside science, Alma Lantz and her research team in Denver, Colorado, uncovered some profound differences.[15] When a meta-analysis was applied to the data, it was possible to determine a measure called "effect size," which is essentially expressed as standard deviations units based on group mean differences. The larger the effect-size value, the greater is the difference between the two groups. Table 7.3

TABLE 7.3

	Effect Size[b]
Factors Distinguishing Female Scientists from Female Nonscientists[a]	
Low need for approval	1.13
Interest in math	1.11
Career commitment	0.92
Oriented toward things	0.91
Self-confidence	0.77
High math aptitude	0.76
Number of math courses taken	0.75
Certainty of career choice	0.70
High IQ	0.68
High grade-point average	0.58
High science aptitude	0.55
Family member in science	0.53
Narrow interests	0.52
High spatial ability	0.52
High number of science courses	0.51
Factors Distinguishing Female Scientists from Male Scientists[c]	
Low concern for job discrimination	0.76
Low need for approval	−0.66
Broad range of interests	0.65
Anticipated time in workforce	0.54
Informal science learning	−0.53
Spatial ability	−0.47

SOURCE: Data based on A. Lantz, "Synthesis of Evidence and Theoretical Explanations of the Underrepresentation of Women in Science," (Unpublished National Science Foundation project, 1981).
[a] There were no differences between the groups on any demographic variables, nor on any attitudes concerning sex roles.
[b] Effect-size is essentially expressed in standard deviation units.
[c] A negative value means that women are weaker on that factor than men.

ranks the major differences between female scientists and others in order of effect size.

The differences between female scientists and female nonscientists are very striking. The most consistent set of differences is in ability. Female scientists have higher grade-point averages and IQs, and high scores on tests of mathematics, spatial ability, and science. The second most consistent set of differences is found in *interest*. Female scientists show a very high interest in math, are oriented toward things rather than people, and their interest is considerably more focused. This interest is reflected in the fact that they take more math and science courses than other women. The last major factor is personal commitment and self-concept. Female scientists are extremely highly committed to a career in science; they anticipate spending much more of their life working at their careers, and they are very certain of their career choice. This goes hand in hand with strong self-confidence and the absence of need for other people's approval.

When the female scientists are compared to male scientists, their profiles are almost identical. Men are somewhat more independent and have had more informal experience with science. Women in this survey have less concern about discrimination in the workplace and anticipate having longer careers. Interestingly, the female scientists had lower scores in math and spatial ability than the males.

When demographic and attitudinal factors were compared, there was no difference whatsoever between female scientists and other women, or between male and female scientists. Perception of female role, parental attitudes, social values, attitudes of male colleagues, and so on, were identical for the three comparison groups. Factors influencing career development such as role conflicts or the amount of career encouragement also were no different among the groups.

This comparison, of thousands of people in fifty-four different surveys over twenty years, reinforces what has been stated here: The strongest predictors for success in math and science are *ability*, interest, and commitment. If a woman wishes to pursue a career in mathematics, science, or engineering, she will pursue it. She will not be dissuaded by people's opinions or conflicts over her proper role. However, this is not to say that social factors play no part in encouraging talented females to follow a scientific career— or to develop skills that are useful in science.

As noted earlier, the only way to determine whether or not social or environmental factors are effective in producing differences in math performance is to carry out controlled experiments. One such experiment is reported by Lynn Fox.[16] Fox is working with the Johns Hopkins project on talented math students and is particularly interested in the impact of social factors on the girls' math performance. Over the years, some of the girls' concerns in learning mathematics had become apparent. On the basis of her information, Fox established an accelerated math program for seventh-grade girls, in which math problems were designed to be relevant to girls' interests. The students, teacher, and assistant were all female. Cooperation was stressed, and the structure of the class was sufficiently informal to promote a good deal of interaction between the students and teachers. Since one of the major purposes of the experiment was to develop the girls' interest in science and to teach them to see the relatedness between math and science, several outside speakers were brought in.

The original sample consisted of thirty-two girls of high math ability all scoring at least 370 on the math portion of the SAT. These were matched in age, math and verbal scores, and father's and mother's education to two control groups of boys and girls who did not attend these special classes. Of the thirty-two girls in the experimental group, twenty-six attended the course but only eighteen completed it. The course was carried out over a three-month period, for two two-hour periods each week. The results were reported for both the original twenty-six and the eighteen girls who attended in the year 1973. In the 1974 follow-up, the experimental group was ahead in algebra, scoring at a more advanced level than either of the two control groups. Ten of the girls in the special class had completed algebra II and were accelerated by one year in math. None of the control students were accelerated.

By 1976 twelve of the original twenty-six girls (48 percent) were accelerated by one year or more, whereas only 9 percent of the control girls were accelerated by one year and 17 percent by one-half year. However, by this time the control boys had caught up and were achieving at the same level as the girls in the experimental class.

According to the 1976 survey, the higher achievement of the girls in the experimental group was not reflected in any greater interest in science; in fact, they showed less interest at this time than the control girls who had been accelerated because of ability. The girls in the experimental class showed a greater interest in science in 1973, 1974, and 1975. By 1976, the control girls showed more interest. The boys were extremely consistent in the reports of interest in science, and both the accelerated and nonaccelerated groups were identical. The interest in science as a career rose from 60 percent in 1973 to 75 percent in 1976.

Fox concludes that the experimental manipulation did not seem to make a difference in choice of science as a career. Yet the intervention did make a difference to a continuing ability in mathematics, as the girls in the experimental group were performing similarly to the control boys and the usual sex difference appears to have been eliminated. Despite this, the girls still seemed less interested in math than the boys. When questioned about their future plans, 60 percent of the girls in the special course planned to complete calculus in high school, in contrast to 70 percent of the boys. Although Fox appears somewhat discouraged about the lack of enduring effects of her intervention, such a short program cannot be expected to have a prolonged effect. Had this approach been continued throughout an entire school year, the results may have been much more dramatic. Even so, the short-term gains were impressive. And it must be remembered from Stalling's report that girls have more difficulty in geometry than algebra, and the intervention focused entirely on algebra.

Fox's experiment is certainly a step in the right direction, and much more research is needed to determine exactly what environmental factors will help promote girls' ability in math. Clearly the all-female setting and the social content of the course made a difference to the girls' freedom to ask "stupid" questions. Yet Fox did not include an experimental group of boys who received particular attention to their needs. This is a critical issue, because it resurrects the moral dilemma once again: Is the goal of education to make all children identical? If the same amount of time and money were spent on *both* boys and girls in math education, would they still end up differently?

The next chapter explores the various other theories that have been put forward to try to explain sex differences in higher mathematics—the visuospatial hypothesis, the verbal hypothesis, the object/person dimension, and the motor/activity theory (discussed in an earlier chapter). These theories are not mutually exclusive, and none is independent of either biological or environmental factors.

8

Mathematics: Why Males Excel

The visuospatial hypothesis is the second most popular theory advanced to explain sex differences in higher mathematics. Unlike the socialization hypothesis, this theory does not attempt to determine the cause of the sex differences, but poses the issue in a new way: If sex differences do indeed exist in spatial ability and if spatial ability is important for aptitude in higher mathematics, can this factor alone account for the sex differences in math? Although this may seem like nothing more than substituting one puzzle for another, spatial ability is a narrower and more accessible concept than "mathematical aptitude." This is especially true in light of Patricia Davidson's suggestion that a student may have one of nine possible learning styles or strategies. Spatial ability is a general capacity to image objects in different perspectives, a *visuomotor* skill.

This chapter reviews the evidence for the relationship between spatial ability and mathematics and also for sex differences in spatial ability. Some workers have attempted to determine whether or not spatial ability is inherited or acquired, and this has led to several studies exploring the genetic factors in spatial ability. Most of this work has focused on a model based on a recessive gene on the X chromosome. Others, including myself, have suggested that spatial ability may be acquired, or at least enhanced, by certain types of behavior in childhood. These issues are still unresolved, but I will discuss the current status of these approaches, as well as the evidence on spatial ability and the brain.

Two additional theories concerning the sex differences in mathematics are unrelated to the spatial hypothesis. The first is the view that females rely excessively on verbal or linguistic strategies and that these are counterproductive when applied to math problems that relate to the visual properties of objects. The second is that the much greater interest in people than in inanimate objects that females show would result in an indifference to advanced mathematics. This would be increasingly true as mathematics became more abstract.

Seeing the World Move When It Isn't

There is no agreed-upon definition of spatial ability. In general, it refers to a capacity to imagine objects or representations of objects in different planes and perspectives. Many of the so-called spatial tasks are actually problems involving imagery in three dimensions. This is true even when the problems are represented in a two-dimensional line drawing, as for example in the Space Relations Subtest of the Differential Aptitude Test (DAT). An item from the test is presented in figure 8.1. You can estimate your own aptitude

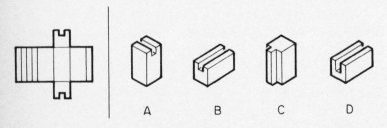

FIGURE 8.1

Fold the image on the left in your mind and determine whether it corresponds to any or all of the figures A–D on the right.

in spatial ability by how rapidly you can solve this problem. Someone with high ability will find the solution in an instant. The score on the spatial relations test is determined by how many problems are solved correctly in thirty minutes.

The speed at which this type of problem can be solved is largely determined by the capacity to visualize the line drawing in motion. In fact, motion in some form or another—the real or imagined motion of one's body in space, the imagined motion of an object about an axis, or the anticipated direction of movement of an object already in motion—is a key ingredient of almost all the tests that claim to be measuring spatial ability. The capacity to visualize the relationship between the motion of one's body and elements or objects in the world makes it possible to frame space in terms of geometric coordinates. This leads to the ability to construct mental maps of unfamiliar towns or landscapes.

Although there have been a few attempts to discover what some of the various spatial tests have in common, there have been no exhaustive analyses of this issue. Therefore, we still do not know whether there are two, three, or more types of spatial ability. However, we are primarily interested in assessing a "spatial" factor in cognitive ability because of the consistent correlation between many of these spatial tests and mathematical problem solving.

The Fennema and Sherman study indicated that spatial ability accounted for approximately 23 percent of the variance in overall math achievement (see table 7.2).[1] This means that spatial ability alone contributes 23 percent to the total score on their mathematics achievement tests. When Sherman tested eighth-graders and followed these children through to the eleventh grade, she found that the scores on the DAT spatial relations test at grade 8 were among the top predictors (along with math ability and the number of math courses completed) for subsequent ability in understanding math concepts and for math problem solving.

Stallings undertook a detailed analysis of the relationship between performance on the DAT spatial relations subtest and a math achievement test battery developed by the Stanford Research Institute.[2] These results are presented in table 8.1, where variance estimates have been added.

Spatial ability is correlated to every subspecialty of higher mathematics but is completely unrelated to arithmetic. As might

TABLE 8.1
*Total Variance Contributed by Spatial Ability to
Various Types of Math*

	Men (%)	Women (%)
Calculus	3	32
Analytic geometry	46	36
Trigonometry	7	25
Geometry	24	27
Algebra II	.02	6
Algebra I	25	20
Arithmetic	.4	.009

NOTE: Based on data from J. A. Stallings, "Comparison of
Men's and Women's Behaviors in High School Math Classes,"
paper presented at the American Psychological Association,
New York, 1979.

be expected, it is most highly related to analytic geometry, a
relationship that accounts for nearly 50 percent of the total score.
These results support earlier research that found that tests of
spatial ability correlate most highly with geometry, less with
algebra, and not at all with tests of computation.[3] Also of interest
in Stalling's analysis is the absence of a relationship between the
spatial relations test and both calculus and algebra II for the boys,
suggesting that in these two disciplines, a nonspatial strategy may
serve just as well as a spatial strategy. However, Stallings's findings
that spatial ability is consistently related to higher mathematics for
the girls confirms Sherman's results that spatial ability is an even
more important marker for females than for males.

The DAT battery was validated on several thousands of school
and college students. When the test battery was published in 1959,
tables were provided showing the correlations between the various
subtests.[4] For males the highest correlations between spatial relations and other tests in the battery were to math achievement,
science, art, and mechanical drawing. For females the highest
correlations were to math, science, and music. Spatial ability
appeared to be more related to performance in mathematics for
females than for males. The strongest relationship between the
spatial relations test and any single aptitude was to plane geometry.

The demonstration of a relationship between spatial ability and
math achievement is conclusive, especially with respect to geometry.
The next question that arises is: Can the sex difference in mathe-

matics be accounted for, at least in part, by sex differences in spatial abilities? This is a much harder question to answer. Furthermore, a positive answer to this question, which seems likely, does not solve the mystery of sex differences in higher mathematics, but raises the further issue of why the sexes differ in visuospatial ability in the first place. Before I attempt to answer this question, let us look at the evidence for sex differences in spatial ability.

Females: Lost in Space?

When the DAT was standardized, scores were assessed independently for males and females. In the spatial relations subtest, the males scored nearly 1 standard deviation higher than the females. Males who were at the 50th percentile scored between 58 and 61, but females at the 50th percentile scored only 43 to 46.[5]

Since 1959 the performance of males and females on this particular test has suffered from a now-you-see-it, now-you-don't phenomenon. In the Madison, Wisconsin, project, the differences between the sexes were not pronounced, and in more recent tests they are tending to disappear. In Sherman's latest analysis of Madison students, sex differences in spatial ability were not reported at either grade 8 or grade 11, despite the fact that at grade 11 the sex difference in mathematical ability was still very strong. By contrast, Stallings reports that sex differences on this test were found in Palo Alto high school students in every class she tested, except algebra II and trigonometry. I failed to find sex differences on the same test in two different studies on over one hundred Stanford students.[6] Nor did I find sex differences on this test in forty Palo Alto high school students. Thirty miles away at the University of California in Santa Cruz, Kristina Hooper, using the identical test, found sex differences to be as robust as ever in a group of over one hundred precalculus students.* This effect cannot be caused by a different experimental approach, because, although I found no sex differences in Palo Alto students, I did

* Personal communication.

find enormous sex differences in a population of English college undergraduates. It is possible that students in certain areas are overly familiar with this particular test. This may be the case in Madison where testing has been going on for several years. Perhaps the students are becoming "testwise" or are being trained to take the test by the classroom teacher.

There are many types of spatial ability, of which the spatial relations subtest is but one example. If males are found to score consistently higher on a number of these tests, then perhaps one can conclude that spatial ability is genuinely a sex-related aptitude. A number of different spatial tests are described in this section. What is of special interest is the age at which sex differences begin to appear. For a long time it was believed that sex differences in spatial ability emerged only during puberty. This is because in the standard pen-and-paper test, such as the DAT spatial relations test, sex differences never appeared much before the age of twelve to thirteen years. Now it seems that the reason for this result was that the test is too difficult for *any* child below this age. Sex differences did not appear because boys and girls alike were failing the test.

Jean Piaget's theory about the stages of development in childhood states that young children internalize mental images or "schemas" by combining sensory information with their actions.[7] He defines the first stage as the "sensorimotor" stage, because children are learning to integrate what they see, hear, or feel with various patterns of motor behavior. When this theory is applied to sex differences, it predicts that differences would appear very early on those spatial tests involving real three-dimensional objects, but would not appear until much later on more abstract material, such as drawings of the same kind of problem. This argument is based on the discovery that very young infants are particularly accurate in detecting differences between real three-dimensional faces and objects but extremely inaccurate when tested with two-dimensional representations, such as photographs and line drawings.[8]

In order to determine whether or not sex differences would appear on three-dimensional spatial tests in young children, my student Cindy Morley and I carried out a series of experiments on over 130 preschoolers aged three to five years at preschools in Santa Cruz. Each child was tested individually.[9] We gave the children two kinds of problems using real objects: two-dimensional

TABLE 8.2
*Two- and Three-Dimensional
Problem Solving.*

	2-D Problem		
	3 years	4 years	5 years
Male	127.0	89	78.7
Female	122.9	105.9	103.3
	N.S.	N.S.	N.S.

	3-D Problem					
	3 years		4 years		5 years	
	Time	Errors	Time	Errors	Time	Errors
Male	47	1.95	36.7	.66	20.25	1.08
Female	53.7	2.17	45.0	1.23	36.16	.33
	N.S.	N.S.	$p < 0.03$	N.S.	$p < 0.05$	N.S.

NOTE: The top table shows the average time in seconds for children to complete three jigsaw puzzles. There were no errors on this task. The bottom table shows the average time and error scores for the same children building a replica of a three-dimensional Lego block pattern. $N = 137$.

jigsaw puzzles and a three-dimensional problem using Lego blocks. Sex differences did not appear on either of two jigsaw problems. In the Lego task, the child had to watch us construct a three-dimensional model of six rectangular yellow and white blocks. The child had a set of the same six blocks and was requested to construct an identical model to ours. Boys and girls were very different in the time it took to complete the problem. Table 8.2 illustrates that no sex differences were found at three years of age, but that they did appear in the four- and five-year-old children.

Gustav Jahoda, a British psychologist, gave a similar task to Scottish children aged seven, nine, and eleven and to Ghanaian children aged ten, twelve, and fourteen.[10] Sex differences were found to be highly significant in both populations at all ages on the three-dimensional block tests. However, there were no differences between boys and girls in either country on tests involving the manipulation of two-dimensional objects, either physically or mentally. The cross-cultural differences were also revealing. The Ghanaian children performed similarly to the Scottish children when asked to construct a three-dimensional pattern of blocks from a replica placed in front of them, but showed striking deficits when asked to construct a similar block pattern from a photograph or line-drawing. The same cross-cultural effect occurred in older children, even after the Ghanaians had been provided with some training on how 3-D objects could be represented in pictures. This offers further confirmation of the theory that the late emergence of sex differences on certain spatial tests may be due to the fact that the tests demand a level of abstraction that is not available until considerable learning has taken place.

Other cross-cultural studies have revealed the same sex difference on three-dimensional problems in young children. I. R. Brooks in New Zealand tested 55 Maori and 55 Pakeha children, aged four years, on their ability to construct a design from blocks. Among the Maori children, the sexes did not differ, but among the Pakeha, males were superior.[11] In Papua, New Guinea, 339 schoolchildren were given several tests devised by Piaget. Males were found to be superior on all tests of conservation of quantity in which children watch liquid being transferred between two beakers of different sizes, or plastic dough transformed in shape, and are asked whether the amount (quantity) has changed. Boys grasped this concept approximately two years earlier than the girls did. Sex differences were not found on other Piagetian tasks such as conservation of length and number.[12]

These results illustrate that, in various cultures around the world, most young boys are *accelerated* with respect to girls in at least one cognitive ability. Therefore, the global development lag hypothesis, discussed in chapter 3, cannot possibly be maintained. If young boys were delayed in overall development with respect to girls, then they would be expected to show a deficit in every aptitude. As this is not the case, it must be concluded that different skills develop at different rates in boys and girls.

Sex differences have been found in younger children on spatial tests that involve line drawings, but only when these are relatively simple. In one of the earliest reports of a sex difference, in 1918 Porteus published his data on the Porteus Maze for 453 children aged seven to fourteen. Although no statistical tests were available to analyze data at that time, Porteus determined that the boys solved these problems faster than the girls. By 1965 Porteus had carried out over two hundred more experiments on his two-dimensional pen-and-paper maze. In 99 of the 105 male-female

Piaget's Water-Level Problem

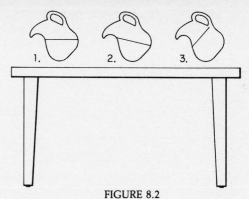

FIGURE 8.2
Choose the flask that depicts the water level accurately.
NOTE: Based on a problem devised by Piaget and Inhelder (1956).

comparisons, the males were superior. Lauren Harris at the University of Michigan has summarized the evidence from the Porteus studies and a number of maze tests of this type, as well as mazes constructed in three dimensions, tactile mazes, and pattern-walking mazes. Sex differences generally appear after the age of seven to eight years, and are particularly noticeable if the subject is asked to rotate the maze in various planes from memory.[13]

One of the most surprising and dramatic sex differences in a spatial task involving a simple line drawing is found on Piaget's water-level test. As can be seen in figure 8.2, the test appears inordinately easy, requiring the subject to indicate the water level in a tilted pitcher either by drawing a line or pointing to one of several drawings that depict the water line at various angles. However, even when the horizontal plane is represented in the drawing, as for instance when the pitcher is resting on a table, females are still inaccurate in this task. It has been estimated that approximately 50 percent of college women do not know the principle involved, and even when they are told they continue to perform more inaccurately than the men. The sex difference in this task appears at around eight to nine years and becomes increasingly large with age. One reason why this test has produced considerable interest is because it is highly correlated with performance on the DAT spatial relations test.[14]

In perhaps the most extensive study on sex differences in Piaget's task, Lynn Liben and Susan Golbeck, two American psychologists, thoroughly examined the strategies adopted by 160 college students.[15] They used two tests to study whether the students could align drawings horizontally and vertically. The women consistently scored below the males on the water-level test, the majority getting two to three correct versus the men's five to six. (Six was a perfect score.) The women performed equally badly when asked to draw a cord and light bulb on a picture of a train shown climbing a steep gradient. When they were asked how they approached this task, most women said that they drew the water line or the light cord with reference to the space *inside* the drawings. They did not take into account the position of the drawing on the page or base their decision on the influence of gravity.

Liben and Golbeck then supplied the correct strategy for an additional 160 subjects, but this still did not eliminate the sex difference in accuracy; only 50 percent of the women were able to take advantage of the additional information. These findings suggest that females do not seem to consider more than one piece of information about the spatial properties of objects or events at the same time.

Oddly enough, this capacity to isolate figure from ground or ignore the three-dimensional properties of two-dimensional drawings actually enhances women's performance on certain tasks. Simon Heywood and Karen Chessell, two English psychologists, devised one such task and tested it on thirty college students (see figure 8.3).[16] Here the task is to estimate the distance between the end points of the acute angles and place a mark on the upper line of the angle that corresponds to the distance. The angles varied from 5 to 120 degrees.

Although all of Heywood's subjects underestimated distance, and the amount of the underestimation increased with the width of the angle, the men underestimated the distance considerably more that the women. This effect was specific to line drawings with angles, as no sex differences were noted in the respondents' estimation of distance between two dots or two sets of parallel lines. As females were more accurate in this task and the size of the angle had a strong influence on performance, one could conclude that females are *less* influenced by three-dimensional cues in line drawings than males. This suggestion is supported by results from a series of tests on visual illusions in which males

Expanding Angles

FIGURE 8.3

For each angle, place a mark on the top line equivalent to the distance between the two ends of the angle.

SOURCE: Adapted from S. Heywood and K. Chessell, "Expanding Angles," *Perception* 6 (1977):571–83. Reprinted with permission of the author and Pion Ltd.

have been shown to be extremely susceptible to the Poggendorf illusion, shown in figure 8.4.[17] Unlike all other illusions, the Poggendorf illusion is produced solely by the angle of the intersecting lines. Sex differences were not found on any of the other illusions, but in those few cases in which an acute angle created part of the illusion, males were more affected than females.

There have been few attempts to determine the extent of sex differences in spatial ability. In an ambitious series of studies, Ernest Barratt at the University of Delaware tested two hundred college men and women on ten different types of pen-and-paper tests of spatial ability.[18] Barratt was interested in relating Lewis Thurstone's earlier work at the Carnegie Institute of Technology to sex differences, which Thurstone did not report. Thurstone, who used factor analysis to study intelligence, claimed to find three distinct and unrelated spatial factors.[19] The first, Factor 1, was the ability to recognize objects when seen from different

The Poggendorf Illusion

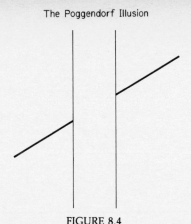

FIGURE 8.4

Estimate how much the intersecting line deviates from a straight line.

angles. This involves imagining the three-dimensional properties of a rigid object and its motion around an axis. Factor 2 was the ability to imagine movement or displacement among the various parts of a static object, and Factor 3, the ability to relate objects in space to one's own body position.

Barratt compiled a battery of spatial tests, which included the original Thurstone tests and other well-known spatial tests, such as the DAT spatial relations test. Males were overwhelmingly superior in nine of the ten tests. When Barratt analyzed the data using factor analysis, three independent spatial factors appeared for the males, confirming Thurstone's results. Space Factor 1, the ability to imagine a rigid object rotating in space, was the strongest factor. The second most reliable factor was like Thurstone's Factor 2; it involved tasks in which the subjects had to imagine parts of an object being folded or unfolded. Factor 3, which involved the ability to imagine that one had walked around an object and was viewing it from a different position in space, was weaker.

The women's data revealed only two factors and these were different from the men's. Factor 1 was a general spatial ability indicating that all ten tests were strongly related. Factor 2 was a much weaker factor and resembled Thurstone's Factor 1. If one took a conservative position, accepting only the strong results, males would have two independent spatial aptitudes: one for visualizing rigid objects rotating around an axis and another for imagining changes in the relative positions of objects or parts of objects. Females would evince only one general spatial ability, with performance on any one test predicting performance on any other. A thorough analysis of these factorial approaches has been provided by Marcel Just and Patricia Carpenter at Carnegie-Mellon University. They report from their research on high versus low spatial visualizers that the high-ability subjects rotate objects around a much greater and more complex set of axes—described as "non-standard." They do not report the sex of their high- or low-ability groups, however.[20]

It is not possible to reach a definitive conclusion regarding this issue from the results of Barratt's research, because there are a number of so-called spatial tests that he did not use, especially those testing spatial abilities in real-world situations. So far we have no way of knowing whether any of these real-world tests relate to the same factors that were uncovered by Thurstone, Barratt, and others. One spatial skill quite distinct from the typical spatial test discussed so far is the capacity to find one's way in unfamiliar towns and to construct mental maps of landscapes.

Studies reviewed by Lauren Harris indicate that, from about the age of ten, boys have a better knowledge of local geography and are more accurate in determining direction, when questioned about a familiar terrain.[21] But this could be due to the boys' greater tendency to explore. In my own research, my student Janet Sparks and I asked fifty college students to draw a map of the University of California campus at Santa Cruz.[22] Because of the layout of the roads and buildings, 75 to 80 percent of all students make their way about the campus on foot, and we found that men and women were equally familiar with the layout of the campus. The students were asked to draw their maps to scale on an eight-by-eleven-inch sheet of paper. Scoring was based on the accuracy of the placement of buildings with respect to geometric coordinates, accuracy of layout with respect to absolute distance or scale, and so forth. The results are presented in table 8.3.

Males were much more accurate in the placement of buildings with respect to geometric layout. Females were more accurate in producing a map to scale, and this resulted in a better judgment of distance. Men consistently underestimated distance with respect to the total area of space available to draw the map. The most striking difference between the men and women's maps was that on many of the women's drawings, roads and paths were virtually

TABLE 8.3
Average Scores for Men and Women on Map Drawings.

	Men	Women	
Number of major roads and paths	11.39	6.11	($p < 0.001$)
Spatial coordinate errors	4.39	6.22	($p < 0.025$)
Relative deviation error (distance)	1.73	1.38	($p < 0.05$)
Extra buildings included	4.33	7.44	($p < 0.05$)

SOURCE: D. McGuinness and J. Sparks, "Cognitive Style and Cognitive Maps: Sex Differences in Representations of a Familiar Terrain," *Journal of Mental Imagery* 7 (1983): 91–100. Reprinted with permission of Pion Ltd.

absent. Yet the women included many more buildings in their maps, showing that the omission was not due to a lack of familiarity with the campus or poorer memory. In order to explore this further, we asked one hundred students to participate in a second experiment in which they were *specifically* asked to draw in all roads, paths, bridges, and so on, between a set of buildings drawn to scale on a sheet of paper. Though the sex difference was reduced by this manipulation, the females still remembered fewer roads than the males, and their total score for all "connectors" showed a statistically reliable sex difference. It is possible that one of the primary benefits of paying attention to the location of roads and paths is that it helps to form an accurate image of a geometric layout.

Another real-world spatial task that produces pronounced sex differences is visuomotor tracking. In this case the image is in motion, and the task is to anticipate or track the movement by using a lever. Videogames are typical examples of this kind of task. Here males are found to excel from the age of five years and continue to do so until the age of seventy.[23] Their superiority is due to *accuracy* at young ages, not speed. However, males' reaction time improves noticeably relative to females' across the school years, thus providing them with a considerable advantage in those tracking tasks that combine accuracy with speed.[24] When the tracking test is increased in complexity, the sex effects are exaggerated. Harris reviews a number of studies that confirm this result.[25] Charles Rebert and his associates at Stanford Research Institute have shown that when boys and girls begin to learn an unfamiliar video game, they perform similarly. Over time, however, the boys become increasingly more skilled than the girls.[26] This may explain why 90 percent of the people in video arcades are male.

From all the evidence, it appears that males excel in visual imagery in three dimensions and that they are much more likely to translate problems presented in two dimensions into three dimensions. Males also exhibit rapid and accurately timed motor behavior in response to objects in motion, and their *memory* for object relations in space is also superior (that is, they do not require that the objects or spatial elements be in view to perform accurately). What produces this ability: A superior visual memory? A visual system designed to code images in three dimensions? A property of visuomotor integration? All of these? None?

Clearly there is some important connection between movement per se and spatial ability. What has never been determined is whether the way one uses one's body in space, or the way one tends to manipulate objects in the world, leads to schemas of three-dimensional objects in motion. Several types of sensorimotor integration must be studied if we are ever to understand the origin of spatial ability.

As an example, here are four basic categories of visuomotor interaction: (1) A static observer views a static world. (Evidence for the types of sex differences found in this situation will be presented later.) (2) An observer in motion moves through a static terrain. Here the cognitive maps study is relevant. Once they begin to move in space, males appear to construct spatial coordinates in three dimensions, whereas females relate landmarks on the basis of proximity: what is "next to," "behind," "near," or "far away." (3) A static observer watches objects in motion. One test of sex differences in this type of situation was carried out by Albert Burg, who developed a dynamic visual acuity test for the California Department of Motor Vehicles.[27] His purpose was to determine whether visual acuity, as tested by an eye chart, was the same when one was standing still as it was when driving an automobile. Burg's results on thousands of California drivers showed that men were overwhelmingly superior in detecting fine detail in targets in motion.

Finally, (4) An observer is in motion in a world of moving objects. This situation occurs in most sports, when driving with other moving vehicles, and in visuomotor games in which the observer's motion must be timed to that of the display. In general, most tests in this category have shown that males are faster and more accurate, and self-correct their movements considerably more rapidly than females.

To date there are almost no data on any of the obvious questions that arise when considering these four types of visuomotor integration. We do not know whether any, or all, or none, relate to the tests on spatial ability just discussed. We do not know the developmental progression of any of these aptitudes. We do not know exactly when and how or why the sex differences appear. However, a few clues suggest that the aptitude males exhibit in tests of spatial visualization may arise because they adopt a different style of learning about the world.

Explaining Sex Differences in Spatial Ability

This chapter began by asking whether the sex difference in higher mathematics could be explained by a sex difference in spatial ability. The answer is a tentative yes. However, this raises the question of *why* there are sex differences in spatial ability. In this section I will review the even more tentative attempts to answer this question. The first theory to be considered deals with the organization of the brain and the assumption that there is some genetic predisposition for males and females to develop different types of neural organization that could be important to spatial ability.

BIOLOGICAL THEORIES

There is some evidence that visuospatial ability has a genetic component. However, all attempts to pin down the sex differences using a genetic chromosomal model have failed. According to this theory, there is a recessive gene on the X chromosome. This gene inhibits another gene on the other X chromosome and somehow prevents the full development of spatial ability. As only females have two X chromosomes, the theory predicts that father-son correlations will be roughly zero and that the highest correlations will be between father-daughter and mother-son. Early findings supported the theory, but more rigorous tests have shown that, at least in its present formulation, it cannot be maintained. The arguments and data are presented in considerable detail by Steven Vandenberg and Allan Kuse, who point out that their studies on twins have revealed strong evidence for a *genetic* component to spatial skills.[28] However, the mechanism is entirely unknown.

In the three-generation family studies on dyslexics presented in chapter 6, Shelley Smith discovered that severe dyslexia is often accompanied by extremely high visuospatial ability, a phenomenon that runs in families.[29] A similar effect has been reported by Joyce Steeves in a study of children classified as dyslexic. She found that approximately 25 percent of 130 extremely delayed readers had quite phenomenal skills in spatial ability and mathematics. These children were actually identical to mathematically gifted children on reasoning tests and superior to them on tests of visual reproduction. Of the twenty-seven gifted "dyslexics," six were girls.[30]

There is undoubtedly a genetic component to high spatial ability, but we do not know how important learning might be to its development. As yet we have no evidence from humans about how this ability might be represented in the brain. One clue comes from research on rats discussed earlier, where Marion Diamond discovered a consistent sex difference in the thickness of the cortex of the posterior part of the brain.[31] In the normal male rat, the right hemisphere is thicker, and in the normal female rat, the left hemisphere is thicker. Interestingly, male rats have superior maze-running ability. Apart from these data, little is known about the neural organization of spatial ability and what might give rise to the sex differences.

Despite the popular view that spatial ability is located in the right hemisphere of the brain, the evidence supporting this con-clusion is contradictory. Several experiments, including my own, have shown that the left hemisphere is actually more precise in detecting differences between objects rotated in space than the right hemisphere.[32] Furthermore, the more complex the spatial task, the more the left hemisphere becomes engaged, and this is true for both males and females. The only consistent evidence shows that the right hemisphere is highly efficient in rapidly analyzing two-dimensional visual patterns.[33]

Joseph LeDoux has recently suggested that part of the role of the right hemisphere in spatial ability is to integrate images of objects with a type of motor performance he calls "manipulospatial" ability.[34] He cites as an example what occurs in patients who have surgically "split brains." This operation severs the corpus callosum, the fiber bundle that transfers perceptual information between the hemispheres, and is performed for intractible epilepsy. Prior to the operation, the patients can draw three-dimensional objects equally well with either hand. Following surgery, only the *left* hand, which is controlled by the right hemisphere, can reproduce a three-dimensional form. The right hand still retains its manual dexterity in writing because it is connected to the left hemisphere, but because the left hemisphere has lost its input from the right hemisphere, it can no longer activate manipulospatial programs.

Although this is an intriguing hypothesis and fits well with the idea of the relationship between motor performance and spatial ability, we are still awaiting an accurate map of all the brain systems involved. Other research on brain-damaged patients has implicated the frontal lobes of the brain in spatial visualization.[35] This does not mean that a biological substrate for "space" may never be found, or that the sexes may not differ in the development of these systems. The major problem is not so much knowing where to look in the brain as in the fact that we do not yet understand spatial ability sufficiently to draw reasonable parallels with biological function.

Additionally, as pointed out in chapter 6, there is no conclusive evidence that male and female brains are lateralized differently. Sex differences in general hemispheric function in either normal or brain-damaged patients have been very hard to demonstrate.[36] It has been observed consistently in brain-damaged patients that right-hemisphere lesions impair males' performance on spatial tasks, while these same lesions leave females' spatial abilities more intact. However, this seems to reflect the preference of many females for solving spatial problems by using a verbal strategy, a *left*-hemisphere function.[37] Thus we cannot determine whether females lack right-hemisphere spatial skills, or whether they have them but fail to develop them. Furthermore, females with left-hemisphere lesions are also less impaired in language ability, but this does not mean that females have no left-hemisphere capacity for language! These results may indicate a more general principle, that females are simply less vulnerable to brain damage.

It is for these reasons that the findings of George Ojemann and his group and the theory advanced by Doreen Kimura, presented earlier, are of interest, because they suggest that male and female brains have the same floor plan but that the neural networks *within* brain regions are organized differently. That this might be a biological predisposition is supported by Diamond's finding that the differences in left and right cortex in male and female rats appear to be independent of the environment in which the animal is reared.

SPACE AND SEEING

A second possible explanation of sex differences in spatial ability is that there is a basic and biological difference between males and females in the way the visual system functions. A number of studies have shown that males have sharper visual acuity and more efficient binocular vision. There is no way these sensory differences could be acquired, as visual acuity and binocular integration are relatively immune to training.[38] Because of these striking differences in visual processing, I theorized that spatial ability may stem from the males' superior visual abilities. However, in a series of studies I have found that although males do indeed have superior visual acuity and more efficient stereoscopic vision, neither of these abilities correlates to tests of spatial ability. Also, Lesley Brabyn and I could find no relationship between tests of depth perception and spatial ability. From studies on over 120 subjects, we concluded that visual acuity, binocular convergence, and stereopsis, or depth perception, do not have anything to do with performance on visuospatial tests.[39]

In another set of studies, Lorraine McLaughlin and I attempted to discover whether there were any sex differences in visual memory.[40] We found that there were none, *unless* the task required a verbal response. Altogether eighty college and high school students participated in the experiment. Each student was shown forty-eight colored slides consisting of unfamiliar landscapes and city streets. Then they were shown twenty-four of these slides mixed with twenty-four new slides and were asked to determine which slides were new and which were old. Because visual recognition memory is nearly 100 percent accurate, only a small portion of each slide was visible. No sex differences were found in either population. However, when the same students were shown a series of twelve similar slides and asked to *write* everything they could remember about all of them, the females remembered many more details about the slides than the males in both the college and the high school groups. Females were particularly accurate in noticing and describing the people in the photographs.

The importance of verbal recall to tests that claim to be measuring "visual" memory has been confirmed in a study by Amy Olson and me on 220 elementary school children aged seven to nine years, reported in chapter 5.[41] The children saw a series of pictures or words, then were tested unexpectedly on recall. The children were asked to write down everything they had seen in any order they chose. In seven out of eight comparisons, the girls remembered considerably more items. However, when we changed the instructions and asked the children to *draw* their answers, the sex difference disappeared. The girls did equally well whether drawing or writing, but the boys remembered more when they drew their answers. This means that the boys are disadvantaged when they have to translate perceptions into words and writing—left-hemisphere motor skills.

SPACE AND MOTION

So far it has not been possible to relate spatial ability to any aspect of visual sensory processing in either males or females. If this holds up, there are only two possibilities left: Either spatial ability develops through an interaction with the environment and is more related to movement or motor behavior than it is to vision, or spatial ability is a cognitive process that is of a completely different order from, and independent of, any primary sensory or motor skills. If this is true, then the sex difference would be due to an entirely different organization of the brain.

The first hypothesis relates to the argument cited earlier, that as boys and girls develop, there is a difference in the way they use the two basic motor systems, the gross-motor system and the fine-motor system. An anecdote will demonstrate the difference between behaviors that are organized by the two systems. A blind girl about twelve years old was brought to an institute for remediation. When the therapists began working with her, they discovered that she moved awkwardly and had never extended her arms beyond her body. She became extremely anxious when she was asked to do this. This had less to do with her condition than with an overly protective mother who brought her everything she requested. This is an extreme illustration of what can occur when the gross-motor system is very nearly eclipsed by the fine-motor system. This child spoke fluently and was very dexterous, but she had never learned to relate her body to objects in space.

The essence of the gross-motor system is that it operates *outside* the immediate body space; because of this, it is strongly influenced by the visual and kinesthetic senses, those senses that send messages to the brain about the position of the joints of the body. By contrast, motion in the fine-motor system is executed with very little regard for what exists in space. Speech runs off unaided by any external visual input or input from the large joints. Even complex fine-motor skills such as piano-playing can be carried out with minimal feedback from the visual and kinesthetic senses. Contrast this with what is required to move around a room, walk across a field, or go roller-skating. When the gross-motor system is engaged, it *must* be related to objects in the world.

Chapter 4 reviewed the evidence for the preeminence of fine-motor control in females. In this chapter, data have revealed a male superiority in control of bodily movement with respect to objects in the world. So far there are no biological theories as to the origin of this sex difference, other than the obvious fact that males must learn to move more muscle mass than females. Another important piece of evidence is that males of all mammalian species commonly engage in rough-and-tumble play, while females rarely do. In cases where a fetus has been exposed to drugs that contain male hormones, the offspring, whether male or female, exhibits a much higher level of rough-and-tumble play than normal children of their sex.[42] As males and females show a preferential bias toward one or the other motor system, it might be expected that they would develop slightly different sensorimotor aptitudes.

Evidence indicates that males are more likely to manipulate

objects than females and that this is related to problem-solving ability. English psychologist Corinne Hutt investigated how preschool children respond when they are allowed to play with a completely novel toy.[43] There was no sex difference in the initial degree of curiosity shown, but there were sex differences in the number of children who did not approach the toy at all (more girls) and a highly significant effect for behaviors involving novel uses of the toy. In one of my own studies, reported in more detail in the next chapter, we did not find any sex differences in the novel use of play material. However, we did not introduce a special toy for this purpose, so the results may not be comparable.

Others have found that two tests of curiosity or exploration were highly related to problem-solving skill in young boys. On the other hand, problem-solving ability in the girls was strongly related to verbal development. Similar research has shown that boys are more likely to play with unfamiliar toys and that the amount of curiosity shown by boys is highly related to the extent to which they manipulated objects.[44]

By and large, the behavioral data are not conclusive regarding the antecedents of sex differences in visual spatial skills. While it is clear that the sex effect appears considerably earlier than was formerly believed, the sex difference seems to have little to do with primary visual functions. Although boys have a tendency to manipulate objects more than girls and be attracted to novel toys, these behaviors have not been tied directly to subsequent spatial ability.

Biases Against Excellence

BENT TWIG

Two remaining theories concerning the development of sex differences in mathematics are totally unrelated to either a socialization hypothesis or spatial visualization. The first is the verbal hypothesis, which was mentioned earlier. Julia Sherman formulated this theory in 1967.[45] Referring to the verbal theory as a "bent twig" hypothesis, Sherman believes that early precosity predisposes a child to rely too heavily on skills that may subsequently be inappropriate to the task. A good deal of support for this idea comes from subjective reports from women engaged in mathematical or spatial tasks; these women frequently describe their problem-solving strategies in terms of a linguistic analysis of the problem. Males are much more likely to be visualizers and to be unable to give verbal descriptions of their performance. This fact was brought home to me when I asked students in a general psychology class to verbalize the solutions to problems in a mechanical aptitude test. The men, by and large, were unable to describe how they solved the problems, whereas the women were highly articulate but their solutions were frequently inaccurate. Male students typically said: "I can see it, can't I?" or "It moves, doesn't it?"

To approach a complex mathematical concept or formulation merely as if it were a symbolic shorthand for a verbal statement is to miss the point entirely. But this is what often happens. Many algebraic statements or geometric formulae represent descriptions of a spatial relationship between points, lines, or objects. Merely knowing the rules provides no insight into the spatial principle involved in the equation. If one has an excellent rote memory, then the algebraic rules will be easily mastered, but their true significance will be missed.

INTEREST: OBJECTS AND PERSONS

Last but not least, it does matter what you're interested in. All the evidence strongly supports the fact that girls are interested in people and boys are interested in objects. Mathematics is largely about objects and rarely if ever about people, or even living organisms.

Females' interest in people begins at an early age. In figure 8.5 I have collated the data from E. W. Goodenough's study carried out in 1957, showing that preschool girls drew more people in spontaneous drawings and also talked more about people when asked to invent a story about a pattern they were shown. It is not too surprising that girls told stories about people, because one might imagine that every story would contain people. What is

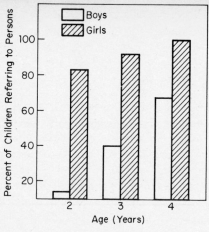

FIGURE 8.5

The percentage of boys and girls who spontaneously referred to persons when asked to invent a story about a mosaic pattern.

SOURCE: Based on data from E. W. Goodenough "Interest in Persons as an Aspect of Sex Differences in the Early Years," *Genetic Psychology Monographs* 55 (1957):287–323, a publication of the Helen Dwight Reid Educational Foundation. Reprinted with permission of Heldres Publications.

remarkable is that boys were able to tell stories that omitted people altogether![46]

Another interesting facet of this sex difference emerged in a study by Norma Feshbach and Michael Hoffman at UCLA in which they asked children to tell stories that were linked to particular events in their lives that made them happy, sad, proud, and so forth. The stories were coded in various ways, including looking at the agents that produced the emotions and the context. What was fascinating was that girls' feelings were almost entirely dependent on social factors, especially contact with parents, whereas boys' emotions were just as likely to be connected with objects. Objects and possessions could make boys happy, sad, or angry.[47]

In one of my own studies I employed a technique called binocular rivalry to determine whether college men and women would report differences in seeing objects or persons. The subjects looked into a viewer that displayed one image to the right eye and a different image to the left eye. The visual fields were separated. This produces "rivalry," in which the item of greatest interest dominates and actually suppresses the less interesting item. The image pairs contained a picture of people and a picture of a common object, such as a wristwatch. Females reported seeing people for significantly longer periods of time than they reported seeing objects, and reported seeing people more than males did. The exact reverse was found for the male subjects.[48]

The hypotheses presented in this chapter may not be definitive, but they are certainly more extensive and perhaps more convincing than a theory relying on sex-role socialization as the sole explanatory principle for a female deficiency in higher math. In chapter 11 some of these issues will be revived when I consider, in light of all the evidence, how mathematics might be taught to encourage *both* male and female talent.

The evidence reviewed so far on children with learning problems has come from studies where the learning difficulty is assessed objectively by achievement tests for reading and mathematics. For hyperactivity, the "learning disability" I will next consider in this book, there are no objective tests. The following two chapters will explore all the ramifications that arise from classifying children's behaviors *without* recourse to objective methodology.

9

Hyperactivity: A Diagnosis in Search of a Patient

As a child of six I entered into a five-dollar wager with my father, who said I couldn't sit still for five minutes. He won. I still recall the confidence with which I entered into the contest and the ensuing anguish of the burning and twitching sensations that began to build up all over my body. This was made all the worse by the acute awareness that five dollars was a lot of money. Eventually, as the burning and twitching overcame me, I leapt out of the chair in total distress.

When I began to review the hundreds of studies on the hyperactive child, this episode came vividly to mind, and I wondered: What would have happened to *me* if I had been six years old today? Although I was an excellent student, my school days were peppered with admonitions: "You'll go to the principal again if you don't stop that"; "Stand in the cloakroom until you are ready to calm down." My favorite was: "Diane, please *crawl* back to your seat." (I still secretly admire the teacher for that one.) I was the child who forgot my parent's permission slip, lunch, and an extra sweater for the trip to the zoo that everyone seemed to know about except me. "Where were you when I told the class, and what were you doing yesterday when I reminded everyone."

Distractibility, considered to be a major concomitant of "hyperactivity," continued with me through college. The library was the least conducive place to study. Every little noise or bit of movement was thrown into high relief against the intense stillness. Instead I checked out books and wrote my term papers from midnight to dawn.

Many of my friends aren't much better off. There is Ted, who insists we all go bowling after a late dinner following the opera, and Harry who runs (never walks) between his office and his laboratory at least forty times a day, and Jim, who is president of three companies and never seems to need any sleep. And there are the dozens of people who cannot tolerate sedentary work or imposed time constraints. They have become professional athletes and coaches, entrepreneurs, foreign correspondents, artists, and scientists. Many of these people might easily fit the category of "the hyperactive child" if they were in school today. It seems to be only very recently that any of this behavior has been deemed socially undesirable.

What is hyperactivity? These sketches have described people who tend to be more active than normal, largely due to a temperamental predisposition. My distractibility was also due to temperament. On the other hand, my inattention and daydreaming in class were a result of a curriculum that moved too slowly. A retreat to a fantasy world was more interesting than anything going on in the classroom. These symptoms, currently associated with the diagnosis of hyperactivity, are a result of temperamental or situational factors.

But hyperactivity can include much more. Some "hyperactive" children are openly disruptive. They don't sneak down the aisle as I tried to do, they stand up and walk, or go to the window, or shout across the room, or imitate animals and trains. Others are quick to become angry and respond with physical violence. In addition, approximately 40 percent of all children diagnosed "hyperactive" have serious learning problems. In other words, hyperactivity has become an umbrella term for various types of behavior that get on everyone's nerves. While any of these behaviors could result from any number of different temperamental and situational factors, physicians commonly attribute them to "organic" causes.

Daniel O'Leary and his colleagues at the State University of

New York at Stony Brook have been studying reactions of physicians and psychologists in different countries to descriptions of hyperactive children. Drawing from a number of references providing descriptions of "hyperactivity," they compiled a list of these symptoms and attributed them to a nine-year-old boy with a normal IQ.:

> Abnormal motor activity with excessive motion, impulsivity, short tolerance of frustration, restlessness, destructiveness, failure to complete assignments and follow instructions, noncompliance, temper tantrums, poor interpersonal relations, labile emotions, short attention span, perceptual impairment, language and speech problems, specific learning disabilities.[1]

When they presented this case description to pediatricians and psychologists in Italy and the United States, there were profound differences in diagnosis. The Americans were considerably more likely to diagnose the child as learning disabled or "hyperactive," and were about equally divided in attributing the problems to organic and to environmental causes. About 30 percent chose drugs as the major intervention. The Italians were more likely to describe the child as having a "personality disorder," saw the major cause of the difficult behavior as situational, and preferred to use therapy or behavioral intervention. Similarly, a study in England showed that the diagnosis of hyperactivity was twenty times more likely for American than for English school children.[2]

The description of the hypothetical "hyperactive child" and the radically different reactions of the professionals from two countries raise the central questions for this chapter. First, it is highly unlikely that any one child would exhibit all of these symptoms. These are symptoms produced by a variety of causes, some organic, some situational, some temperamental. There is no evidence that any of these symptoms consistently cluster to define what physicians call a "syndrome." Clusters of symptoms are typical of organically produced diseases but not of behavior problems. If the Italians and American physicians were polled on their opinion of how to diagnose and treat the symptoms of pneumonia or scarlet fever, there wold be nearly unanimous agreement. But when confronted with symptoms of hyperactivity, they do not agree, even remotely, on the diagnosis, the cause, *or* the treatment. More to the point, there is no agreement among physicians and psychologists *in the United States* on any of these factors.

Another problem is the relationship between hyperactivity and learning disabilities. The literature is about equally divided between researchers who insist on studying "pure" hyperactivity, where children score in the normal range on IQ and achievement tests, and those who claim that hyperactive children are notorious for their persistent academic failure. Recent studies have attempted to discover whether the current selection procedures are confounding hyperactivity with learning disabilities. Two studies found that when children are selected on the basis of hyperactivity scales alone, 30 to 50 percent have learning difficulties. A third study indicated that 40 percent of children with learning disabilities were also hyperactive. These studies reveal serious methodological flaws in the construction of hyperactivity scales.[3]

What this means is that some "hyperactive" children misbehave as a consequence of learning difficulties, some because of boredom, some because of the physical constraints of the classroom, and some because they are inherently more active and distractible than other children. Most of these highly active and distractible children are boys.

I have previously pointed out that a number of boys are being misclassified as learning disabled because of inappropriate test norms for reading and spelling. This is quite apart from the philosophical implications of value judgments implicit in our attitudes about learning to read and write. The same criticism can be made about hyperactivity questionnaire norms, where the problem is further exacerbated because the diagnosis "hyperactivity" or "hyperkinesis" is based on questionnaires that lack clinical validity and for which there is no agreed cut-off point for what constitutes "normal" or "abnormal" scores. In addition, as I have mentioned, the scales are never used to select students who produce excessively low scores; hyperactive children are considered abnormal, but *hypo*active children are not, a completely invalid procedure.

As a whole, epidemiological studies over the past thirty years have shown that parents and teachers generally rate about 20 to 30 percent of all children aged six to twelve years as overactive and inattentive.[4] It has become increasingly common to view these children as in need of clinical or medical treatment. Over the past decade the incidence of "hyperkinesis," or hyperactivity, has reached epidemic proportions in the United States. According to a report released in 1971 by the U.S. Department of Health, Education and Welfare, an estimated 5 percent of the school population was being treated for moderate to severe hyperkinesis.[5] By 1974 the estimated proportion of children with this disorder had risen to as high as 15 percent.[6] Estimates from clinicians and psychologists reveal that hyperactivity has infected anywhere from 5 to 20 percent of our school-age population.[7] Daniel O'Leary conservatively estimated that between 600,000 and 700,000 children are being treated with medication such as Ritalin.[8] The discrepancies in estimating the incidence of this disorder reflects the ambiguity surrounding the definition, description, and diagnosis of hyperactivity in children. Nevertheless, hyperactivity has become the single most common behavior disorder brought to the attention of child psychiatrists.[9]

A disorder afflicting so many people, at so young an age, should command the serious attention of scientists and medical practitioners bringing the utmost in logical and inductive reasoning to bear on the issues. But this has not been the case, leading some researchers, clinicians, and pediatricians to begin to voice alarm that the epidemic is running out of control, not because it is *real*, but because a myth has caught hold of the lay population and is expanding to include their own members.

Influenced by clinicians who believe that hyperactivity is real, parents often describe their "hyperactive" child in the same tone of voice one would use for someone with epilepsy or spina bifida. What is tragic and alarming is the fact that these parents believe their child is suffering from a grave neurological disorder. Yet evidence reveals that this assumption is not even remotely near the mark. Before investigating the experimental evidence in detail, it is necessary to demonstrate that the diagnosis *"hyperactive"* is based on a number of logical fallacies, which I call the seven fallacies of hyperactivity.

The Seven Fallacies of Hyperactivity

1. *Hyperactivity Is a New Disease.* The first fallacy relates to the sudden appearance of the disorder. It is difficult to think of a single physical disease or mental disorder where the symptoms were unknown *before* the remedy was discovered. Of course, parents and teachers had been dealing with noisy, difficult, restless, distractible children since the dawn of the human race. But suddenly this behavior in otherwise normal children began to be considered symptomatic of a disease or of brain damage. The history leading to this conclusion is difficult to unravel and contains the following five strands.

Drug companies devote a large percentage of their resources to discovering new drugs. Any new compound that has a measurable effect on either physiology or behavior is heavily promoted in terms of research and, ultimately, marketing. Psychostimulants like amphetamine, methylphenidate hydrochloride (Ritalin), and pemoline produce changes in motoric behavior in animals and humans (hyperactive or not). Any child who has difficulty in motor control, especially those who find it hard to sit still in classrooms, runs the risk of becoming a target of a marketing effort.

The medical model still aims at cure rather than prevention, focusing on disease rather than health, and finds the simplest remedy to be the prescription of drugs. Doctors are innundated with marketing material from drug companies. Furthermore, the medical approach is based on a philosophical stance that everyone falls into one of two categories: "sick" or "well." Since being sick is attributed mainly to physiological causes, drugs are the obvious therapeutic choice rather than attempts to deal with behavior or psychosocial factors.

Parents are made aware by the media and literature, through clinics and parent-teachers' associations, of what an "ideal child" should be like. Generally, their own never quite matches up. The tendency then is to ascribe the cause of any deviation from the norm to factors outside their control and most preferably to an underlying physical problem. If their child has a "disease" curable by drugs, then the child's deviant behavior is not their fault.

173

This same attitude affects teachers who have to deal with these children in the classroom. It is much easier to believe that the children are "sick" than to have to accept the responsibility for controlling their behavior. Furthermore, as will be discussed later, most early-grade teachers (when hyperactivity causes the greatest difficulty) are female, and hyperactive children are almost exclusively male. It is conceivable that as part of a shift in social attitudes, female tolerance of male behavior patterns is decreasing.

Finally, as a nation we are becoming increasingly devoted to "normalization" as a cultural value. Everyone must be the same, conform to the same rules, develop the same kind of skills and intellect, and ascribe to identical values. Sitting still in a classroom, paying undivided attention to an adult for six hours every day is good; anything else is bad.

2. *There is such a thing as a "normal" child.* In any physical disease or disorder, there is a difference between being well or being unwell, infected or healthy, rundown and depleted or fit. Even psychotics experience moments of lucidity and can contrast these to periods of hallucination or severe depression and so forth. Where, however, is the boundary between hyperactive children and everyone else? The children exhibit no apparent discomfort, feel perfectly well, have no physical disease and no sign of neurological disorder. What then is wrong with them? What is wrong is that their behavior *seems* to deviate from the norm. The question at issue is, first, what measure does one use to determine a "hyperactivity" score (there are no standardized tests), and second, where on the curve does one draw the line demarcating normal from deviant behavior? To diagnose hyperactivity one has to determine exactly where along the normal curve the line is to be drawn. Any decision would represent a statistical, never an absolute, value. As was shown in chapter 3, if the rationale currently employed was applied to diagnose *hypo*activity as well as *hyper*activity, 36 percent of all school-age males would be considered "abnormal."

3. *Hyperactivity can be diagnosed.* Diagnostic tools will be reviewed in considerable detail later, but in summary, it is no exaggeration to state that *diagnostic scales for determining the incidence of hyperactivity are behavioral indices only.* As currently diagnosed, hyperactive children have no demonstrated brain dam-

age; few, if any, have perceptual-motor problems; no signs of disease have ever been discovered; and there is considerable controversy as to whether they are even more active than any other child their age. If one extracts the consistent markers common to the various hyperactivity scales, one ends up with two major factors: inattention, and behavior inappropriate to social context or problems of self-control. The children exhibit behaviors that parents and teachers find hard to ignore; therefore, they *seem* more active because they are so obtrusive. As noted earlier, these children are a nuisance.

Parents and teachers diagnose these children, since it is they who fill out the hyperactivity scales—and their ratings simply reflect the degree of their tolerance for annoying behavior. Clinicians and medical practitioners accept these ratings sometimes without question; and children who are maximally disruptive are put on drugs.

In double-blind drug studies on hyperactive children, the children classified "hyperactive" can be given drugs whether they have received them before or not. To make this seem a valid procedure, they are thereafter referred to as "patients." If children show behavioral changes following the intake of a psychostimulant drug, they are designated as "responders"; in some diagnostic approaches "responsivity" constitutes an indication of the disorder. This means that *the response to a drug forms the basis of the diagnosis.* As no control (normal) child can be given drugs, almost every drug study on hyperactive children is invalid because there is no comparison to a control group. In fact, recent data have shown that the proportion of drug "responders" in a group of normal children is identical to that of a hyperactive group.

4. *Hyperactivity can strike anyone.* No, it cannot. It strikes mostly males, and does so in a ratio of from six to one to nine to one (or 86 to 90 percent). So rare are hyperactive girls that few experiments on hyperactive children include them. For some reason, this difference between the sexes never seems to strike anyone as peculiar. Yet a fundamental question must be asked: Is the sex ratio due to some abnormal or deviant process, or does it arise because of some *normal* process? Searching the literature for sex-related diseases such as color-blindness and hemophilia reveals that such disorders affect less than 1 percent of the population.

Diseases or disorders affecting up to 15 percent of schoolchildren such as colds, upper respiratory infection, mumps, and measles, do not single out males as their exclusive victims.

However, if one looks at male-female differences in *normal* physical and physiological functioning, these sorts of ratios abound. A statistical sample of extremes in height, weight, strength, lung capacity, and so forth, would include largely men. There are no women among the top fifty sprinters in the world. It is therefore more likely that the high proportion of hyperactive males represents a real sex difference in *normal* behavior.

5. *The hyperactive child has a maturational lag.* Because six-year-old hyperactive boys bounce around like four-year-olds and appear to act as four-year-olds, some people conclude that their brains are developmentally slowed down. There are two things wrong with this view, despite the fact that it is more appealing than the notion that these children have brain damage.

First, as the majority of hyperactive children have normal intelligence, learn to read at the normal age, and show adequate skills in arithmetic, what precisely is "lagging"? If they run around the room paying no attention whatsoever, then it is nothing short of miraculous that they can learn to read and write in passing, without studying at all! This would seem to indicate a developmental acceleration rather than a lag.

Second, baboons, gorillas, and chimpanzees are considerably more advanced than humans at earlier ages. A developmental "lag" reflects a superior level in cultural evolution. We know that a slower-developing brain is an indication of greater brain plasticity and more potential for learning. It is not necessarily true that the doctrine of efficiency—faster is better—should be applied to people. Aside from this, we have already seen that hands-on exploration may benefit the development of visuospatial ability. This type of behavior is not promoted in current classroom settings but is, perhaps, the most appropriate and necessary for the "hyperactive" child.

6. *Distractibility is bad.* We have very little notion of how early childhood experiences lead to the development of different cognitive systems. Distractibility is always discussed in relation to hyperactive children in negative terms. The positive aspects of distractibility are that a child stays open to experience, maintains his or her curiosity, and feels free to explore the world. Before we

prevent children from allowing the environment to direct their attention, it is important to understand the implications of the need for a variety of stimulation and experience, especially the need to investigate and explore. Similarly, the positive aspects of high activity or unrestrained activity are exuberance, vitality, energy, and health. While self-discipline must be acquired, it should not be at the expense of curiosity and exploration.

One of the only consistent research findings is that hyperactive children perform poorly on vigilance tasks, which require subjects to pay undivided attention to a series of quite meaningless, repetitive patterns. So far the evidence has shown that this type of task bears absolutely no relationship to any relevant academic pursuit; yet researchers consistently assume that these tests measure some unidimensional aspect of "attention."

7. *Hyperactive children have no opinion.* Even schizophrenics are asked to describe their hallucinations. In reading well over one hundred papers, I have found only a few studies in which the authors bothered to discover what these children think and feel. I have come across no reports on what these children like to *do.* In all of the studies that have investigated attitudes and feelings, the children interviewed had been on an extensive drug regime or had been diagnosed as "hyperactive" for several years. By and large, these children indicated that they were under considerable stress, and they consistently exhibited low self-esteem. Only one experimenter questioned whether these feelings might be *produced* by the psychosocial factors involved in the drug regime itself and by being labeled hyperactive. Everyone else assumed that the depression, anxiety, and lack of self-confidence the boys exhibited was *caused* by "hyperactivity."

As professionals, our primary concern must be to adopt more stringent criteria for classifying children in need of clinical or medical care. The major difficulty with using terms like "hyper-activity" or, recently, "attentional deficit disorder" as if they constituted a disease entity or syndrome, is that fidgety behavior and inattention are symptoms of a host of different situations and conditions.

Excessive, unremitting hyperactivity is a consequence of brain damage or a biochemical imbalance in less than 1 percent of the population. Such brain damage could be inherent or produced by prenatal exposure to toxins (including alcohol) and childhood exposure to lead.[10] (It is important to note that studies have not confirmed any connection between intake of carbohydrates or sugar and hyperactive behavior.)[11]

By contrast, fidgety behavior or the inability to concentrate can be produced by boredom or stress. Children with persistent learning problems begin to worry, then to panic, and eventually to give up entirely. For either the gifted or the poor scholar, six hours is a long day. If work is finished too soon or not at all, then misbehavior is likely to occur.

Equally likely is that hyperactivity is one end of a continuum of a perfectly normal temperamental trait more typical of males. Children also differ in "cognitive styles." One child may learn by listening to explanations, while another may need more hands-on exploration—behavior more typical of a "hyperactive" child.

In the research that will be reviewed in chapter 10, these factors, plus a number of other ones, such as IQ, perceptual-motor skills, and severe conduct disorders, are confounded. Yet millions of people are convinced that the diagnosis of hyperactivity has a solid medical history behind it. The above analysis alone is not convincing. In the following sections I take up the history behind the diagnosis of hyperactivity, and the development and use of diagnostic scales.

Symptom or Syndrome?

In 1937 American psychiatrist Charles Bradley outlined the organic behavior syndrome in children and its amphetamine treatment.[12] Twenty years later psychiatrists Maurice Laufer, Eric Denhoff, and Gerald Solomons followed up Bradley's initial idea with an article describing a hyperkinetic behavior syndrome in children.[13] They listed seven symptoms and their descriptions: hyperactivity, short attention span and poor powers of concentration, variability, impulsiveness, inability to delay gratification, irritability, explosiveness, and poor schoolwork. Laufer, Denhoff, and Solomons proposed that the syndrome "may be due to organic causes," for it was commonly found in epileptic, cerebral-palsied, and brain-damaged mentally retarded children. According to the authors, *"apparently* anything which produces dysfunction of the diencephalon [a part of the brain stem] and the diencephalocortical connections before birth, during birth, or in the first five years of life *may result* in this syndrome" (emphasis added). (The reader is asked to pay particular attention to the words "apparently" and "may result." This is another way of stating that the authors do not know the cause of the disorder.) They suggested that this impairment can make the central nervous system abnormally sensitive to stimulation from both internal and external sources. This was seen as a possible explanation of the hyperkinetic child's heightened response to physical stress (such as hunger, a full bladder, coldness, and so on) or sensitivity to distracting stimulation.

However, when neurological examinations were carried out on children with this "syndrome," no consistent abnormalities were discovered. This meant that the particular cluster of behaviors outlined above was not reliable. Next, Laufer and his colleagues postulated that abnormal electrical activity of the brain (as evidenced by EEGs) may be indicative of disturbed behavior, although the abnormalities are nonspecific. They concluded that it was their impression that these abnormal EEGs reflected the presence of a large number of children with the hyperkinetic syndrome . . . but they also stated that there was no close correspondence between EEG and abnormality, as many of the children in the series with well-marked symptoms of the hyperkinetic syndrome had normal EEGs, and that a number of the children without the hyperkinetic syndrome have had abnormal EEGs. The difficulty of establishing any neurological correlate of hyperkinesis in children will be discussed in the next chapter.

Despite the fact that neurological examinations and recordings of brain-wave activity revealed no coherent pattern for the hyperkinetic group, the notion of a syndrome was not abandoned. Instead, the diagnosis of hyperkinesis came to be based primarily on the child's history, taking into account possible birth traumas and parental descriptions of the child's behavior. However, just as neurological examinations have proven inconclusive, so, too, have other diagnostic tests. At this time there is no objective measure for the hyperkinetic syndrome apart from the child's developmental history and the subjective reports of parents and teachers. Consequently, Laufer, Denhoff, and Solomons proposed: "A favorable response to amphetamine is supportive evidence for a diagnosis of the hyperkinetic syndrome." A "favorable response" is taken to mean anything that reduces movement and problematic behavior.

Thus the diagnosis is based on a patient's reaction to medication. The danger in this practice is obvious. If typically solemn people were given lithium (a drug used for severe manic-depression) and it was found to reverse their temperament, making them more light hearted, would such a change in character label the person "manic-depressive"? A "favorable response" to a drug does not indicate pathology. A common example is found in the enormous individual variations in the reaction to alcohol. As sociologist Peter Conrad has pointed out, stimulant drug treatment was available long before hyperkinesis became a designated syndrome.[14] It appears that it was not until Laufer, Denhoff and Solomons created the term "hyperkinetic syndrome" in 1957 that the drug treatment found a patient population. Thus it is highly probable that the rise in the incidence of hyperactivity since the early 1960s is in part a direct consequence of an available medication.

Once the myth of a "hyperactive syndrome" took hold, the proliferation of vague definitions and numerous characteristics associated with hyperactivity led to a profusion of descriptions of the disorder. In response to the confusion, a report was prepared by a team of national authorities in 1966 for the Department of Health, Education and Welfare.[15] They uncovered thirty-eight terms alone used to describe children characterized by extreme overactivity. In an effort to contain this explosion in terminology, "minimal brain dysfunction" (MBD) was chosen as a unifying concept. "Minimal" referred to the fact that the brain damage could not be determined; the speculated involvement of the "brain" was indicated by "soft" neurological signs of impairment in some hyperactive children; and "dysfunction" avoided the issue as to whether these behavior disorders have an organic basis.

The study group went on to delineate ninety-nine signs and symptoms characterizing minimal brain dysfunction. Once again, no one challenged the notion that a syndrome *exists*, and all that has been accomplished is an exercise in semantics. On the basis of this fixed assumption, the team set out the ten most common characteristics of the 99 symptoms that had been cited by various authors in order of frequency. These were:

1. Hyperactivity
2. Perceptual-motor impairments
3. Emotional lability
4. General coordination deficits
5. Disorders of attention (short attention span, distractibility, perseveration)
6. Impulsivity
7. Disorders of memory and thinking
8. Specific learning disabilities (reading, arithmetic, writing, spelling)
9. Disorders of speech and hearing
10. Equivocal neurological signs and irregularities in the EEG

It is important to understand precisely what occurred. The task force decreed that the expression "minimal brain dysfunction" was the umbrella term for a number of disorders and learning disabilities that may or may not include hyperactivity. What has happened in practice is that "MBD" and "hyperkinesis" have come to be used *interchangeably*, as hyperactivity was often the major presenting symptom among those applied to diagnose both learning disabilities and behavior disorders. "Hyperactivity" has since come to stand for either.

In the following decade, psychologists and clinicians set out to explore the nature of MBD or hyperkinesis. By the mid-seventies, the level of sophistication in research and logical analysis had not noticeably improved. In 1974 Domeena Renshaw published a book entitled *The Hyperactive Child*, in which she makes a distinction between hyperactivity as a symptom and hyperkinesis as a syndrome.[16] (This may be called having your cake and eating it.) "Hyperactivity is a symptom. The hyperkinetic 'syndrome' (HK) is a collection of clinical behavioral manifestations, forming a clinical entity with a wide spectrum from mild to severe" (p. 4). According to Renshaw, hyperactivity is a common "symptom" in childhood that occurs normally from the ages of two to five years and is characterized by overactivity, restlessness, and distractibility. By about three and a half or four years old, according to Renshaw, a child develops the ability to sustain attention for five to ten minutes. As the child grows older, stress, excitement, fatigue, or emotional tension can manifest itself as hyperactivity. In these cases where hyperactivity is a reaction to environmental conditions, its occurrence is as spontaneous as its recovery, when the conditions are altered.

On the other hand, Renshaw sees the hyperkinetic syndrome as "a recognizable entity" that can be detected as early as two years. The severity of symptoms appears, however, to be determined subjectively, by the family's tolerance of the child's behavior. The actual "diagnosis" is based on the persistence of at least half of the following twenty-two symptoms:

1. Ceaseless, purposeless activity
2. Short attention span
3. Highly distractible
4. Highly excitable; labile emotions
5. Uncontrolled impulses (talks, hits, leaps, etc.)
6. Poor concentration (overincludes all stimuli)
7. Heedless of danger/pain
8. Poor response to reward/punishment
9. Destructive; aggressive; lies; steals; has temper tantrums
10. Constant clash with environment
11. Accident-prone; clumsy; poor motor coordination
12. Speech problems
13. Strabismus (squint)
14. Perception difficulties; audio-visual problems
15. Mixed L-R dominance (ex: R-handed/L-eyed/R-legged)
16. Irregular developmental milestones (no crawling then walking)
17. "Untidy" drawing, coloring, handwriting
18. Nothing completed spontaneously, needs excess reminders
19. Inability to cope with phase-related activity
20. Poor socialization; quarrelsome; no respect for others
21. Sleep disturbance
22. Needs constant supervision

(pp. 82–83)

The clustering of at least eleven of these signs is considered essential to the diagnosis, though it is impossible to see how any group of these symptoms could cluster to produce a single disorder. Also, according to Renshaw, the child's response to drug therapy is also seen to be of particular importance in diagnosing the syndrome. Once more, twenty years after Laufer, Denhoff, and

Solomons' article, subjective reports and a "favorable" response to stimulant drugs are the basis for diagnosis.

Meanwhile, there have been a few attempts to study these behavioral symptoms experimentally, using appropriate control groups and statistical analyses. A study by Mark Stewart revealed that several of the symptoms found in hyperactive subjects were also present in control subjects. Among the most prevalent in the control sample were overactivity (33 percent), talking too much (20 percent), fidgetiness (30 percent), teasing (22 percent), and bed wetting (28 percent). The main difference between two groups was the number of symptoms displayed. Out of a possible fifty-five behavioral symptoms investigated by Stewart, hyperactive subjects displayed an average of twenty-two, whereas only three (overactivity, fidgetiness, enuresis) were common in more than one-quarter of the control subjects.[17] These findings suggest that behavioral problems are common in children; however, those children diagnosed as "hyperactive" appear to have more problems than most. Overactivity was the only symptom manifested in *all* hyperactive subjects. Of course this result is to be expected. If you select children on the basis of the number of behavioral anomalies, then it is not surprising that the children are different from others who do not exhibit these anomalies. What was revealing about this study is that the control group exhibited a number of behavioral problems as well. Even hyperactivity was found to be present in 33 percent of the control subjects.

Using factor analysis, which allows the experimenter to examine the relationships among a large number of different measures, John Werry at the University of Auckland tested 103 children diagnosed as hyperactive on a number of different neurological and behavioral tests.[18] He found ten totally unrelated factors, all of which had the symptoms of "hyperactivity." These were labeled by Werry as:

Factor I:	Motor Incoordination
Factor II:	Impaired Drawing Ability
Factor III:	Dysgnosia-Dyspraxia
Factor IV:	Psychopathology—Poor Environment
Factor V:	Immaturity
Factor VI:	EEG Abnormalities
Factor VII:	Neurological Impairment
Factor VIII:	No clear defining criterion

Factor IX: Impaired Cognitive Performance
Factor X: Abnormal Paranatal Status

Werry's findings are particularly interesting for two reasons. First, they illustrate the enormous range of behavioral and neurological disorders that result in a common symptom of "hyperactivity." Second, his factor descriptions bear almost no relationship to the subjective and ad hoc lists of symptoms that have been discussed so far. Furthermore, all but Factors IV, V, and VIII are readily quantifiable measures, for which it would be an easy matter to construct robust diagnostics. Yet, despite this, the diagnostic tests have not appeared, and instead Werry's name has been associated with a commonly used paper-and-pencil scale frequently employed as the *sole* criterion for the diagnosis of hyperkinesis or MBD. It is clear from the nature of Werry's research that the Werry-Weiss-Peters scale was originally designed as a preliminary screening tool to select children for more rigorous testing. This would enable clinicians to determine subsequently which factor or factors most characterized a particular hyperactive child. However, in practice, in almost every piece of research and in clinical assessment, this important second step is omitted.

In one of the few attempts to present a rational analysis of the problem, Dorothea Ross and Sheila Ross in their outstanding book reflect on the distinction between "symptom" and "syndrome," and concude that detailed studies reveal no evidence for a unitary cluster of characteristics. Instead, hyperactivity should be viewed as a nonspecific symptom whose significance depends on a variety of factors including age, sex, social and environmental factors such as parental discipline, situational appropriateness of the behavior, and ability to inhibit the hyperactive behavior on command.[19]

The extreme difficulty in establishing any coherent diagnosis for hyperactivity is a clear indication that there is no such thing as a syndrome of "hyperkinesis." Yet despite this obvious fact and the abundance of evidence supporting it, the term "hyperkinesis" continues to denote a single behavioral disorder that is typically treated with stimulant drugs. Despite Werry's findings, the diagnosis is entirely determined by subjective reports of behavioral problems provided by teachers and/or parents, and largely derived through questionnaires. A closer look at these so-called diagnostic scales will reveal even further confusion surrounding a diagnosis of hyperactivity.

Diagnostic Scales

The original hyperkinetic syndrome outlined by Laufer, Denhoff, and Solomons seems to have originated as a description of retarded and brain-damaged children. The seven symptoms they outlined, in fact, define a developmentally retarded child, whose immaturity is a by-product of gross intellectual impairment. However, a complication arises when these same descriptions are applied to children with normal intelligence. How does one quantify qualitative behaviors? For instance, how immature is "immature"? What is a "short" attention span and what is normal? How irritable is irritable?

This confusion is clearly reflected in the descriptions provided by various authors in the field and by the rating scales themselves. The Werry-Weiss-Peters scale describes only one problem, repeated with monotonous redundancy: Is the child unable to inhibit inappropriate motor behavior in most situations? (see table 9.1.)

As time has passed, various scales have been developed solely on the basis of the author's own particular biases and assumptions. (There is a good financial inducement to developing test batteries.) The tests represent a multitude of factors describing a polyglot population, all of whom appear similarly hyperactive. Some define the hyperactive child as exhibiting behavior that gets on everyone's nerves. The "nuisance level" criterion is most glaringly obvious in the scale designed by Stewart, Thach, and Freidin. (See table 9.2.) Hyperactivity in this context is taken to infer highly aggressive behavior and a tendency toward criminality.[20]

At the opposite extreme, the Department of Health, Education and Welfare checklist of the ten most common symptoms of MBD includes all the attendant difficulties in every form of learning disability, but excludes high aggressivity and socially deviant behavior.

Renshaw's list of symptoms incorporates all of these, and her diagnostic specification based on the persistence of only half of the symptoms in the list therefore gives rise to various distinct populations. Some of these are antisocial and aggressive, some learning-disabled, while others exhibit none of these problems but suffer from perceptual-motor difficulties or gross-motor impairment.

The Conners Teacher Rating scale is one of the most commonly

TABLE 9-1
Werry-Weiss-Peters Activity Scale

	No	Yes—A Little	Yes—Very Much
During meals			
Up and down at table			
Interrupts without regard			
Wriggling			
Fiddles with things			
Talks excessively			
Television			
Gets up and down during program			
Wriggles			
Manipulates objects or body			
Talks incessantly			
Interrupts			
Doing home-work			
Gets up and down			
Wriggles			
Manipulates objects or body			
Talks incessantly			
Requires adult supervision or attendance			
Play			
Inability for quiet play			
Constantly changing activity			
Seeks parental attention			
Talks excessively			
Disrupts other's play			
Sleep			
Difficulty settling down for sleep			
Inadequate amount of sleep			
Restless during sleep			
Behavior away from home (except school)			
Restlessness during travel			
Restlessness during shopping (includes touching everything)			
Restlessness during church/movies			
Restlessness during visiting friends, relatives, etc.			
School behavior			
Up and down			
Fidgets, wriggles, touches			
Interrupts teacher or other children excessively			
Constantly seeks teacher's attention			
Total score			

SOURCE: From J. S. Werry, "Developmental Hyperactivity," *Pediatric Clinics of North America* 15 (1968): 581–99. Reprinted with permission.

TABLE 9.2

Symptoms on which the Diagnosis of Hyperactive Child Syndrome was Based

Overactivity (including unusual energy and restlessness) and Distractibility (including short attention span, never finishing work and projects) and any six of the following:

Fidgets, rocks, etc.	Disobedient
Climbs on roof, etc.	Doesn't follow directions
Runs over furniture	Doesn't respond to discipline
Always into things	Defiant
Heedless of danger	Wakes early
Runs away	Hard to get to bed
Constant demands	Wets bed
Easily upset	Many accidents
Impatient	Lies often
Won't accept correction	Takes money, etc.
Tantrums	Neighborhood terror
Fights often	Sets fires
Teases	Reckless, daredevil
Destructive	Fears

SOURCE: From M. A. Stewart; B. T. Thach; and M. R. Freidin, "Accidental Poisoning and the Hyperactive Child Syndrome," *Diseases of the Nervous System* 31(1970): 403–7. Reprinted with permission of the Physicians Postgraduate Press Inc.

used scales for selecting children for clinical referral and for laboratory experiments. In 1978 Keith Conners and his colleagues, Charles Goyette and Richard Ulrich at the University of Pittsburgh tested 570 children with an average age of about ten years on a revised version of this test compared with an earlier version.[21] Parents were instructed to fill out the questionnaire items from the parents' scale and teachers to fill out items from the teacher's scale.

These data were then put on computer and a factor analysis was carried out. This procedure determines which of the many questionnaire items are correlated, that is, specific answers to some questions are highly predictive of answers to others. The questionnaire items for the parents clustered on five major factors: (I) conduct disorder, (II) learning problems, (III) psychosomatic symptoms, (IV) hyperactivity, and (V) anxiety. The factor structure for mothers and fathers was similar. The factor structure for teachers was simpler: Only three factors, (I) conduct disorder, (II) hyperactivity, and (III) inattention, were emphasized.

A shortened form called a Hyperactivity Index was compiled

from the parents' and the teacher's scales in what seems to be a completely arbitrary manner. The parents' items included: excitability/impulsivity, fidgety and "up and going," from Factor IV (hyperactivity); destructive behavior from Factor I (conduct disorder); fails to finish things, distractible or poor attention span, and easily frustrated from Factor II (learning problems); labile mood changes, which was part of Factor V (anxiety) for the mothers, but not the fathers. "Disturbs other children" was part of Factor I for fathers but not for mothers. "Cries easily" was also included, though was not part of any factor for mothers or fathers.

The items from the teacher's scale included three related to the conduct disorder factor: temper outbursts, pouting or sulking, and sudden changes of mood. Four items are related to hyperactivity: fidgety, "up and going," disturbs other children, excitable/impulsive. Other items selected from Factor III were "fails to finish tasks," and "easily frustrated." Yet, despite the computation involved in accumulating these data, it is hard to determine just what the Hyperactivity Index is supposed to be measuring. If it is desirable to establish a scale for hyperactivity, the scale should not include items from factors that relate to conduct disorder, attentional problems, or anxiety.

Mother/father and parent/teacher correlations were also computed, the results of which demonstrate how unreliable questionnaire data can be. (Bear in mind that these ratings were all made on the same children by their fathers, mothers, and teachers.) The highest correlation for mothers and fathers for any factor was for Factor I, conduct disorder. The correlation was 0.57. Computing the variance (0.57×0.57) indicates that the agreement between fathers and mothers on their child's behavior accounts for only 32 percent of the score. Another way of stating this relation is that fathers and mothers agree only about one-third of the time. The agreement on the remaining factors was much poorer. The correlation for the total Hyperactivity Index was 0.55, or 30 percent agreement. When teacher ratings and parent ratings were compared on conduct problems, learning and attentional problems, and hyperactivity, the correlations were 0.33 (11 percent agreement), 0.45 (20 percent agreement), and 0.36 (13 percent agreement) respectively. The correlation for the hyperactivity index as a whole was 0.49, or 24 percent agreement.

Another way of expressing these relationships is to say that on average, mothers and fathers disagreed about the severity of their child's behavior about 70 percent of the time, and both disagreed with the teacher's opinion about their child 75 to 85 percent of the time. Teachers and parents also disagreed on their attitude toward what constitutes appropriate behavior for sex and for age. Parents were considerably more likely to attribute problems in conduct and schoolwork to the fact that their children were boys and hyperactivity to their being younger children. Teachers attributed conduct problems to age and hyperactivity to both boys and younger children.

Despite the unpredictability of this test, the Conners' scale has been the most widely used instrument for the "diagnosis" of hyperactivity. Many, if not most, psychiatrists, physicians, pediatricians, and psychologists have based their interventions largely on the basis of a child's scores on this scale. These interventions often include the prescription of psychostimulant drugs.

In 1980 the *Diagnostic and Statistical Manual of Mental Disorders (DSM-III)*, published by the American Psychiatric Association, created a new diagnostic category called "Attentional Deficit Disorder" (ADD).[22] The criteria include distractibility, daydreaming, and failure to finish work or projects. ADD can also be accompanied by hyperactivity, which involves fidgeting, failure to stay seated, and excessive running and climbing. Note the sleight of hand by which a previous diagnosis "hyperactivity," which used to subsume problems of attention, has been reversed, so that "hyperactivity" has become a secondary symptom of an "attentional disorder."

Teachers and parents are solely responsible for rating children on these attentional and hyperactive behaviors, because, as the *DSM-III* manual notes, they are rarely exhibited in a one-to-one situation, such as the clinic! (This fact might trigger some suspicion that these behaviors are situationally specific and that we might blame the situation rather than the child.) Thus psychiatrists have put the onus for diagnosis directly on the shoulders of parents and teachers, who have absolutely no training in diagnosing behavior disorders. The *DSM-III* does not specify how parents would know whether their particular child was more or less "distractible" or "runs excessively" because they have no basis of comparison. Robert Rubenstein and Ronald Brown tested children diagnosed "ADD without hyperactivity" and "ADD with hyperactivity" on a huge battery of tests, involving behavioral measures, achievement tests, and other hyperactivity scales.[23] None of these tests singly or in combination could distinguish children placed into these two categories any better than chance.

Hyperactive Children: Bad Boys or "Just Boys"?

As indicated, all diagnostic scales consistently select many more males than females as hyperactive. Because of this lopsided sex effect most studies on hyperactivity rely almost exclusively on male subjects. Thus not only do the tests themselves lack construct validity, but they fail to establish norms that are based on sex. A further problem with most hyperactivity scales is that they are not based on norms at all. That is, there are no norms for any of the categories defined by the questionnaire items.

As a result, it is impossible to distinguish between hyperactivity as a symptom of a more serious disorder or as a behavioral trait of a proportion of normal boys. Given the extremely high estimates for the incidence of hyperactivity, it seems likely that much of what we are seeing is just one end of a continuum of typical male behavior. My own research has shed some light on this issue. In an observational study carried out on preschool children during free play, Cindy Morley and I obtained some interesting results on the way in which boys and girls spontaneously time their behavior.[24] In over one hundred hours of observations, individual children were monitored for twenty-minute periods. Everything the child did in that time period was faithfully recorded by either a male or female observer and subsequently categorized for specific behavior patterns.

Figure 9.1 illustrates the scores for the average duration in minutes for each of these categories. Perseverance, for example, was calculated as the longest time a child spent on any *one* activity during the period of the observation. The average time for the girls was twelve minutes, for the boys, eight minutes. Girls spent twice as much time in play organized by the teacher (usually, but not always, female), whereas males spent twice as much time in

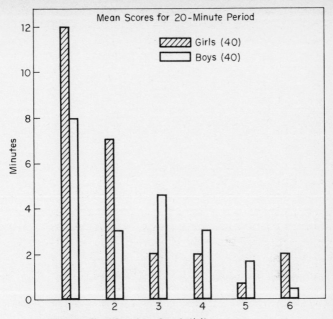

FIGURE 9.1

The average time in minutes during a twenty-minute period in which boys and girls engaged in various behaviors. (All sex comparisons are significant at $p < 0.01$.)

unsupervised play—constructing things or watching other children.

Figure 9.2 illustrates the frequency of occurrence of certain behaviors. Boys are found to carry out four and one-half different activities in twenty minutes, girls only two and one-half. Particularly interesting is the number of interruptions of ongoing play. Boys interrupted what they were doing three times more frequently than girls. Behaviors in categories 7 to 9, which were intended to tap destructive and aggressive behaviors, occurred extremely infrequently. None of our observers ever saw any serious misbehavior, and no child at this excellent preschool was considered deviant, hyperactive, or difficult to control. Therefore, a sex difference of

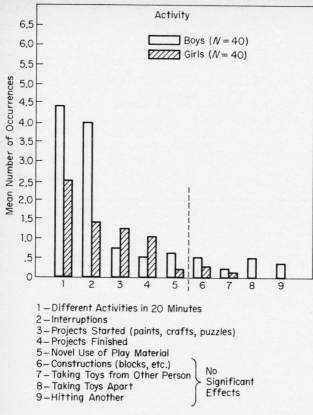

1 — Different Activities in 20 Minutes
2 — Interruptions
3 — Projects Started (paints, crafts, puzzles)
4 — Projects Finished
5 — Novel Use of Play Material
6 — Constructions (blocks, etc.)　⎫
7 — Taking Toys from Other Person　⎬ No Significant Effects
8 — Taking Toys Apart　⎪
9 — Hitting Another　⎭

FIGURE 9.2

The number of occasions during a twenty-minute period that boys and girls engaged in various behaviors. (Comparisons 1 to 5 are significant at $p < 0.01$; comparisons 6 to 9 are not significant.)

the magnitude we discovered is all the more remarkable and illustrates that when children are left to their own devices, *boys time their actions differently from girls.*[25] In a classroom setting, the routine and structure favors the timing patterns of girls far more so than that of boys. Imposing these unnatural temporal constraints on young boys can disrupt their normal rhythms and produce frustration and tension.

Despite the innumerable difficulties in determining just which child should be diagnosed as hyperactive and the fact that the questionnaires used in this process are invalid, psychologists and psychophysiologists have spent hundreds of hours in an attempt to pin down behavioral and physiological correlates of "hyperactivity." These experiments are reviewed in the following chapter. The outcome of these endeavors can be revealed beforehand: Essentially nothing has been found. For this reason, chapter 10 could be skipped entirely, except that it does provide a data base that proves that hyperactivity per se, independent of low IQ, learning disabilities, and highly aggressive or antisocial behavior, is not a valid diagnostic criterion. Furthermore, Russell Barkley and Charles Cunningham's extensive review indicates that stimulant drugs have failed in all cases to effect any improvement in academic ability.[26] Chapter 10 details how an enormous number of research programs can be maintained in the face of no evidence.

10

Hyperactivity: A Patient in Search of a Diagnosis

Chapter 9 showed that it was not possible to establish a valid diagnosis of "hyperactivity" by using questionnaires, for questionnaires reveal as much about the degree of a parent's or a teacher's tolerance for annoying behavior as they do about the child. For this reason, psychologists have attempted to approach the problem in a more objective way. If the questionnaire data are imprecise, then controlled laboratory experiments are the solution. The procedure has generally been to take a group of annoying children classified as "hyperactive" by their teachers and compare them to other children classified as "normal." The children are matched for age, sex, and IQ. Then researchers attempt to discover if there are any differences between the two groups on objective tests.

The major question is how to determine which tests to employ. Two general approaches have been tried. The first is to select tests borrowed from the clinic or from a neuropsychological battery on the basis of the symptoms that hyperactive children are supposed to exhibit, such as abnormalities of motor behavior or attention. A second solution is to find *any* test that distinguishes between the two groups. When such a test is discovered, it is thereafter considered to be a marker for "hyperactivity." So far, tests that are considered markers are mainly vigilance tasks. These are boring, repetitive tasks requiring fixed attention to a set of meaningless patterns.

Psychologists are usually at pains to rule out learning problems as a factor in their selection of hyperactive children. In addition to controlling for IQ, many psychologists also consider the children's performance on various reading and math achievement tests. This means that the two groups are often well matched on ability. The rationale for this procedure is that the psychologist wants to measure "pure" hyperactivity, independent of low IQ or learning disabilities.

But what is the logic behind these procedures? If children were merely considered to be naughty or disobedient, they would be sent to the principal and reprimanded. If this did not work, the parents would be brought in and some remedy would be sought. But this is not what everyone believes to be the case about a "hyperactive" child. The implicit assumption behind these efforts is that "hyperactive" children have some organic disorder. If psychologists can discover objective tests for such a disorder, then these test scores can be used both in diagnosis and for the prescription of drugs.

However, the "diagnosis" has already taken place! Children in all of these laboratory experiments have been preselected by the very scales that psychologists are seeking to replace. In reality, all that is being accomplished is a greater understanding of what disobedient children do differently than obedient children. And if these disobedient children have no learning problems and no health problems, why should it be assumed they have an organic disorder? As the children are performing well in school, but misbehaving, then the obvious solution is to change their behavior, not to give them drugs or test them in laboratories.

The purpose of any testing or intervention must, in the long run, be to help the child acquire academic and social skills. Therefore, the following critical questions must be kept in mind throughout this chapter:

1. Does the current practice of diagnosis and treatment of hyperactivity make any difference to the child's progress in learning appropriate or necessary skills?
2. Is there a relationship between any of the tests that hyperactive children find difficult or tedious and any definable academic skill?
3. Does the diagnosis of hyperactivity and its treatment make the child happier and more able to cope?

4. Is there any evidence that drugs are more effective than behavioral techniques for improving academic performance and moderating inappropriate behavior?

If any of these questions are answered in the negative (and I believe all are), then there is a powerful argument for abandoning our current practices of diagnosis and treatment.

Activity Levels

"Hyperactive" means "to be more active than most." But there are many ways to be active. A highly active person might complete a task at a greater than average speed. If the task were carried out correctly, this would be an indication of efficiency. On the other hand, someone could be highly active for no purpose, just moving for the sake of moving or going haphazardly from one thing to another. This kind of behavior is not very useful for accomplishing a task, but is entirely appropriate for exploring new sights and sounds on a nature walk. Hyperactive children can be viewed in much the same way as cocker spaniels. Rushing about in the woods and on the beach is perfectly acceptable, but the same exuberant activity is not so welcome indoors. What this means is that it is impossible to determine whether activity levels are normal or abnormal independent of context.

To date, all that is known is that hyperactive children tend to be more active than their peers, but this activity is considerably more noticeable in social groups and highly structured classrooms. As noted earlier, psychiatrists often find that children referred to them exhibit no excessive activity in a one-to-one interview or testing situation. Several studies have been carried out to determine whether direct behavioral observation can demonstrate differences between hyperactive and nonhyperactive children. Some of these studies employ trained observers who do not know whether children have been diagnosed hyperactive. Other studies use mechanical devices such as stabilimeters, which tally the absolute amount of motion over fixed time periods. The results from all of these studies have been equivocal, with about half finding no difference and half finding a difference. Situational specificity is a key factor.[1]

In the study carried out by Daniel O'Leary and his coworkers at Stony Brook discussed in chapter 1, children rated hyperactive were observed in two types of classrooms along with a control group.[2] The hyperactive children did not moderate their behavior between an open and closed classroom setting, whereas the control group became considerably more passive in the confined setting. In the open classroom the two groups did not differ in the amount of activity that was observed. What also proved revealing about this study and others using objective measuring techniques is that parent and teacher ratings are *unrelated* to the amount of actual activity that can be observed or measured.

The hyperactive child is described as deviating from the average or normal child. But the major problem is that "average" is left undefined. Ross and Ross noted in their recent book on hyperactivity that a purely quantitative concept of hyperactivity cannot be maintained because of its lack of validity. There are no activity "norms" for children and, due to situational factors, the goal of establishing activity-level norms may never even be possible.[3] Thus, should we be able to quantify hyperactivity, which is imperative if activity levels are to be employed as a diagnostic criterion for an organic disorder, there is always the problem that the amount and type of activity is context-specific. This means that a set of activity-level norms would have to be established for a variety of contexts. So far we have made almost no progress toward these goals.

What is unquestionable is that those stimulant drugs used as a treatment for hyperactivity significantly reduce activity in children. However, it is now known that such drugs act similarly on *non*hyperactive children. A team of researchers at the National Institute of Mental Health led by Judith Rapoport reported in 1978 that dextroamphetamine dramatically reduced motor activity in fourteen normal ten-year-old boys.[4] They state: "After drug administration the children appeared unusually inactive, not simply less restless" (p. 562).

Apart from the significance of this finding for invalidating "drug responders" as a diagnostic criterion, it raises considerable problems for behavioral diagnoses. Even assuming there were data or a valid method for constructing a normal distribution of activity levels, where on the curve should one draw the line between demarcating pathological behavior from normal behavior? Second, why not give all children drugs who fall above the mean on activity level and make the entire class more malleable?

Jerome Schulman and his colleagues have taken a different approach to assessing activity levels in children.[5] They proposed a model in which each individual regulates his or her total bodily movement over a long period of time around some optimal or "modal" level. The individual can deviate from his or her own particular pace as situations in the environment alter. The results of their research revealed that children display characteristic activity levels over time that are marked by substantial individual variations. These variations occur both between and within certain specific environmental situations. In more recent studies researchers have been able to confirm that this model applies well to the hyperactive child.[6] That is, the activity levels of these children are highly specific to a given situation. This fact is largely responsible for the difficulty in establishing normative activity levels for children. In reviewing the limited number of studies in which this has been attempted, Dennis Cantwell summarizes: "Unfortunately, results have been inconclusive and there is a serious question whether hyperactive children actually have a clearly greater amount of daily activity or a different type of motor activity than non-hyperactive children" (p. 5). Yet another serious flaw in a purely quantitative conception of hyperactivity, according to Ross and Ross, is that the important information lies in the qualitative aspects of the activity behavior, including its relevance, goal-directedness, and appropriateness.[7]

Most studies have reached the same conclusion: Hyperactive children may be somewhat more active than other children, but there is an additional aspect to their behavior that is problematic. Measuring activity levels alone does not differentiate between two equally active children, one who enthusiastically engages in class-work, moving from project to project, and one who energetically creates havoc without ever accomplishing anything constructive.

For this reason it is difficult to differentiate between normal activity and excessive or pathological activity. Nearly twenty years ago John and Corinne Hutt pointed out that hyperactive children are noticeable because they have greater difficulty in adapting their behavior and level of activity to various physical and social constraints.[8] As a result, these children often display situationally or socially inappropriate behavior. Within this framework, the hyperactive child can be thought of as a social deviant, moving and acting in a manner contrary to societal expectations and norms.

But what *is* normal activity for young children? Evidence from archaeology indicates that the earliest "homes" of the human race were open campsites. Anthropologists studying peoples in traditional cultures indicate that for young children, normal activity is often almost continuous play, interspersed with a few chores. In the most typical of the hunter-gatherer societies, this play continues well past puberty (which occurs considerably later in these societies than in our own). Returning from six months in the wilds of New Guinea, anthropologist Peter Reynolds described his amazement at the feats of athleticism of the young children.[9] They ran, swam, and climbed with the assurance of circus acrobats. Further, he noted, almost no discipline was enforced and none was required.

This observation is echoed in Pearse and Crocker's report on the Peckham Experiment, which describes the impact of a neighborhood community health project, set up prior to World War II in Peckham, a borough of South London. The center was dedicated to the promotion of health through preventive medicine, and functioned as a health and recreational center for the entire family.

All observers have been astonished at the untiringness of the children moving freely in their chosen occupations. Many who on Saturdays or in the holidays come to the Centre at 2 P.M. and leave at 6 or 7 P.M. spend the whole day in one activity after another without rest or pause even for food. A boy of 5½ still unable to swim was seen to dive from the spring-board into 10 feet of water twenty and more times in half-an-hour. And that not just in a frenzy, but day after day, with great purpose in response to his subjective urge to master the dive according to his capacity, content to rely each time on some struggling effort to bring him to the side of the bath. Or we could cite a boy of under 4 years old who spent four hours, day after day without a break, on a pair of roller skates, till he had achieved that particular balance. The records compiled from the children's cards show that these rather outstanding examples could be matched by hundreds of others showing great constancy of effort—which is indeed the rule and not the exception in the Centre children. . . . We did not in the beginning plan the children's activities on the basis we have just described but attempted to form groups and draw up time-tables and made schemes for the regular distribution of the children to activities of their choosing. *All this the children very largely ignored,* for it must be remembered that they were free to do so. Observation very quickly led us to abandon such methods and to evolve the present scheme by which the child can move in spontaneity of action within the general social framework.[10] (pp. 200–202, emphasis added)

It is possible that children who refuse to abide by adult admonitions to sit still and conform to rules set by adults for their own convenience are the very children who know what is good for them. By contrast, children who are overly conforming and remain for hours in sedentary postures may not. Who is to say which behavior is "normal"?

Pearse and Crocker touch on the issue of attention and perseveration when they observe that when children are engaged in something "suitable" to them, their whole attention and effort remain on the task. A large majority of children showed "a great constancy of effort" when doing what they wanted to do. This fact must be kept in mind in studies that attempt to measure attention. It does matter what you are asked to pay attention to. In attempting to discover any behavioral correlate of hyperactivity, especially those involving attentional control, psychologists have focused on a number of psychomotor tasks, often called vigilance tasks, developed during World War II to study fatigue in radar operators. So far there have been few attempts to discover what these tests have to do with progress in school or anywhere else.

"Attention Deficit Disorder"

Problems in the control of attention could result from deficiencies in the regulation of the central nervous system, which could produce distractibility, failure to sustain attention to a task, inability to plan actions, and a diminished attention span. However, similar difficulties could be created by an environment that is either too overwhelming or insufficiently compelling. This means that research on attention in hyperactive children suffers from the objection that the task is critical to the outcome of the study. That is, children will persevere at tasks that are "suitable," challenging, and interesting, but will rapidly lose interest in boring tasks or tasks that are beyond their particular aptitudes. Most of the attentional tasks, such as vigilance tasks, that have been employed in hyperactivity research are tiresome and dull. It is scarcely surprising that the children who seem most independent of adult control tend to perform poorly on these tasks.

The major goal of the studies on attention in hyperactive children has been directed to the question of how the reports by parents and teachers of distractibility, short attention span, and lack of perseverance can be operationally defined through controlled experiments. In every experiment on attention, one assumes that the subject is "paying attention," otherwise the experiment would be impossible to carry out. Because one can only measure how well a subject performs in the tasks, it can never be determined whether these manipulations are measuring attention or something else. The results obtained from such experiments could just as well be attributable to perceptual ability or to motivation. In all tasks requiring a rapid response, the results could also be due to individual variation in motor performance.

These problems are endemic to all research on attention, but are especially critical in studies on hyperactive populations. Are these children performing differently from their nonhyperactive controls because they do not like to conform to the activities and rules established by adults, because they are disinterested and not motivated to do well, or because they cannot maintain attention? Thus even when hyperactive children are found to perform identically to normal controls, might they have been *superior* if they were really involved? As few researchers control for motivation and rarely ask their subjects whether or not they found the tasks interesting, motivational factors cannot be ruled out. Even if one puts aside these difficulties, the more fundamental problem of how to make sense of the equivocal results arises.

For these reasons the selection of an appropriate task has been a confounding factor in many studies on attention in hyperactive children.

BEHAVIORAL STUDIES ON ATTENTION

Much of the research on the performance of hyperactive children on behavioral tests has been carried out through a collaborative effort between psychologists at McGill University and the Montreal Children's Hospital. In several of these studies, experiments have used the Matching Familiar Figures Test (MFFT) designed to measure impulsivity. Impulsivity—arriving at a premature decision—is assumed to reflect a deficiency in attentional control. In this test, children are expected to match a standard pattern or figure to one of six possible alternatives. Early results showed that hyperactive children appeared more impulsive (faster response times with more mistakes).[11] However, further research did not confirm these findings. Susan Kroener compared the performance of hyperactive children to nonhyperactive children who were also classified as either impulsive or reflective (slow and accurate).[12] She developed several conceptual levels for the solution to the tests by increasing them in complexity and found that hyperactive children were no more impulsive than the nonhyperactive impulsive children. In addition, the hyperactive children were found to use *higher*-level concepts in problem solving than either the impulsive or reflective control children. The hyperactive children also benefited from strategy instructions, whereas the nonhyperactive impulsive children did not. She concluded that "these findings argue against the idea of a central conceptual or perceptual deficit in hyperactive children."

Susan Campbell studied reflective, impulsive, and hyperactive boys.[13] As was expected, reflective boys had significantly longer reaction times and fewer errors on the MFFT than either of the other two groups. However, there was no difference between the hyperactive and the impulsive boys. The same results were found on the Children's Embedded Figures test, in which the subject has to locate a hidden figure that is camouflaged by extraneous patterns. According to Campbell, the failure to detect a difference between hyperactive and normal impulsive boys on either of these cognitive measures suggests that "the school problems of this hyperactive group cannot be explained in terms of inefficient cognitive strategies."

The MFFT measures not only impulsivity but also perceptual ability, that is, the capacity to discriminate between minor variations in patterns. Donald Sykes and coworkers in Montreal set out to discover whether or not hyperactive children would have greater difficulty if they were required to memorize something at the same time they were asked to match the patterns.[14] In this study twenty hyperactive boys and twenty control subjects looked at patterns, geometric shapes, and colors. The children were allowed to initiate each trial by themselves. The results showed that the hyperactive boys were identical to their controls on all measures of solution speed and error scores.

One of the more consistent findings in the literature is that children diagnosed as hyperactive are inefficient in tests of reaction time. In experiments of this type the subject is asked to watch a screen or listen to a loudspeaker and to press a key as quickly as possible each time a particular event is detected. Hyperactive children have been found to be marginally slower than their controls in the average speed of their response. However, the major difference between the groups has been the tendency for hyperactive children to be more variable in their response times, as well as to tend to press for a target when it did not appear.[15] Such errors of commission and variability are reduced by stimulant drugs in children previously diagnosed as hyperactive.[16] These results are in sharp contrast to the uniformly slow reaction times observed in mentally retarded children, children with genuine cerebral dysfunction, and those with severe learning disorders, precisely those children who are eliminated by the selection procedures.[17]

One of the reasons hyperactive children have increased variability and error scores may well be due to motivational factors. A clue that this might be the case is found in a study by Nancy Cohen, another member of the Montreal team, in which children were *paid* to respond rapidly and accurately.[18] Under these conditions the hyperactive children's performance was identical to that of the control group on all the measures taken. However, when the payments were withdrawn in the second half of the experiment, the hyperactive children's performance began to decline steadily while the control group maintained their previous levels of performance.

A motivational hypothesis could equally well explain hyperactive children's poor performance on one extremely boring vigilance test called the Continuous Performance Task (CPT). Here subjects see or hear twelve letters chosen randomly from the alphabet and are told to press a key each time there is an X followed by an A. Hyperactive children make more commission errors, more multiple presses, and score fewer correct detections. More relevant to a motivational theory, their performance is found to decline markedly over trials, unlike the control groups, who maintain or improve their performance. Based on the results of a series of studies that included the CPT, Donald Sykes and his Montreal colleagues concluded that in all tasks where the child is in control of the situation (internally paced tasks), hyperactive children perform just like everyone else. But when the task is controlled by the experimenter (externally paced tasks), hyperactive children do worse.[19] Once again, this conclusion supports the view that hyperactive children, who are not easily regulated by adults, are more independent, which may result from a need for self-governed action.

Finally, no consistent differences have been observed in other tasks specifically chosen to reflect the capacity to maintain attention such as the Embedded Figures test, mentioned earlier, or the Stroop test, in which the subject has to rapidly name colors from a list of color words that are printed in colors different from the color name, such as the word "yellow" printed in green.[20]

Hyperactive children are alleged to be highly distractible. If this is the case, then tests of distractibility—presenting loud or bright distracting cues during a task—ought to disrupt hyperactive children more than their controls. However, there is no evidence that hyperactive children are more distractible than other children. Susan Campbell and coworkers were unable to find any differences between hyperactive children and their controls in two tests of distractibility, and scores were not improved by stimulant drugs.[21] Donald Sykes asked hyperactive children and their controls to carry out a vigilance task, which was disrupted at random intervals by a loud noise.[22] The noise did not disrupt performance in either group. Similar results have been found in a number of other studies.

In a detailed examination of this issue, David Bremer in Hawaii and John Stern in St. Louis asked hyperactive children and a control group to read passages of material while they were occasionally bombarded with loud sounds (bells or electronic beeps) and flashing lights.[23] Distractibility was measured by monitoring eye movements with small electrodes. Hyperactive children did indeed pay more attention to the distractors, but this did not affect their performance on the reading task. Furthermore, in the quiet condition when no distractors were presented, hyperactive children did not look up from their reading any more frequently than the nonhyperactive group, showing that under normal conditions they are no more distractible than other children.

In summary, if hyperactive children have a deficiency in attentional control, such as high distractibility or inability to sustain attention, it has been difficult to demonstrate in controlled experiments. Instead, what these studies reveal is that hyperactive children are considerably less motivated to continue performing repetitive tasks, unless they are paid to do so. These results strongly suggest that what is being measured by diagnostic scales is a tendency for hyperactive children to fail to apply themselves to tasks they do not prefer. What has been uniformly neglected in all of this research is the question of whether children diagnosed as hyperactive can apply themselves to tasks they *do* prefer, such as football, skateboarding, and video games.

BEHAVIORAL STUDIES ON COGNITIVE TASKS

If hyperactive children have problems in controlling their behavior and maintaining attention to a task, these difficulties ought to be reflected in scores on cognitive tests or in academic performance. That is, if their poor performance on vigilance tasks is indicative of some *central* deficit in attentional control, then performance on any tasks requiring sustained attention, such as reading, spelling, math, problem solving, and so forth, should be equally weak. We have already seen from Bremer and Stern's study that reading is not affected, provided hyperactive children are tested with children matched for reading age.

Over fifteen years ago the Montreal group headed by Virginia Douglas studied hyperactive and nonhyperactive children in a concept-formation task.[24] The children were expected to discover which category (plant, animal, and so forth) would be rewarded by a marble. After ten consecutive correct responses, the problem was reversed. No differences were found between the groups when a marble was given for every correct response. But the hyperactive children performed less well when a marble was given for *every other* correct response. One year later this difference between the groups in their reaction to continuous and partial reward was still in evidence. This finding seems to indicate that either hyperactive children are frustrated by partial reward or lose interest faster in this type of situation. However, there is no evidence that they cannot do the problems *should they wish to do so.* The researchers argued "quite strongly against the currently held opinion that they [hyperkinetic children] suffer from basic deficits in the fundamental cognitive operations involved in the concept formation process" (p. 392).

Roscoe Dykman and his research team at the University of Arkansas found a similar effect in a series of studies that combined the need for sustained attention with the development of a cognitive strategy. They investigated the performance of three groups of boys: hyperactive, learning disabled, and a control group. They used a task originally developed by neuropsychologist Karl Pribram to demonstrate the effects of lesions to the frontal and temporal lobes in animals. The purpose of the task is to guess which pattern on one of twelve panels is "it" (the novel condition), and stay with this for five trials and then switch to a new pattern.

Children were awarded a penny each time they picked the correct panel. Initially only two patterns appeared, but as the task progressed additional patterns were added. Altogether there were thirty-eight problems, and every child completed at least 540 trials, taking well over an hour. For half of the children, each *new* item that was introduced became "it," (called the novel condition), and for the other half, a different target item was randomly selected by computer (random condition).

Dykman analyzed his data by looking at the first twelve trials and the final twelve trials for each of the two conditions—novel and random. In the initial trial with only two patterns, where the child had to guess which pattern was "it" and work out a problem-solving strategy, hyperactive children solved the problem faster than the other two groups. In the overall analysis of the novel cue condition, there was no difference between the hyperactive group and the control group on any of the measures such as time to solution, search rate, and after-search lapses (which involved failing to press the correct panel five times). One hyperactive child had to be eliminated from this analysis because he discovered a way to beat the game. Instead of pressing five consecutive times and moving on to search for a new pattern, this child pressed only four times, made a mistake, which reset the computer to repeat the trial, and then pressed again four times. He earned more money than any other boy!

It was in the more difficult random condition that the differences emerged. During the first twelve trials hyperactive children performed exactly like the control group, but in the last twelve trials their performance began to deteriorate. They began to play with the apparatus and extraneous panels, and subsequently they took longer to solve the problems than the controls. (Throughout, the learning-disabled boys were inferior in performance to both the hyperactive and the control boys, but this result could be due to the fact that they also had lower IQ scores.) When the boys were asked how long it had seemed to take to play the game, two-thirds of the control were accurate (one hour), as opposed to half of the learning-disabled group but only one-fourth of the hyperactive group, who imagined the game had lasted much longer. Eight hyperactive boys stated that they had wanted to quit early, as opposed to one boy in each of the other groups.

Taken together, these findings confirm the results on studies of attention. Hyperactive children do not like to continue in repetitive tasks. During such experiences, hyperactive children's subjective impression of time is considerably altered. However, there is no evidence that hyperactive children are any different from other children in their ability to do problem-solving tasks or to develop appropriate cognitive strategies. In fact, the evidence could be used to support the suggestion that they develop them faster and more effectively than normal children. From this series of studies the authors conclude:

> After a decade of studying hyperactive and LD [learning-disabled] children, we have come to expect that either group will perform less well than age and I.Q. matched controls on almost any task or test demanding sustained attention. However, we have been frustrated in attempts to find tasks which separate the two clinical groups. By keying on hyperactives who read adequately and reading-disabled or LD children who were not rated hyperactive, we had thought to uncover clear-cut cognitive, psychological, sociological and performance differences. Such has not been the case. (pp. 295–96)[25]

In a companion experiment Dykman and his group looked at

the effect of methylphenidate on performance in this task for boys classified as hyperactive, reading disabled, and attention disordered.[26] The groups were identical in the placebo condition on all measures. The psychostimulant drug had profound effects on reducing extraneous responses and after-search lapses, but this effect was equivalent for all three groups. The reduction in unnecessary responses resulted in an improved solution rate overall, with an increase of two to four problems solved in the same length of time. Once again, stimulant drugs are found to produce the same effects in children not diagnosed as hyperactive.

There is some evidence that verbal memory improves with stimulant drugs but most researchers have attributed this to somewhat enhanced attention during testing, rather than to some enduring change in memory capacity.[27]

Obviously, if hyperactive children are selected on the basis of having no deficits in school subjects such as reading, spelling, and math, problems in academic tasks will not be expected to emerge in studies on the hyperactive child. This raises the question of the purpose of the diagnosis. All along it has been alleged by the media and marketing material that unless hyperactivity is treated, the child will fail in school. The remedy is supposed to be drugs. Drugs do indeed calm most children down (including nonhyperactive children), but do they improve academic skills? The answer is clear: *They do not.*

Russell Barkley and Charles Cunningham reviewed available short- and long-term studies on the impact of a drug regime on academic performance.[28] In the seventeen short-term studies they considered, which ranged from two weeks to six months, they found no significant changes in a wide variety of reading, spelling, and math tests in most (82 percent) of the fifty-two tests involved. In the remaining 18 percent of the studies where some improvement was noted, the effects were inconsistent even within the same experiment. Long-term studies showed much the same result. Many hyperactive children were doing poorly in school despite the fact that they were taking stimulant drugs. Especially important are studies carried out by Judith Rapoport and her group at the National Institute of Mental Health. Here hyperactive boys on and off drug regimes were compared at the end of one and two years. No differences were seen in tests of reading, spelling, or math between the drug groups or those children on placebo at the end of one year. One year follow-up showed that those children who had never taken drugs were performing identically with those children on a drug regime.[29] Results of several additional studies indicated that neither the amount of drug dose nor the length of time the drug was used was in any way related to objective tests of achievement.[30] When teachers were asked, however, they considered drugs to have improved children's academic ability, even though objective tests showed that this was not the case. As Russell Barkley and Charles Cunningham remark: "The data surveyed point to a significant discrepancy between objective measures and the subjective opinions of teachers and parents on achievement performance" (p. 90).[31]

Russell Barkley found the following tests to be uninfluenced by stimulant drugs: Wechsler IQ (nine experiments), Wide Range Achievement Test (three), Illinois Test of Psycholinguistic Abilities (one), Burt Reading Test (one), Goodenough Draw-A-Man (five) and Loney Draw-A-Car (one), Primary Mental Abilities (one), Bender Visual Motor Gestalt (six), and short-term memory (one).[32]

Follow-up studies taken many years after diagnosis have uniformly shown that hyperactive children fail in school to a much greater degree than would be predicted by their ability. Later in this chapter I will address the paradox that whereas hyperactive children seem to be identical to other children on objective academic tests, they continue to perform poorly in school.

Before turning to this important subject, we must look at a final category of research on the hyperactive child—the studies investigating the physiological measures that are known to correlate with "attention."

PHYSIOLOGICAL CORRELATES OF ATTENTION

Psychophysiology is the study of the accompanying peripheral physiological changes that reflect central brain states regulating psychological processes. The classical example is the change in the electrical activity of the skin (skin conductance) produced by certain psychological states. When overall skin conductance levels increase, this indicates that the subject is aroused or stressed, a fact that has proved useful in the lie detector test. Other measures, such as heart rate changes, are also highly specific to various types of attentional control, such as distraction, attention to the environment, and concentration on a problem.[33]

Research on physiological indices in hyperactive children, have led several investigators to view the hyperactive child as *hypo*-aroused, that is, *less* responsive on physiological measures than normal controls. This effect was contrary to expectations, because these children were believed to be overaroused due to their alleged distractibility. As distractibility implies excessive reactivity to extraneous stimulation, the findings were described as "paradoxical." This paradoxical effect could reflect some dysfunction in the children's attentional control mechanisms, but it is more likely to represent their lack of interest in the distracting events. So far, no experiments have been designed that allow one to make a clear distinction between these two hypotheses. Until this occurs, one cannot accept at face value many researchers' conclusions concerning the meaning of the differences in physiological responses between hyperactive children and their controls. Any statistical difference is almost inevitably taken to have negative connotations for the hyperactive child. Despite the fact that there is no way to determine anything about the results except that the two groups are different, words like "deviant" or "abnormal" are always applied to the hyperactive subjects and never to the control group.

Quite apart from this very fundamental problem, the results from studies measuring physiological responses in hyperactive and control groups present an extremely inconsistent picture.

Three physiological indicators have been employed to study hyperactive children. Two of these indicators, skin conductance and heart rate, correlate with certain states of attention with 100 percent predictability in all individuals. If hyperactive children have deficits in attention, consistent abnormal values in these indicators would surely be highly important. In skin conductance measures, the ongoing, or basal, level of this index varies with a number of factors, such as anxiety, disinterest, or relaxation. An initial "phasic" component is a precise indicator that the central nervous system has processed a new or surprising event in the environment, a prime indicator of distraction. When the same event is repeated many, many times, this component drops out (habituates), reflecting the time it takes for the memory systems of the brain to code that new event. An example of a skin conductance response is presented in figure 10.1.

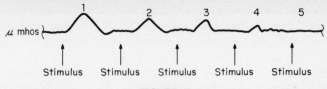

FIGURE 10.1

A typical skin conductance response to an abrupt stimulus. Conductance is the inverse of resistance and is measured in mhos instead of ohms. Phasic responses diminish and disappear if the same stimulus is repeated many times, a process called "habituation."

A second indicator is reflected by changes in heart rate that accompany sustained attention or problem solving. When paying attention to the environment, heart rate slows noticeably, indicating sustained attention. During problem solving, on the other hand, the environment is shut out. This is reflected by a dramatic increase in heart rate, which varies according to the difficulty of the problem. For example, the heart rate accelerates during mental arithmetic.

Last, based on Laufer, Denhoff, and Solomons' earlier work, many subsequent studies have also attempted to pin down the EEG correlates of performance in children diagnosed as hyperactive.

SKIN CONDUCTANCE AND ATTENTION

James Satterfield and Michael Dawson at U.C.L.A. studied hyperactive children and normal controls during a period of relaxation.[34] They discovered that basal skin conductance levels were lower in the hyperactive children (suggesting they were more relaxed). When the researchers presented a series of tones, the phasic responses of the hyperactive group were smaller in amplitude than those of the control children. However, there were no differences between the groups in responses to the remaining tones in the series. In other words, coding in the central nervous system would appear to be identical. Stimulant drugs were found to increase nonspecific phasic responses, those responses that are unrelated to events in the environment, but the drugs had no effect on any of the other measures. In 1972 Satterfield and his colleagues divided hyperactive children into two groups according to whether they were responsive or unresponsive to stimulant drugs.[35] Among those children who were off drugs, the "good responders" had lower basal skin conductance levels than the controls, whereas the "poor responders" had higher levels than the controls. Both hyperactive groups were identical to normal undrugged controls when they were under medication.

These results have often been quoted as indicating that hyperactive children show "abnormal" physiological responsivity when compared to normal children. Quite apart from the nonsense of this position, Satterfield's results have been almost impossible to replicate. In an extensive review of the psychophysiological research, James Hastings and Russell Barkley concluded that of the ten studies on skin conductance levels, seven showed no differences between hyperactive and normal children, and the remaining three were all from Satterfield's laboratory.[36]

In an early study from the Montreal group, Nancy Cohen and Virginia Douglas found no differences whatsoever between hyperactive children and a matched control group on either basal skin conductance levels or in phasic responses to a repeating series of tones. The only difference between the groups was that the hyperactive group had a response to the first tone in the tone series, that was smaller in amplitude than that of the control group.[37]

Cohen and associates went on to investigate the effect of a stimulant drug on a population of hyperactive children, tested on and off the drug.[38] Apart from any task-related effect, the drug elevated basal skin conductance levels by 36 percent overall. In contrast to Satterfield's results, in this study stimulant drugs decreased the amplitude of the skin conductance responses to the tones the children were told to ignore, but had no effect on the phasic responses to the tones the children were told to attend to.

In a subsequent study Philip Firestone and Virginia Douglas reported that both the hyperactive children and the control group had identical basal skin conductance levels, which increased in both groups by the same amount as they carried out a timed task. The hyperactive group showed somewhat less phasic responsivity to a warning signal, but apart from this effect, no other differences were found.[39]

Other researchers have similarly failed to find any differences in skin conductance measures. Dykman and his colleagues saw no difference between his MBD (minimal brain dysfunction) population and their controls in basal skin conductance.[40] During a timed task in which children were asked to press a key to a particular tone, the MBD children had a greater increase in basal skin conductance (opposite to the findings just cited) than the controls. Their performance on the task was also worse.

Finally, in a comprehensive study carried out by Theodore Zahn and his colleagues, forty-two MBD children referred for persistent hyperactivity and inattention were tested along with fifty-four controls in a reaction-time task.[41] Baseline levels of skin conductance did not differ between the groups throughout each resting phase. The phasic conductance responses in the MBD group were found to be lower in amplitude, with slower onset and longer recovery times. Stimulant drugs increased the overall levels of skin conductance, exactly as Cohen and associates found. However, the drugs also increased the *sluggishness* of the phasic responses, contrary to prediction. The authors explained this unexpected result as due to the drugs' effect in lowering peripheral skin temperature, which in turn affected the phasic responsivity.

To summarize these results, hyperactive children revealed overall basal skin conductance levels that are no different from any of their nonhyperactive controls. When phasic responses are measured, hyperactive children very occasionally produce a smaller initial phasic response to the first of a series of events, suggesting that the initial response to an event in the environment produces *less* arousal in hyperactive subjects than in control groups. The remaining responses in the series show few differences between the groups, although in one study Carol Spring and her associates reported that hyperactive children produce a more *rapid* habituation of phasic responses than the control group.[42] That is, in hyperactive children the phasic responses return to baseline levels faster than in normal children, which indicates either more efficient coding by the central nervous system of hyperactive children or their disinterest in the stimulus.

Stimulant drugs produce dramatic effects on skin conductance baselines, elevating them to abnormal levels, but have no consistent effects on the phasic responses. In other words, the changes indicate that the drugs would enhance the levels of arousal or stress but have no impact on distractibility or coding speed of new information.

The data on skin conductance responses indicate that hyperactive children are, if anything, *less* responsive to input from the environment than normal children—that is, *less* distractible, completely the opposite of what has been suggested from their behavior. This indicates that children diagnosed as hyperactive may *appear* to be distractible because they respond to events in the environment that are interesting to them rather than what is relevant to the particular demands in the classroom at the time. In short, they are not paying attention to what the teacher requires, but rather to something else more compelling.

HEART RATE AND ATTENTION

As noted, heart rate slowing, or deceleration, is a primary indicator of sustained attention to events in the environment, whereas heart rate acceleration indicates that the environment is being temporarily blocked or inhibited while the person is engaging in problem solving or cognitive effort.[43]

Early studies on hyperactive children that measured heart rate responses indicated that there were no differences in basal heart rate between children classified as having MBD and controls.[44] In one of these studies Dykman had children discriminate between two tones. The MBD children showed greater slowing of heart rate, indicative of *more* sustained attention. However, Alan Sroufe and his group at the University of Minnesota report that their 21 MBD subjects showed significantly *less* deceleration during a reaction-time task, results that are opposite to Dykman's.[45] Using a double-blind design, subjects who took methylphenidate exhibited a greater degree of heart rate deceleration in this task than subjects who did not, indicating more sustained attention. Others have found equally contradictory results.[46]

Stephen Porges and his associates were among the few investigators to make an attempt to interest the children by challenging them to compete in racing toy cars.[47] However, as they included no normal control group in their experiment, the results pertain only to hyperactive children either on methylphenidate or a placebo. They found that basal heart rate was strongly increased by the drug. However, during the initial portions of the game the two groups had identical heart rate changes. The only effect that emerged in this study was that during the final stages of the game, the group on a placebo showed an increase in heart rate, whereas the drugged group did not. This could indicate an abnormal effect of the drug in that the children on the placebo showed excitement (heart rate increase) as the game was nearing completion but that the drugged group were too passive to care. Despite this possibility, the authors conclude that the heart rate increase found in the placebo group is an "abnormal" autonomic response. Without a control group, this conclusion is completely unwarranted. The drug had *no* effect on the children's performance in this task, and its major effect was to grossly elevate basal heart rate. Cohen also found this drug effect in the study cited earlier; a mean heart rate increase of 15 percent across all subjects was recorded, and in one subject there was an increase of nearly 100 percent.[48]

Zahn's study reported heart rate baselines were equal between hyperactive children and their controls.[49] These same hyperactive children exhibited noticeable elevations in heart rate when they were given either d-amphetamine or methylphenidate. Those hyperactive children who received no drugs had heart-rate changes that were more sluggish in response to the demands of the experiment.

So far the results from the experiments on heart-rate responses show no consistent differences in deceleration during sustained attention between hyperactive children and their controls, or between hyperactive children on a drug or a placebo. However, the results do show the profound effects that stimulant drugs produce on the cardiovascular system. The adverse side effects of abnormal reduction in skin temperature under stimulant drugs cited by Zahn and associates and the elevated levels of skin conductance should be paid more attention. Furthermore, these abnormal shifts in baseline call into question any results obtained on subsequent physiological changes when children are tested on stimulant drugs because all changes in physiological responses are strongly determined by the initial baseline levels.

EEG: BRAIN WAVE ANALYSIS*

Since the advent of computer analysis of brain electrical activity, less serious attention has been given to studies that report brain wave abnormalities using raw records of ongoing EEGs, a technique

* The following discussion of brain wave analysis (pp. 208–17) is highly technical in content and directed more to researchers in the field.

found to be seriously deficient when compared to computer analyzed data. A study by J. R. Hughes indicates[50] the difficulty in providing meaningful EEG correlates of hyperactivity from the older method. He selected 214 hyperactive underachievers, eight to eleven years of age, IQ above 89, and matched them for age, sex, and classroom. Three independent clinicians evaluated their EEGs. Based on the EEGs, 41 percent of the hyperactive group were classified as "abnormal," but then so were 30 percent of the "normal" control group!

Computer analysis of brain waves is generally restricted to two techniques. In what has come to be called event-related potentials (ERP), brain waves are triggered by the abrupt onset of an event, such as a light flash, which then is repeated over many trials, sometimes up to one hundred. These brain waves are averaged together, or superimposed, so that the main features emerge from the background "noise" to produce a prototypic wave form for each particular event. These averaged wave forms are often consistent over days and are peculiar to each individual, almost like a fingerprint. Certain peaks and troughs are thought to reflect different aspects of perception and attention. For example, the amplitude of a wave occurring at about 300 to 400 milliseconds appears to reflect the detection of a novel event, similar to the phasic component of the skin conductance response. The timing and complexity of these peaks and troughs are particularly influenced by the age of the individual.

In the second type of analysis, an ongoing EEG is monitored during a task and the total amplitude (power) for each frequency is stored in the computer for the duration of the task, usually about one to two minutes. These "epochs" are then analyzed by computer and broken down into frequency bands, such as 8 to 12 cycles per second, the alpha band. Precise analysis has shown that all frequencies are present at all times in all brains; the only aspect that varies is the amplitude of each frequency. For the most part, studies that employ this methodology have focused largely on the alpha band power. The "alpha state" corresponds to complete relaxation. When the power in this band of frequencies is reduced over some portion of the brain relative to the rest, it is assumed that this portion is actively involved in processing.

Modern EEG research using computer techniques is still in its infancy, and most of the factors influencing electrical shifts in the brain remain undiscovered or uncontrolled. While computer analysis offers an enormous advance over what has been described as the "eyeball analysis" of raw EEG records, the precision required to determine just which attentional states are reflected by just what aspect of the EEG cannot yet be determined.

For this reason, EEG research on hyperactive children is imprecise and unfocused, which makes it difficult to summarize the data in any meaningful way. Readers should bear in mind that the results are contaminated by differences in task variables, drug versus no drug conditions, age effects, and frequently no control groups.

A few experimenters have investigated EEGs using frequency (or spectral) analysis. In one of the first studies, James Satterfield and his team of workers looked at EEG power (the amount of power in each frequency band) in six hyperactive children who responded best to drugs and five subjects who did not respond, and compared them to eleven controls.[51] Hyperactive responders were found to have higher mean power in the alpha band (8–12 cps) while they were resting as well as more artifacts in the recordings produced by extraneous movement than either the nonresponder group or the control subjects. Stimulant drugs did not affect alpha power. Subsequent research showed that in a group of fifty-seven hyperactive children, those with more slow wave activity (1–7 cps) showed the best response to stimulant drugs in terms of teaching ratings.[52] In an experiment the next year, the authors rated 18 percent of 120 hyperactive children as having normal EEGs. However, there was no relationship between teacher and parent ratings and the degree of abnormality of the EEG.[53]

In a study involving conditioning to tone-light pairs and reaction time, E. Grünewald-Zuberbier and his colleagues tested eleven hyperactive children selected from an institution for maladjusted children and a control group.[54] Hyperactive children had higher power in both the middle-frequency alpha band and the higher frequency beta band (12+ cps). Alpha amplitude returned to its resting levels faster in hyperactive children following attention to an event in the environment. No other differences were found in the EEG during a series of different tasks.

In the Satterfield studies the hyperactive subjects had higher amplitude activity in the low- to mid-frequency bands, but in the last study hyperactive children had higher amplitude or power in the mid- to high-frequency bands. As neither group of researchers reports the details for the entire frequency range, but rather describes only those areas where an effect was obtained, one must conclude that these results completely cancel out. Another interpretation could be that hyperactive children have higher power across *all* frequencies, both slow and fast. If this is the case, then the results again would cancel, because the only way to compare subjects is in terms of *relative* changes between the frequency bands since there are enormous individual differences in the absolute levels of power for each particular frequency. In other words, the studies of amplitude change in EEG have shown nothing whatsoever.

The data from the studies using event-related potentials are summarized in table 10.1. Each experiment is set out showing the major difference in some portion of the brain wave between hyperactive children and controls or between hyperactive children on and off drugs.

The event-related potential, composed of various peaks and troughs, can be measured in three ways: first, it is determined whether the electrical changes shift electrically in positive or negative direction with respect to a baseline; second is latency, measured as the length of time in milliseconds from the onset of an event to a particular bump in the ERP record; and third is amplitude, measured in millivolts, of each of the bumps. Because of the enormous individual variation in the arrangement of these peaks and valleys, it is extremely important that researchers present exact details in both latency and amplitude. Many studies do not meet this simple requirement and instead report peaks and troughs by number, N1, N2, P1, P2, P3, et cetera, which reflects only the direction of positive or negative electrical activity. The numbers are supposed to represent hundredths of milliseconds, but in fact they do not, as each shift in brain potentials varies with the task and with each individual.

As an example, figure 10.2 presents an ERP from one individual that reflects activity of the brain while the subject saw red squares 90 percent of the time and green squares 10 percent of the time. The two wave forms are superimposed, so that the differences can be more clearly seen. This indicates how variable wave forms can appear in the same individual.

In the following analysis of the ERP research I have tried to

Amplitude Differences in Evoked Potentials: Summary of Results.

Authors	Task	Polarity Shifts in Milliseconds					
		80 90 100	120	140	200	250	300
Satterfield et al. 1972	Auditory clicks				Drug $H_R > H_N$		
Satterfield 1973					$H < C$		
Buchsbaum and Wender 1973	Light flashes			$H > C$			
Hall et al. 1976	Light flashes		$H = C$		$H = C$		
Halliday et al. 1976	Target flash				placebo $H_R < H_N$	$H_R = H_N$	$H = C$
Prichep et al. 1976	Target clicks Uncertain target				$H < C$	$H > C$	$H > C$
	Certain target				$H = C$		
	Certain vs. uncertain				H less difference to C		
Zambelli et al. 1977	Dichotic tone detection	C diff hemispheres H no diff hemispheres					
Satterfield 1979	Tones 6–11 years		$H \uparrow$ with age	$C \downarrow$ with age H no change			
Buchsbaum and Rapoport 1979	Light flash probability estimation	$C \downarrow$ with age $H_R \downarrow$ with age $H < C$		C no change with age H_R no change with age	$H < C$		

H = hyperactives   C = controls H_R = hyperactive drug responders H_N = hyperactive nonresponders

Amplitude differences: < less than   > greater than   = equal

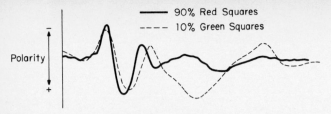

FIGURE 10.2

Averaged event-related potentials (ERPs) from one scalp electrode for one individual watching a series of highly probable stimuli (red squares—solid line) interspersed with infrequent stimuli (green squares—dotted line). The subject was counting the green squares.

provide the clearest possible assessment of the data, but because of the absence of any standardized method for reporting results and the general tendency to report *anything* that shows group differences, out of the hundreds of effects produced by ERP, the data present an extremely confused picture.

In some of the studies reviewed earlier that measured power alone, the authors also reported on ERPs. In the Satterfield studies the general finding was that hyperactive responders showed higher amplitude than the control group for the waves P2 to N2, which presumably refer to waves other researchers call P200 to N200. As no information is provided on either milliseconds or millivolts, it cannot be determined whether the positive or the negative peak is larger, nor precisely when these effects occurred. The same difficulty is present in the ERP information report from the study by Grünewald-Zuberbier, Grünewald, and Rasche, who state that "initial" amplitude responses to signals are smaller in hyperactive subjects. If "initial" stands for early, then their results could refer to P1 to N1 peaks at around 100 milliseconds.

Monte Buchsbaum and Paul Wender compared a control group of twenty-four males and females to twenty-one male and three female hyperactive children.[55] Despite the authors' statement that these controls were matched for age and sex, there is no possible way this could have been achieved. Because of the unequal sex ratios and the fact that there are large differences between the sexes in ERP amplitudes, their findings are highly suspect.[56] What they do report is that hyperactive children (that is, males) had larger amplitudes for the peaks N140 to P200 to light flashes.

Hyperactive subjects also showed a greater increase in the amplitude of these waves as the intensity of the light flash was increased. Amphetamine did not change the N140 to P200 amplitudes in hyperactive "responders," but decreased the amplitude of this component in "nonresponders" in the high-intensity condition only. Auditory ERPs produced by tones were more "variable" in hyperactive children than in controls. No details of amplitude differences were given, so presumably none were found. Amphetamines appeared to decrease "variability" in auditory ERPs.

In 1976 R. A. Hall and his colleagues reported an attempt to replicate the Buchsbaum and Wender study—this time using twenty-six hyperactive children and nineteen controls, all male.[57] In two experiments that examined the amplitude effects for the peaks P120 and N150, as well as N150 to P200, when children had to pay attention and also when they were relaxed, the authors could find no differences between the groups. No differences appeared in the slope of the amplitude changes to increasing levels of stimulation, nor were there any differences in latencies of the various peaks between groups. They concluded that their results warrant a very cautious view toward the hypothesis that hyperkinetic behavior in children is the manifestation of neurological defects as measured by ERPs.

Roy Halliday and several coworkers at Langley Porter Institute carried out two studies on active and passive attention using hyperactive children identified as good and poor responders to Ritalin.[58] Unfortunately they included no control population. Amplitude differences between the two groups were found only at N145 to P190, and these were complex. In general, responders showed lower amplitude scores both off the drug and on placebo when compared to the nonresponders, with the amplitudes increasing when they were put on methylphenidate. However, nonresponders showed the highest amplitude on *placebo* compared to their own baseline and the lowest amplitude when they took no drug; their results while on the drug were intermediary between the two. The authors do not discuss these strange results. Apart from the fact that they make no sense, the general findings are at variance with those of Buchsbaum and Wender and with Satterfield, who both report *lower* amplitudes in the N1 to P2 range for hyperactives, no drug effects on these waves in "responders" but *decreasing* amplitudes for "nonresponders" who are on drugs.

221

Also paradoxical in the Halliday study was the finding that nonresponders showed a huge decrease in variability between active and passive attention in response to Ritalin, whereas the so-called responders showed no reaction to the drug whatsoever! In the two experiments carried out by Halliday, the two nonresponder groups behaved so differently from one another that they resembled two distinct populations.

In their study Leslie Prichep and his colleagues employed a passive versus an active (certain versus uncertain) attention task to auditory clicks.[59] Three groups participated—placebo–placebo, placebo–drug, and a control—consisting of a total of twenty-four males, eight to eleven years of age. The major effect was that in the uncertain attention condition, the hyperactive boys showed a reduced positive component at P186 and an increased negative component at N250 in response to the second of two clicks. The P295 component (essentially P300, the "orienting wave") was significantly larger in hyperactive children in response to the second click in conditions of certainty (when no information is provided by the signal). In general, fewer differences were found in the ERP wave forms produced by the certain versus uncertain signals in the hyperactive subjects, especially at latencies of P186. Drug effects were seen only in conditions of uncertainty, elevating the amplitude of N100 and P200. No drug effects were found for any measure in conditions of certainty.

What these results imply is that the brains of hyperactive children respond equally to relevant and irrelevant input and show less responsivity to input considered to have a high degree of information (uncertainty). Of course these same results could be obtained if the child felt that the information provided by the task was uninteresting (uninformative), despite the authors' assumptions to the contrary.

Also studied was a slow negative brain wave called the Contingent Negative Variation (CNV), which appears in similar situations as the heart rate deceleration response does, during attention to the environment. Prichep found that there were no group differences on this measure, nor was the CNV affected by stimulant drugs. As the CNV is a measure of sustained attention, Prichep's results confirm those found on heart rate deceleration measures, indicating that both the autonomic physiological and the EEG correlates of sustained attention do not distinguish hyperactives from their normal controls.

In contrast to all the studies cited so far, Andrew Zambelli and colleagues found differences in the very early components of the ERP in a task in which subjects had to detect certain tones played to one ear or the other.[60] The ERP wave forms of hyperactive boys (fourteen years of age) were similar in amplitude for the two ears for tones they were told to ignore and those they were told to detect. The control groups showed significant differences between the ears for these relevant and irrelevant signals. This difference appeared early at about 80 milliseconds, as a negative wave. No other group differences were found. This result was replicated on twelve-year-old boys.[61]

All phases of the event-related potential have now been implicated: very early components in detecting signals, middle components in passive attention to simple lights or tones, and late components where there is uncertainty in the situation. Unfortunately, not one of these findings either has been or can be replicated.

In 1979 at the New York meeting of the American Psychological Association, Monte Buchsbaum and Judith Rapoport reported on a most important experiment.[62] It is one of the few studies carried out in which a large population of *normal* children were tested on and off amphetamine drugs. The results were immensely complex, showing ERP component, electrode placement, age, and drug effect interactions. Three important findings emerged.

First, hyperactive children (who showed larger N140 to P200 amplitudes in the Buchsbaum and Wender 1973 report) were now found to have *smaller* N140 to P200 amplitudes. This was the most significant finding of the study. These results were obtained in off-drug comparisons to the control group.

Second, at the older age levels (ten to twelve years), the ERP of normal and hyperactive children showed little effect of amphetamine drugs. Differences were found only in the younger group (six to nine years).

Finally, drug effects acted differently on the two values studied (P100 to N120 and N140 to P200), *only* at ages six to nine and only for posterior electrode placements. Normal children on the drug showed an enhanced N120 amplitude, whereas there was

223

no drug effect for the hyperactive children. The reverse finding, a drug effect at P200 for the hyperactive children, did not occur for the normal group. Yet there was no drug effect at P200 for hyperactive children in the same laboratory in 1973.

To summarize: Buchsbaum and Rapoport's results completely contradicted their own earlier findings. Differences in the groups' response to the drug were dependent on age and the site of electrode placement, and specific to wave forms known to vary between individuals by 20 milliseconds or more. At the same meeting Satterfield reported that 20 percent of all children exhibit no wave form complex P100 to N120 whatsoever.[63] In fact, Satterfield reported on a further variable, that of an *increasing* amplitude of the P100 to N120 component in hyperactive children with age and the opposite effect in nonhyperactive children. This age shift, going in opposite directions for the two groups, cuts across the boundary of Buchsbaum's groups, which were from six to nine years and ten to twelve years.

In reviewing the psychophysiological literature, it became apparent that no matter what result was obtained, whichever category fit the hyperactive group was the one deemed abnormal. If heart rate went up in hyperactive children in one study, this was a "deviant" response; if it went down in another, this was equally "deviant." This sort of science smacks more of a medieval witch hunt than of a sincere desire to get at the truth.

Drugs, Labeling, and Academic Performance

What are the implications of all these data? First, and most critically, normal children "respond" to stimulant drugs. In a series of studies from the group at the National Institute of Mental Health headed by Monte Buchsbaum and Judith Rapoport on normal adults and children and hyperactive children on and off amphetamine, normal children had the same drug-related changes as hyperactive children on a number of tasks. These include EEG changes, activity levels, and tests of vigilance, reaction time, and memory. In general, the effects were more pronounced at younger ages (at about six to nine years), with the drug having considerably less effect on performance of adults.[64] Concluding from the results of a study with a large battery of tests, Monte Buchsbaum, Judith Rapoport, and their associates state:

> Our data do not strongly support the concept of a unique stimulant drug response in [hyperactives]. Generally, differences in the effects of a stimulant drug between normal and hyperactive children are much less striking than those between hyperactive boys and adults. Speculations about the pathophysiology of the hyperactive syndrome that have been based on a drug response have suffered from the lack of such a control group.[65] (p. 942)

These findings completely abolish a diagnosis based on a favorable response to stimulant drugs. They also raise the issue that has been voiced many times in this volume: If problem children are found to "improve" in performance when given a drug, should *all* children therefore be given drugs, to make them even more manageable?

As already noted, stimulant drugs have a profound effect on the autonomic nervous system, lowering skin temperature, raising skin conductance levels, and elevating heart rate; they also have resulted in a decrease in appetite and weight loss. The noticeable changes in behavior and the dramatic effects on the peripheral and central nervous system are reflections of the drug's action on the brain. We know that amphetamine has a chemical affinity with dopamine and norepinephrine, major neural transmitters in many regions of the brain, but we have no idea how amphetamines operate to modulate brain activity when performing cognitive or perceptual tasks.

There is little evidence that a regime on amphetamines produces any noticeable increase in academic performance, and much evidence to the contrary. Duane Riddle and Judith Rapoport conducted a two-year follow-up study on seventy-two hyperactive boys at eight and ten years, all of whom had been treated with amphetamines and 65 percent of whom were still on medication. These boys showed either a static performance in reading skills and math from age eight to ten, or a decline.[66] Their achievement in no way reflected their potential as indicated by IQ scores taken at age eight. Passivity does not guarantee learning.

All studies are consistent in revealing that psychostimulant drugs have no effect in improving school performance or social adjustment at any age, and the length of time on drugs is totally unrelated to improvement in academic performance. Geoff Thorley's exhaustive review showed that the follow-up studies were equally consistent in suggesting that children diagnosed as hyperactive in childhood have an exceedingly poor prognosis for academic achievement and social adjustment.[67] Using only well-controlled studies as a data base, Thorley's review indicated that hyperactive young adults have no more incidence of severe problems such as psychosis, criminal behavior, or drug abuse than normal controls. Four studies also showed no evidence that hyperactive children had fewer friends, despite the fact that teachers believed they did.

What the hyperactive population does exhibit, even as much as ten to twenty years later, is the same behavior that produced the initial diagnosis: higher levels of activity and poorer performance on boring, repetitive tests. However, what is most revealing about these studies, and most serious, is that hyperactive young adults have considerably lower self-esteem and feel more depressed, nervous, and "worthless" than normal controls. Research from Douglas and her associates in Montreal indicates that these young adults fail more grades, get lower marks, and are more frequently expelled from school. A similar finding was revealed in a four-year follow-up at UCLA by Linda Charles and Richard Schain.[68]

The discrepancy between the objective measures of academic achievement and the consistent report that children diagnosed hyperactive are overwhelmingly prone to academic failure requires that we look closely at the follow-up studies on academic performance. The first study from the Montreal group carried out in 1971 failed initially to match the controls and hyperactive children on IQ.[69] When they attempted to adjust for this by eliminating subjects who could not be matched, hyperactive children scored lower on a composite rating of ten academic tests. However, the authors concluded that the "hyperactive children, 4 years after diagnosis, were as poor in classroom performance as they had been 1 year after diagnosis" (p. 219). The inescapable conclusion from this statement is that there was a large proportion of learning-disabled children in the hyperactive group.

The same problem was in evidence in two other Montreal follow-up studies where the hyperactive group showed inferior performance on spelling and verbal tests. Follow-up studies from the National Institute of Mental Health showed that the hyperactive children were significantly inferior in number and reading skills.[70] Thorley points out the significant methodological problem of the failure to match by IQ at the outset of a longitudinal study, but he neglects to mention a more serious problem: the confounding of hyperactive children and children with learning problems.

This leaves only one remaining finding from all of the follow-up research: Hyperactive young adults have low self-esteem and feel "worthless." This feeling of depression and worthlessness could arise because of some serious learning difficulty, in which case the primary goal would be to solve the learning problem, and not to put the individual on drugs.

However, almost every research report ignores the most obvious causal implications of the data—that it is entirely possible that the ensuing psychological and even academic difficulties are a direct result of the *diagnosis* and not a result of the "disorder." Children who are underachieving despite normal IQ and no learning difficulties might be suffering because they have been labeled "hyperactive," because they are disliked by their teachers, and because they have been put on drugs. Extensive research by Carol Whalen and Barbara Henker shows that one of the most dramatic effects of being placed on a drug regime is the attribution of the behavior problems to factors beyond the child's control. During extensive interviews the children revealed that they felt helpless in handling their own behavior. Drugs had become a crutch.[71]

The antagonism of teachers to students who are disruptive in the classroom is highlighted by a fascinating study carried out by Gabrielle Weiss and two colleagues in Montreal.[72] They compared nineteen-year-old hyperactive males who had been part of a longitudinal study with a control group on rating scales sent to teachers and to employers. The scales covered seven areas, including perseverance, ability to get along with others, independence, and work habits. The hyperactive group scored lower than the controls on all seven measures on the teacher ratings and lower on two additional ratings for math and verbal skills. Yet their employers rated these same young men as *identical* to the controls on the seven measures. There was a highly significant difference statistically on each comparison between teacher versus employer response for the hyperactive group. The greatest discrepancy was in the category "fulfills assigned work." There was no significant difference between the two sets of ratings for the control group.

Clearly, hyperactive children and young adults know how to get on the wrong side of teachers. Given a responsible position with a high degree of structure and consistent reinforcement (a salary), they seem to do just fine. This suggests that with children considered hyperactive, it might be more productive to work on behavioral control rather than to prescribe drugs. Daniel O'Leary echoes this suggestion and points out that once children are put on a drug regime, the assumption is made that all will be well. Parents and teachers report that the children are more manageable, and any further attempts to teach the children better ways to handle their behavior and to improve their school performance are abandoned. O'Leary discusses several studies, including those from his own laboratory, that have shown that behavior therapy directed toward improving academic skills improves both classroom behavior and academic performance. The results of these interventions are in stark contrast to the consistent failure of a drug regime to produce enduring changes in self-control and academic achievement.[73]

Nearly a decade ago Peter Conrad wrote about his extensive interviews with children, parents, and doctors in various clinics.[74] On the basis of their reports he concluded that there are three major contributors leading to an increase in the diagnosis of hyperactivity. The first is the drug companies, who market and circulate brochures on drugs and support research. The second are the media, who have contributed enormously to the situation by sensationalizing "data" that were never there in the first place. Last are teachers, many of whom seem eager to label a child hyperactive, get him or her on medication and out of their hair. According to Conrad's study, the most frequent discrepancy in rating scores between parents and teachers was that parents found no behavior problem while teachers found a great many problems. This discovery is confirmed and amplified in the comparison of teacher and employer ratings.

Research on hyperactive children has been underway for over two decades, which should have been sufficient time to pin down some of the key behavioral or physiological traits that are common to this group. Research papers now number well into the thousands. Not all the research has been presented here, but the studies that were reviewed represent a cross-section of those conducted over the past twenty years. More recently, there has been a proliferation of quite extensive and highly focused reviews. These review papers have consistently stressed the problem of the poor methodology and especially the absence of appropriate matched control groups in much of the research on hyperactivity. Many workers, such as Russell Barkley, Daniel and Susan O'Leary, Carol Whalen, and Barbara Henker, are becoming increasingly critical of the current approach to diagnosis and of the failure to assess the psychosocial effects produced by labeling children and the impact of a drug regime.

Something should be done to avoid diagnosing perfectly normal children as "hyperactive." Hyperactivity—severe, uncontrollable, and pathological motion—is a symptom of brain damage that occurs in a minute proportion of the population, most typically in the elderly. Parkinsonism is a prime example. Exuberance or irritating behavior in classrooms cannot possibly be the same thing and could not be an indication of brain damage in up to 20 percent of all schoolboys.

Three groups can and should take action. The first is the research community, which must begin to challenge the notion that after twenty-five years of research the only problem is methodological. Despite the fact that there has been overt criticism of the entire research area, no one has suggested that we abandon the attempt to pin down a disorder that does not exist. Every article closes with the words: "We need more research." *Why?*

The second group are the medical practitioners—clinicians, psychiatrists, and pediatricians—who are often pressured by parents in response to complaints by teachers to put their child on medication. Drugs do not work. They help teachers and parents, but they do nothing for children except increase the likelihood that they will fail to take responsibility for their own behavior. Far more effective outcomes could be achieved with family counseling and by establishing a regime of consistent reinforcement for desired behaviors.

Finally, the key to any real progress is the parents. In the following chapters I take up the issue of remediation and the ways in which parents can help determine how to meet the needs of their children in the most beneficial way.

PART III

Three Ounces of Prevention

11

Schools: Dis-Abling or En-Abling?

Father: Where did you go?
Son: I did not go anywhere.
Father: If you did not go anywhere, why do you idle about? Go to school, stand before your "school-father," recite your assignment, open your school bag, write your tablet, let your "big-brother" write your new tablet for you. After you have finished your assignment and reported to your monitor, come to me, and do not wander about in the street.[1]

Four thousand years ago in a Sumerian schoolboy's story, a father admonishes his son for his poor attempts in school. The father goes on to point out that the art of becoming a scribe is extremely difficult, but worth the effort, because literature is the most exacting and rewarding of the arts. In the father's view, the son's failure to pursue his studies is entirely due to a lack of application. Near the end of the essay, the father makes some unexpected remarks.

Father: Night and day you waste in pleasures. You have accumulated much wealth, have expanded far and wide, have become fat, big, broad, powerful and puffed. But your kin waits expectantly for your misfortune and will rejoice at it because you looked not to your humanity.

Apparently his son has accumulated a good deal of wealth that he does not share with his relatives! Not only is this "schoolboy" a mature adult, but it seems that his financial acumen is less important to his father than his education.

In another set of tablets dated about the same period, a scribe and one of his pupils bait one another concerning their respective aptitudes for scholarship. Failure in school is attributed as much to stupidity as to a lack of diligence. Although it is not certain whether the argument is more in jest than truth, the participants display much concern for the details and trappings of literacy and numeracy.

> Girnishag: You dolt, numskull, school pest, you Sumerian ignoramus, your hand is terrible; it cannot even hold the stylus properly; it is unfit for writing and cannot even take dictation. Yet you say you are a scribe like me.
> Enkimansi: What do you mean I am not a scribe like you? When you write a document it makes no sense. When you write a letter it is illegible. —You are one of the most incompetent of tablet writers. What you are fit for, can any one say?
> Girnishag: Why, I am competent all around. —But you are the laziest of scribes, the most careless of men. When you do multiplication, it is full of mistakes. In computing areas you confuse length with width. Squares, triangles, circles and sectors—you treat them all without understanding.—
> Enkimansi: Me, I was raised on Sumerian. I am the son of a scribe. But you are a bungler, a windbag. When you try to shape a tablet you can't even smooth the clay. When you try to write a line, your hand can't manage the tablet . . . You sophomore [literally "galamhuru," or *sophos-moros*, "clever-fool."], cover your ears! (pp. 241–42)[2]

The ancient Sumerians, the first inventors of writing, valued literacy. But it was a literacy for the elite. The entire school population consisted of the sons of high-ranking politicians, lawyers, and merchants, the most able and talented members of the community. Yet it is apparent from these quotations that to become a man of letters was no easy matter, and success at this endeavor was not inevitable. To a Sumerian, failure meant either a lack of persistence or stupidity. In our democratic society, failure is more often ascribed to brain damage or to differences in socialization, factors beyond the pupil's and even the teacher's control. No one must be blamed.

Whatever the attributions for success or failure, it is a fact that for over four thousand years some pupils have succeeded in their schoolwork and others have not. Some young men have an aptitude for making money, but are dis-able in matters of scholarship. Some kings are dis-able to rule, and some parents dis-able to discipline their offspring. In the final analysis, dis-abilities boil down to a question of *values*, and values are determined by practical considerations. What a society requires of its members to enhance the well-being of the maximum number of citizens will be valued. Similarly, in hierarchical societies, what enhances prestige, status, and power will be valued.

Besides indicating that learning disabilities are at least four thousand years old, two important lessons are to be learned from the Sumerian texts. First, the Sumerians found themselves in the midst of a technical revolution—the invention of writing. This had enormous consequences for social change, not only for economic and political reasons, but also because it led to a flowering of human creativity. Second, in any complex civilization, written language is the key to power. A literate citizen is the transcriber and purveyor of all the accumulated knowledge of a culture. An illiterate citizen can easily be duped and pushed into menial pursuits.

Children need to be literate, to acquire numeracy, and to respond appropriately to social context to have any success in today's world. The major message of this book has been that we should not punish the child because of these cultural demands. Nor should we create unnecessary psychological pressures because we have failed to discover how children learn and how they should be disciplined. So far I have presented evidence on how and why learning problems arise and the importance of sex differences in children's ability to master specific skills. In this chapter I will describe training methods that could considerably reduce or even eliminate most learning and behavior problems.

It is beyond the scope of this volume to review all the many remedial programs for reading, math, and behavioral training. Instead I have chosen to focus on three particularly outstanding programs developed in the United States over the last two decades and tested in schools and clinics. In each of these programs the researchers have made some attempt to approach learning problems scientifically. The most appealing asset they share in common is that they strive for 100 percent success. A reading program must be able to teach everyone to read, not merely a proportion of children at a specific grade level. The programs are the Lindamood reading method, developed by Pat and Charles Lindamood at the Lindamood clinic in San Luis Obispo; a new approach to mathematics training developed by Patricia Davidson at the University of Massachusetts; and the token economy for behavioral management pioneered by psychologist Daniel O'Leary at Stony Brook. These remedial and/or training programs are the best I have seen for teaching reading, mathematics, and behavioral control. They are impressive not only because they *work*, but because they work for the right reasons. That is, they make perfect sense in terms of the psychology of pedagogy as well as in terms of all we know about how the brain processes information. Before beginning this analysis, I want to return to Sumer and briefly trace the history of schools and how writing and reading were originally taught.

Historical Trends in Teaching Writing and Reading

Writing was invented wherever societies became so cumbersome that it was necessary to create divisions of labor between the citizenry. Written records were originally designed to keep track of who owned what crops or owed what debts. In the agricultural societies of Egypt, China, and Sumer, the simple pictograms that represented a particular category of food (barley, wheat, rice) or that designated the giver and receiver (a signature) exploded in number. As the number of symbols expanded, it not only became more and more difficult to remember them, but there was also a strong impetus to pass on this new knowledge. It was soon necessary to invent "schools" where the men (and subsequently their sons) who controlled the distribution of these surplus goods and services could learn this new technique. Over time it became apparent that by expanding the number of symbols one could eventually encompass the entire language. This meant not only that precise records could be kept of all current transactions, but transactions over time, events over time, and ultimately myths, legends, and histories could be permanently set down.

However, pictograms are an inefficient mode for a written

language, as the Sumerians recognized very early. Many Sumerian words sounded alike but had different meanings, which were determined by context. Thus the Sumerian word for water was identical to the Sumerian word for the preposition "in." As a simple solution, the water pictogram was adopted for both. Once people realized that it is far simpler to learn a manageable set of phonetic *rules* than to memorize thousands of pictograms, the entire script gradually became phonetic. As a result of the superiority and flexibility of the Sumerian cuneiform alphabet, other pictorial systems in the Near East fell into disuse, and the Sumerian alphabet eventually became the universal alphabet, largely through its adoption by the Babylonians.

The Sumerian texts were transcribed onto clay tablets. Many of these texts were "schoolbooks" that have been found in an incredible abundance in various parts of the Near East. The texts provide a transparent picture of a typical schoolboy's day. First, each child had to learn to prepare his own writing material, the clay tablet itself. Next, the "school brother," presumably a monitor, wrote out the day's exercises for each student individually. The student was then expected to copy the exercises and finally to recite them aloud. It is important to note that writing always preceded recitation and that the student recited only what he had written. There was a direct connection between writing and reading.

By the time Maria Montessori began her school at the turn of the twentieth century, reading was often taught before writing, or simultaneously as an independent activity. This is still the common practice in most schools today. Montessori had the profound good wisdom to reinstate the ancient practice of learning to write first, accompanied by *recitation* of letter sounds (phonemes). In her method, reading followed as a process of discovery. We now have considerable evidence that the fostering of any skill, no matter how much it may seem to be an internal process (like silent reading), is acquired more rapidly and efficiently if there is motor involvement. Writing develops the connection between the visual symbols and the fine-motor system. Recitation involves the oral-facial musculature and provides feedback to the auditory system.

Montessori described her approach vividly in her book *The Discovery of the Child*.[3] Children were expected to master the written alphabet and to match each letter to its individual sound or phoneme. When this capacity was well established, Montessori would initiate a game during one of their frequent nature walks or trips to the zoo. As the children made their way, various objects were pointed out to them: a tree, a flower, a house, a cow. The children were challenged to name the individual letters in the words for the objects they saw. Next they were asked if they could write those letters in the sand or dirt with a stick. Soon some children were writing down the names for everything in sight.

Soon thereafter the children realized that what could be written could also be read. Montessori recognized that the process is completely reversible. That is, if you learn to sound out words, translate them into phonemes, and see the results as you write them down, then it is easy to transcribe the visual patterns of words back into sound. For the brain, reading is the mirror image of writing: The same neural code underlies the visual and auditory patterns. Furthermore, Montessori had observed that when children *discover* something for themselves, like reading, it is not only more memorable but considerably more exciting. When you discover something you "own" it. Reading becomes something that you do rather than something that is done to you. Montessori's fundamental insight, remarkable not only for its neurological sophistication but for its psychological wisdom, has been kept alive largely by Montessori teachers. Unfortunately, I know of no rigorous test of the Montessori method.

Another method with a long history was inspired by Samuel Orton and developed by two teachers, Bessie Stillman and Anna Gillingham in the United States. This approach was formalized and published in a book by Beth Slingerland and has subsequently become known as the "Slingerland" method.[4] Currently many schools (mostly private ones) use the Slingerland method, in which the approach is similar to the Montessori approach. It stresses extensive work on phonetics and integrating phonetics with fine-motor control developed both through writing and manual exercises. Because the Slingerland method has been fostered by the Orton Society and thanks to the tradition of this society to emphasize experimental methods, we have more data on the success of the Slingerland approach than we have on the Montessori method. Most studies show that it offers a considerable improvement over the traditional classroom techniques as well as those employed in remedial classrooms.

Both the Montessori and the Slingerland approach share a similar pedagogical style. Children are taught in small groups of mixed ages and can choose from a variety of activities at any one time. Each step of a particular skill is carefully explained, and the child works without pressure toward a specified goal. Every goal is clearly attainable and skills are carefully broken down into a stepwise progression. Older children, or those who are quick to learn, help those who are slower. This has additional benefits because teaching helps to clarify one's thinking. It has often been said that teaching is one of the best ways to learn.

Recently I visited a Montessori elementary school that had children ranging in age from six to thirteen years all in the same room. As in Montessori preschools, the children were totally absorbed in their own particular learning experience. There was that unique combination of freedom along with order and respect for others. Almost every child was eager to share with me the excitement of his or her particular endeavor. It did not surprise me that for the eight years the school had been in existence the head teacher had virtually no problems with misbehavior and very few children with learning difficulties, despite the fact that many students had been transferred there precisely because of learning or conduct problems in the public schools. The teacher particularly emphasized to me that she was convinced that Montessori's method of teaching only phonetics and writing, leaving the children to discover reading by themselves, was one of the key factors in the school's success.

Unfortunately, neither of these outstanding methods has been adopted by our public schools. One of the more obvious reasons is that when dealing with large numbers of children, it is simpler to classify them by age and set up schedules. It is far less trouble, at least for the authorities, when everyone does the same thing at the same time in the same sequence. Schools that are organized in this fashion function exactly like assembly lines in factories; as one critic has noted, the main purpose of going to school seems to be to get to the next grade. To implement a Montessori or Slingerland approach in a modern school means that each child entering school would be randomly assigned to one of several classrooms and remain with that group until they finished school. They would leave their "homeroom" only for special lessons such as science, music, or art. Elementary school teachers would have to be trained to understand how the entire learning process unfolded for specific subject areas and be able to work with all ages. It would not be possible, as is currently the practice, for teachers to specify that they "only want to teach fifth grade because they like ten-year-olds."

Recently some school districts, such as San Francisco Unified, have begun a new experiment in what is called "Outcome Education." This type of program is similar to the Montessori approach. Children move at their own pace toward a set of very precise objectives in all the major areas, such as language arts, math, and social studies. The essence of the approach is that the child aims for mastery of specific skills and does not progress until that mastery is obtained. Children can move ahead at different rates in different subject areas. This is a very encouraging first step, and it is to be hoped that it will eventually lead to major changes in our current system of age-graded classrooms. As this approach is so new, we do not yet have any reports of students' progress.

The Missing Piece of the Puzzle

The Montessori and Slingerland methods work very effectively for most children enrolled in these programs. But there are still children—even some trained by these methods—who fail to learn to read and write. These children grow to adulthood as complete illiterates and suffer immeasurably as a result. Because these unfortunate people fail to learn despite years of special training, even though they may be highly intelligent and motivated, educators, psychologists, and neurologists have come to believe that these "dyslexics" have defective brains. But, *if* they could be taught to read and write, it would be hard to argue that their brains were truly defective. It might mean instead that a fundamental connection in the brain between some basic sensory and/ or motor processes was never established.

If this was true, then how could we ever know? And if we found out, what could be done about it? It takes a courageous person to tackle an impossible problem, but it takes genius to solve it. The hallmark of genius is not only deep intelligence but the refusal to accept current dogma and to care passionately enough to persevere. Such a person is Pat Lindamood, director of the Lindamood Center at San Luis Obispo in California, who refuses to let her charges fail.

Lindamood was trained initially as a speech therapist and reading specialist. She became equally well versed in the major techniques that had been developed to deal with speech pathology and reading failure. Yet every one of these methods, when applied to the children and adults she saw in her clinic (75 percent of whom were male), consistently failed to enable these students to become self-generating and self-correcting in their spoken and written language skills. Each method had part of the truth but the underlying principle needed to unite them was completely elusive.

Lindamood reasoned that the deficit she saw in these children and adults must be due to either the lack of control by the motor systems of the brain over the oral-facial muscles, to problems in speech perception, or in the failure of the brain to make a connection between the two. However, all the methods that she was trained to use required verbal responses from the student. When students had defective speech, one could not determine whether they had difficulty discriminating between the various speech sounds or whether they could perceive them perfectly well but could not reproduce them.

One day two girls were referred to her who had very severe, but quite different, problems. One was a twelve-year-old girl, classified as retarded, whose speech was virtually unintelligible. Several earlier periods of speech therapy had been completely unproductive. The girl was now beginning to avoid social interaction and school instruction. When she was asked to imitate different consonant sounds, the girl could only imitate those that were grossly different in production, such as "t" and "g," but not those that were similar, like "f" and "th."

The other girl, about the same age, did not have a speech problem, but had a severe reading and spelling disability. She had been failed twice and was either to be failed again or placed in a class for the retarded. This girl, obviously very depressed, refused to look at Lindamood for five days, much less even attempt to answer questions. Suddenly a chance remark triggered her confidence, and she looked up with an expression of hope mixed with despair. All the years of failure were written into that glance. Lindamood realized that if she couldn't capitalize on that faint ray of hope, her young charge would never believe and never try again. That night Lindamood woke with a flash of insight. She saw an image of a row of colored blocks. She had the solution, the way to break through, without asking her students to speak. The girls could indicate their perception of the number, sameness/ difference, and order of spoken sounds with colored blocks! She woke her husband, Charles, a psycholinguist, and for the rest of the night they formulated the essential details of the procedure. Within a year of this discovery, the retarded girl with unintelligible speech became completely intelligible. She then learned to read and write sufficiently to send and receive simple letters and finished high school in the special education program. The other girl also learned to read and write, and completed high school in regular classes while working in a motherless home as housekeeper and caregiver for two school-age children.

What the Lindamoods discovered by their method was that most speech and reading problems are due to the inability to *perceive* speech sounds in sufficient detail. This can prevent the child from being able to recognize their identity and order in words and their representation in written language. The problem is perceptual and conceptual. A person with this dysfunction is unable to think about sounds in words. This interferes with the ability to self-correct speech errors and/or to recognize the correspondence between spoken and written forms of words. The test for this dysfunction, which involves the use of colored blocks, came to be called the Lindamood Auditory Conceptualization (LAC) test and was described briefly in chapter 4.[5]

The test begins with the most simple case of discriminating between two very different sounds and leads on to building sequences of four sounds in syllables. Throughout the test all the student has to do is place or arrange the correct number of colored blocks in the correct sequence. On each trial a particular sound is represented by only one color, but from one trial to the next there is no fixed relationship between any particular color and sound. The teacher pronounces a short word such as "pip" and then assigns colors to the sounds or asks the student to assign them. "P" might be green and "i" red. Blocks of these colors are then placed in the same order in which they appear in the word: green-red-green. If the child was asked to make "ip," then he or she would be expected to remove the first green block. If the teacher asked for "pop," then the child would be expected to select another color (any would do) and exchange it for the red block.

The Lindamoods have found that their auditory conceptual test is not only very discerning of the underlying cause of a language problem, but it can segregate good and poor readers and spellers with astonishing accuracy. In contrast to language-delayed children, poor readers often have no problems in hearing and producing speech. Their difficulty lies in the sensitivity required to segment the individual phonemes within syllables and to *remember* the order of the various sounds. This inability is reflected in the LAC by confusion when two or more phonemes are combined in a syllable. Poor readers frequently add a block when a sound is omitted, or the reverse, or incorrectly substitute or shift blocks, because the sounds are not sufficiently distinct.

The LAC is a training method as well as a diagnostic tool. It is used to help students to learn to distinguish between sequences of sounds by first beginning with very simple tasks, such as telling one sound from another. Only when all of the phonemes essential to English can be distinguished are the sounds then combined into two sounds, then three, and then four. Throughout, one of the keys to the method's success is the detailed questioning by the teacher. In training people to use her method, especially when working with classroom teachers who are not wholly convinced by her approach, Lindamood has found that it is this "questioning" process that is most difficult to implement. The teacher must always be exactly at the place where the child is, so that the child can describe his or her own impressions, thus providing a clue as to how fast to move ahead. This fine-tuning is, of course, the hallmark of good teaching, but the point is important, as the Lindamood method is not merely a bag of tricks that can be employed without some background and understanding.

Although, the Lindamoods found their techniques helped most people they worked with, they did not supply the complete answer. Some students were still unable to judge the identity, number, and order of sounds in either syllables or words. Never one to admit failure, Pat Lindamood went on to discover the final missing piece of the puzzle.

She began to explore the student's perception of how the individual sounds are produced. In other words, she directed her attention to the oral-facial muscles. To her surprise, she found that students who could speak perfectly clearly often hadn't the remotest idea of the position of their lips, tongue, and palate when executing the most rudimentary sounds. Somehow the sensation produced by these articulatory muscles was not being perceived at all. Although the feedback from the muscles must be going to the brain, the students were not experiencing this at a conscious level. She asked: Would it make a difference if this feedback became conscious, and how can this be accomplished?

First she asked students to feel the position of their lips, tongue, and palate when producing various simple sounds. If they were unable to do this, she imitated the position for them, so they could use *visual* feedback to access the kinesthetic image. Later she discovered that it was sometimes more effective when students saw their own mouth and tongue positions in a mirror, and she subsequently had drawings made to represent various classes of sounds in the English language. In order to categorize these motor patterns she invented descriptive names: lip poppers, lip coolers, tongue tappers, sliders, for various postures used in speech.

Now students had visual, auditory, and motor-kinesthetic feedback all combined to the same objective: producing and perceiving speech sounds. The discovery is classic neurophysiology. Things become memorable in direct proportion to the amount and the variety of input to the brain. The efficiency of memory is dependent on this complexity or richness of input, as this governs the way neurons in the brain become connected. When all of the sensory modalities are engaged in one process, then that process will be enhanced. In addition, if there is a deficiency in one sensory modality (for example, phonemic discrimination) then this can be accessed through another sensory modality, *even,* as Lindamood has shown, by the sensory feedback from the muscles themselves. Lindamood's breakthrough has reinforced what I have been saying all along: "Dyslexics" have a poor aptitude for auditory discrimination, especially of speech sounds. Their problem is no more fundamental than that of a person who has trouble identifying individual pitches in music. Some children cannot carry a tune. Their problem is almost entirely due to the fact that they either do not hear and/or cannot remember the differences between the individual notes as they are trying to reproduce them. Yet we do not say that someone who is tone-deaf has a defective brain. (Though of course they do have "statistically abnormal" brains, because most of us can sing in tune perfectly well.)

As Montessori has shown, even some mentally retarded children can be taught to read. But the child who is mentally retarded is uniformly slow in processing all types of information and abnormal EEG patterns indicate brain pathology. It is an entirely different matter to infer that children have brain damage simply because they are deficient in phonemic analysis. During our evolutionary history we have developed the capacity to respond to speech sounds at the level of the syllable. No society needs phonemic analysis unless it has a writing system, and writing systems are inventions of human cultures, not properties of human brains.

There is still another chapter to our story. Why should a child need to fail at all? Why should it be necessary for anyone to come to the Lindamoods' clinic? If the Lindamood method is successful as a remediation technique, then it should also work for prevention. For several years Pat and Charles Lindamood attempted to interest school districts in a preventive program for reading failure. They were unsuccessful. All the usual objections were marshaled: It was just another reading method; it was too cumbersome; it required too much time for teacher training. Finally, in 1976, they were able to carry out an experimental program in Santa Barbara County, California.[6] At the same time the Arco School District in Butte County, Idaho, began to use the Lindamood concepts to prevent reading failure. In Santa Barbara their method was tested against the Slingerland phonetic method and the Sullivan program, which places the major emphasis on the syllable. The results of tests carried out in the fall and spring on 174 second-grade children are presented in table 11.1. Scores are provided for the fall (pretraining) and spring (posttraining) testing using the Peabody and Woodcock reading achievement batteries. These are shown for each of the three methods plus a control group that had the usual classroom training with a basal reader.

As can be seen from the table, all of the methods were superior

245

TABLE 11.1

Average Reading and LAC Scores as a Function of Training Programs

	Program			
Test	Lindamood	Slingerland	Sullivan	Control (Basal Reader)
Peabody Total				
Fall	77.3	70.6	78.6	70.6
Spring	106.3	91.3	102.4	86.5
GAIN	29.0	20.7	23.8	15.9
Woodcock Total				
Fall	90.2	75.9	95.8	73.2
Spring	172.6	141.3	153.8	117.5
GAIN	82.4	65.4	58.0	44.3
LAC Total				
Fall	52.3	50.6	54.8	37.1
Spring	113.2	69.2	74.2	66.0
GAIN	60.9	18.6	19.4	28.9

The LAC test predicted 77 percent of the variance on the Peabody test and 80 percent of the variance on the Woodcock test. The Lindamood method was superior to all other methods at the 0.001 level of probability.

SOURCE: Analysis (unpublished) by R. Calfee. Cited in P. Lindamood and C. Lindamood, *LAC Test Manual* (Allen, Texas: DLM Teaching Resources, 1979), p. 51. Reprinted by permission.

to the control method. But, in addition, the Lindamood method clearly surpassed both the Sullivan and the Slingerland techniques. This finding is supported by the data from Idaho; there first-grade students using the Lindamood technique were well ahead of published norms on the Woodcock Reading Mastery Test. After only seven months of work, the children had gained the equivalent of over one year in reading skills. Students who were trained by the Lindamood method moved from the district's normal average at the 60th percentile to the 86th percentile on the Woodcock battery. When the children were tested on the Iowa Test of Basic Skills, they were found to be at the 89th percentile after one year and to remain at this high level in the succeeding year, during third grade. The typical Arco child had scored at the 46th percentile over the previous four years.

In every subtest of the Woodcock battery, the scores of the Lindamood-trained children were significantly superior, with statistical values well beyond 1 in 1000. These subtests include letter identification, word identification, word attack, word comprehension, and passage comprehension. Additionally, the children moved up from the typical performance level of the 30th percentile in vocabulary and spelling to the 85th percentile for vocabulary and the 78th percentile for spelling.

By 1983, Pat and Charles Lindamood had convinced a local school district on the basis of these results that their method might work in Santa Maria. To prove their point they launched the most rigorous test of the method to date. The first-grade teacher was trained in the Lindamood method. Starting in September 1983, the children were trained for four months only in auditory conceptualization, oral-motor feedback, and matching phonemes to the written symbols. They were not given any books. In January 1984 they received books for the first time, and in May they were compared to another first-grade class—one that had always received the top reading scores in the district. Despite the fact that the authorities had tipped the scales against the Lindamoods' success, the results were astonishing. On average their students were two years ahead of the class taught in the traditional way, one year advanced in spelling, and six years advanced in word-attack skills. Eight children tested at the college level on word-attack, in which the student has to read pronounceable non-words. The Lindamood-trained children were *all* at least a year above grade level, and all scored at least 70 percent accuracy level on standard reading tasks. The results were unprecedented. The classroom teacher said she had never experienced anything to compare to this in twenty-five years of teaching. Furthermore, she found that six of her eight top readers were boys, and this was a "first" also in her teaching experience. These results are illustrated in Figure 11.1.

The most remarkable result was that so many of the Lindamood-trained children had such a dramatic enhancement in reading and spelling. All of the experimental children were reading at least at third-grade level, sixteen children were at or above the fifth-grade level, and four were at the seventh-grade level on the standard form of the reading test. This represents a spread of ability of about five years, precisely the age spread that Binet reported in the Paris schools where children were advanced because of ability.

In striking contrast, only three of the control group were at or above fourth grade in reading. This means that the progress of the brighter children, who could have done so much better, was

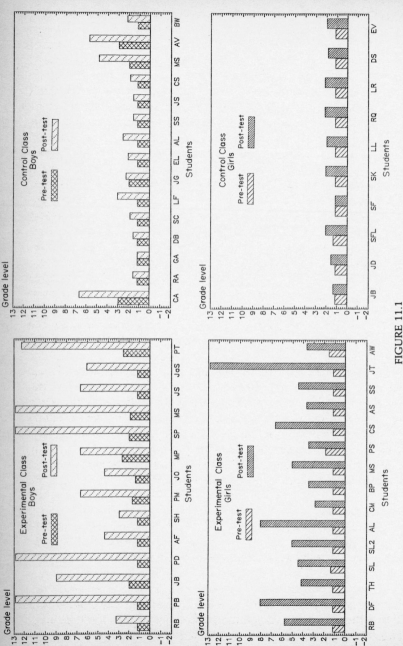

FIGURE 11.1

Scores of the first-grade students in the Lindamood-trained class (Experimental) compared to the class trained in the traditional way (Control) on the Word Attack subtest of the Woodcock Reading Battery.

curtailed in order to insure that the entire class reached the same level of performance.

This fact reveals one of the major pitfalls of the age-graded classroom and points to a critical flaw in our educational system: *excellence can rarely be achieved by ensuring that everyone is average.*

I once asked Pat Lindamood what proportion of her students failed to learn to read. She looked surprised and answered: "None of them." Then she remembered that she had been asked this question before, by someone who was to introduce her at a workshop. When she replied that everyone learned to read at her clinic, at least to a level that enabled them to function effectively, her hostess said that no one would believe this. Instead, when she introduced Lindamood, she lowered the estimate to an 85 percent success rate. I won't be party to the same conspiracy because I have watched the Lindamood teachers in action, and I have personally reviewed all of the data from the Santa Maria study. Her method works. The children and adults who attend her clinic all succeed in learning to read and write, even those who have severe language handicaps. Their training just takes longer. Even adult "dyslexics" who have attended the Lindamood clinic after years of persistent failure and who were unable to read the simplest words have subsequently gone on to complete high school and college.

We are currently experiencing a crisis of confidence in our educational system. This is not surprising, because any of the reading methods discussed work better than those employed in our public schools. Pat Lindamood has provided us with a nearly infallible method, a technique that can bring us to the unimaginable goal of 100 percent literacy. There is no reason why these outstanding methods cannot be presented in our teacher training colleges and implemented in our classrooms.

Mathematics: Preventing Math Phobia

Mathematics has become the cornerstone of the technological age, a fact that has spurred an acceleration in mathematics training. High school students are now expected to master mathematical skills that were formerly taught at the college level. This acceleration has thrown the sex differences in performance into high relief, and feminists have focused on female deficiencies because of the implications for occupational mobility. College mathematics courses designed for men and women with "math phobia" have proliferated, but with little attempt to systematize the appropriate techniques or to carry out relevant experiments. Anecdotal reports indicate that the "phobia" can be diminished and that these students can make progress, but we still have little understanding of *why* they have difficulty in the first place, *when* remediation should begin (isn't college too late?), and *whether* these students ever develop sophisticated mathematical expertise.

Learning mathematics is considerably more complicated than learning to read. Reading is based on some reasonable degree of language competence. But we have little understanding of what competencies underlie the study of mathematics. Similarly, in a writing system the symbol-sound correspondences are limited in number and invariant, while in mathematics the symbol systems change, reflecting differences in the problem set and in complexity.

Mathematics has been defined as the science of quantity and space. This means that a fundamental understanding of quantity and space, similar to the knowledge of a language, is essential to learning mathematics. Quantity and space refer initially to objects and object relations in the world, but these relationships are abstracted by representations in pictures and symbols. Mathematics, therefore, begins in the world, yet for thousands of years children have been taught by the symbols alone. We now know that people cannot fully understand mathematics in its symbolic or abstract form unless they have first experienced concrete examples and pictorial representations. In addition to this problem, quantity and space have multiple properties and can be categorized in many different ways. The more complex the categories and their interrelationships, the more a symbolic shorthand becomes essential. The symbols are initially framed on a specific number system. Yet oddly enough, the conceptual basis of a number system (base ten, base eight, base two, and so on) is rarely dealt with in the classroom.

Training proceeds in the absence of any of these necessary concepts. Children begin by learning a set of symbols in a particular order (a counting system), along with some rules for manipulating them. Rules such as "add" and "subtract" instruct the student to move forward or backward in the counting system. Children often perceive the counting system as extending to infinity, with no defining criteria other than the fact that numbers repeat in some fixed order. The implication that the counting system is based on units of ten often never penetrates, *even* when children can demonstrate that they can "count by tens." This ability breaks down the moment you ask the child to count by tens from seven or thirteen or twenty-four. With the introduction of multiplication and division the memory load may become excessive, especially as children must now deal with the concept of multiples rather than with single units. More problems arise with proportions and partial numbers, such as ratios, fractions, percentages, and decimals. In these areas a firm understanding of the concept of number and of a number system is crucial.

By the time students encounter algebra they are dealing with a complex set of rules that constitutes a code within a code. The first major change from arithmetic is the addition of a set of symbols that can stand for *any* number. In arithmetic the symbol-quantity correspondence is fixed; for algebraic symbols it is more arbitrary. Also important is the spatial position of the letters in the equation, which constitute a set of rules for representing relationships in the world. These higher-order rules make it possible to organize several types of arithmetic operation in a simultaneous form—a recoding. This means that the obvious number-quantity correspondence is lost or hidden.

Furthermore, this recoding can be abstracted into higher-order codes that, to the initiated, can come to have meaning. For example, the formula: $Y = bX + a$ is often described in textbooks as an equation for a straight line. But this is not the actual *meaning* of the equation, and the description is misleading. What the equation *means* is that two variables, X and Y, stand in a particular relationship to one another, such that increments of one variable are related, or proportional, to increments of the other. It is the characteristics of these increments and their relationship that produce a "linear" function.

The process of increasing complexity has now been extended across fourteen to fifteen years. Students with a high degree of intelligence and superior rote memory skills may be able to compensate for any disadvantage in their early training. Other students will not. Many have lost interest long before algebra enters the curriculum. Earlier I discussed the fact that females generally have more difficulty than males with the mathematics of space but are equal to males in the mathematics of quantity. If this is a problem arising from early experience, then when does the problem begin? What steps might be taken to overcome it? While we are at the frontier of understanding how children learn mathematics, we have enough evidence to know what is lacking and why children fall short of success. The next section focuses on the most promising approach to this problem.

A Rare Combination of Talents

Mathematicians are notorious for their inability to communicate verbally what they know. When they are put into the classroom, they often communicate only to the initiated or the gifted. Some math teachers have outstanding pedagogical skills but only a rudimentary knowledge of math. Few people combine both aptitudes, and fewer still have the capacity to grasp the psychological factors involved in learning. One of these rare people is Patricia Davidson, Professor of Mathematics at the University of Massachusetts in Boston.[7]

Davidson always knew that she wanted to teach, but it was her precosity in mathematics that gave her vocational calling a focus. Her aptitude for mathematics was encouraged and fostered by an old family friend who challenged her with conundrums and also by her brother who insisted she develop expertise in mechanics. Together they repaired most of the equipment on the family farm. He used to prod her with the repeated question: "How would this work?" Her ability was recognized and nurtured by an outstanding Jr. High math teacher in her farming community in Vermont. By the time she was in high school she was the obvious substitute whenever a math teacher fell ill. Her perfect score on the Math SAT led to a full four-year scholarship to Middlebury College. Another perfect score on the Graduate Record Exam in mathematics led to more scholarships and her master's and doctoral degrees at Harvard University.

Most students with such phenomenal talent in mathematics become mathematicians, but Davidson remained true to her vocational calling. During her work for her master's she taught in the Harvard-Newton program, and following this at Brookline High School, but it was her experience tutoring children on a one-to-one basis that revealed just how badly children were being taught math. She gained further insight into the problem working as a copy editor for math textbooks. By the time she began her doctorate, she was able to focus her full attention on the problem of remediation in a study of junior high school slow learners. And at the end of this period, she had formulated her strategy.

At Harvard, Davidson developed a curriculum resource center and became a world-renowned expert in cataloguing manipulative material for teaching mathematics. She put her ideas into practice as the math coordinator for the Newton (Massachusetts) Public School District, where she taught in the classroom, conducted teacher workshops, and experimented with her new ideas. Her comprehensive bibliography of manipulative devices published in 1968 put manipulatives—materials that can be manually structured or ordered—firmly back on the map.[8] In contrast to pictures or symbols that stand for objects or numbers, manipulatives, which are the heart of Piaget's "concrete" stage of mathematics, provide children with visible, tangible demonstrations of the principles of number and the spatial properties of objects. Montessori also recognized their importance and designed some useful materials to teach the concepts of number and geometry. Davidson has worked to determine exactly which manipulatives should be applied to which domain of mathematics and for what reasons.

Missing Links

The essence of Davidson's approach is illustrated in figure 11.2. She repeatedly points out that Piaget was right: Children need to proceed from the concrete to the pictorial to the abstract (the

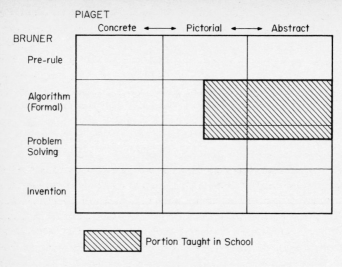

FIGURE 11.2

Davidson's matrix of mathematical concept learning. Ideally a child should begin in the upper left-hand corner and proceed across each row.

SOURCE: Reproduced with permission of Patricia Davidson.

column headings in figure 11.2 that describe the type of representations of a particular problem). However, it is equally important that one knows what to do at each of these stages of learning; in other words, what is the purpose or function of the representation? Davidson has adapted Jerome Bruner's four levels of analysis for developing problem-solving skills.[9] The first deals with the prerule stage, where concepts are formed and an understanding of spatial relationships, such as grouping or iteration, can be realized. The second is the formalization of rules or algorithms to express relationships between objects. Next there is problem solving, where the rules are used for a specific purpose, to achieve a goal in the world. And finally, there is individual invention, where the student can create new problems and new solutions. The shaded portion of the figure indicates the area in which schools concentrate their major efforts. However, if any level of math is not taught by moving from the concrete to the pictorial to the abstract, then failure is considerably more likely.

A further important point is that the transition from concrete to pictorial to abstract is not automatic. These transitions must also be taught. This can be achieved by using pictorial representations in conjunction with concrete examples and by adding in symbols when the child is working with pictures. These comparisons between different forms of the same problems are made many times so that the connection between concrete, pictorial and abstract is clearly apparent. Making such comparisons give children a concrete anchor for the symbols and creates in them the capacity to image objects and their relationships in space. For example, Davidson has invented a series of games called "Chip Trading." The chips are concrete items but can be represented by drawing colored dots. Children can match colored number cards to the colored dots and can then finally match the colored numbers alone. Perhaps one of the most interesting aspects of thinking about math education in this fashion is that it led Davidson to realize that the whole of various areas of mathematics, such as geometry, can be taught entirely in the concrete mode. This is especially invaluable for students who arrive in college geometry classes with no conception of the concrete underpinnings of the discipline.[10]

Davidson began her exploration of the appropriate methodology by asking some fundamental questions: First, what is the concept being taught (addition, place value, or the concept of number)? Second, given the age of the child, what is natural for him or her to like to do? Young children like games of chance, but they like to win. They love things that disappear or can be hidden, and they like to feel things with their eyes closed. This means that you can adapt teaching materials to the concept being taught by inventing games the children will enjoy. In attempting to answer such questions, Davidson created a number of extremely fascinating and useful games, borrowing on old themes and adding some new material and ideas. The Chip Trading series has its basis in the abacus and is particularly useful in teaching the base-ten number system and the concept of place value. Cuisenaire rods, which are colored rods of different lengths, were originally designed to help children develop the concept of number. Davidson has extended their use to encompass the whole of mathematics, but finds them especially useful for teaching spatial reasoning and problem solving.

One of Davidson's most fundamental insights is that children use many different strategies to solve the same problem. This did not surprise her, because she does this herself all the time. Part of her success in taking math examinations was due to the fact that she checked every answer by using an entirely different method. But it does surprise most of us, and it certainly surprises children when they realize that there are many ways to approach a problem. In an attempt to systematize the differences between children's learning styles, Davidson has found that there are two fundamental groups of children. The first use what she has described as Learning Style I, and the second, Learning Style II. Basically, the former use a sequential analytic approach, whereas the latter think in a more holistic fashion.[11]

As an example, let's follow the thinking of someone with Learning Style I doing a simple addition problem: $8 + 6 = ?$ The child stores "8" away and proceeds to count-on by 6, that is: 9, 10, 11, 12, 13, 14, often using fingers to keep track. A more sophisticated version would be to get to 10 (that takes 2), count off two fingers, which leaves four fingers, and $10 + 4 = 14$. The child with Learning Style II will try to work within a base-ten number system, showing that he or she has an overview of what a number system represents. This child will collect terms in the largest possible multiple unit, in this case "5." So the process would go: $8 + 6$ is $5 + 5$ and 3 and 1 left over, that is, $10 + 4 = 14$. Another holistic approach is to collect terms using "doubles," $8 + 6$ is $6 + 6 = 12$, plus $2 = 14$. Or take the example of a multiplication problem: $9 \times 7 = ?$ The Learning Style I child will interpret this as repeated addition: 9 "sevens" are $7 + 7 + 7 + 7 + 7 + 7 + 7 + 7 + 7$. The child can get to 14 and then count-on by fingers, or make seven slashes on paper and count the slashes over and over again. A Learning Style II child might begin using Cuisenaire rods and a centimeter measure, or discover the multiples pattern on a "Hundreds Chart" (a matrix of 10×10 squares numbered from 1 to 100). The pattern of multiples of 7 is "go back three spaces" ($10 - 3 = 7$) and down one row. Patterns of other multiples are illustrated in figure 11.3.

Both types of children will ultimately reach the point where these simple problems become automatic. They will have memorized the solutions. But the second approach shows the better grasp of what a number system represents and has the advantage of basing numbers on strong concrete and pictorial images. This approach can be taught. It need not occur haphazardly. Similarly, the Learning Style I child has the advantage of being more able

Hundreds Tables

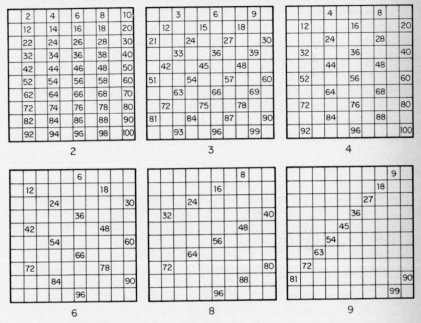

FIGURE 11.3
Patterns of multiples of simple numbers on a Hundreds Table

to verbalize solutions to problems. Such children are considerably more comfortable with word problems and with handling detail.

Davidson and her collaborator, Maria Marolda, have speculated that Learning Style I children have a more left-hemisphere orientation and Learning Style II children more right-hemisphere involvement. It is equally probable that the verbal and sequential thinker (Learning Style I) is more likely to be female, while the spatial and holistic approach (Learning Style II) is more typical of males. If this is true, then we might have a clue that sex differences in mathematical reasoning are present from the very beginning. This means that if the female is not taught to use concrete and pictorial information that develops the capacity for imaging, pattern making, and estimation, her understanding of the essentials of geometry will be minimal.

Davidson is a geometric thinker. I am not. During our interview

I asked her what geometric thinkers thought about. What do they see in the environment? Many of us who were mystified by geometry and higher math cannot understand why we should devote an entire year of study to triangles and circles. Her reply made me realize that geometric thinkers have a very different view of the world. First, everything they see is bounded in two-dimensional space. That is, it has contour and surface. Second, these boundaries are transformable into new planes and combinations in two and three dimensions. Objects move around in space, even in one's imagination. Her words here are better than mine:

> There is pattern everywhere. Even though nature doesn't use rulers, this doesn't mean that patterns in nature are not geometric. For example, one can see ratios, such as the Fibonacci series or the spiral, in nature. Patterns can have congruence, similarity, or symmetry. Congruence means that an object has the same size and same shape. Similarity means that objects have the same shape but not necessarily the same size. And there are many types of symmetry: reflectional, rotational, or translational, where the same thing can appear in a different location. There is tessilation, which means filling a plane with similar objects, like tiling patterns on the floor. Measurement per se is geometric and includes length, angle, and rotation. Metric geometry imposes measurement on one-, two-, and three-dimensional space, going from measurement of length, to perimeter and area, to volume. There can be congruence between two-dimensional and three-dimensional representations of objects. *The awareness of geometric properties is the basis for teaching algebra, geometry, and trigonometry that come much later.* (Emphasis added.)

Remediation Starts with Teachers

Davidson doesn't think that she is special. She firmly believes that all people can learn mathematics if they are taught properly. The problem is how to develop teaching methods for both the schools and teacher training programs that the teachers can use and understand. As almost no one is taught mathematics properly, the problem seems almost insurmountable, at least in the short term. Davidson and the handful of people with her talent are a scarce commodity. Nevertheless, these people are tackling the problem, and the most successful venue has been teacher workshops and, more recently, workshops for administrators who set policy in schools and teacher training institutions. Davidson believes that workshops provide three very important learning experiences that books or curriculum packages cannot achieve.

First, they give the teacher a theoretical framework for the nature of learning. Through an understanding of brain function, the psychology of learning, and the nature of pedagogy, teachers are given the basis for releasing their own talents as innovators. Many excellent teachers know intuitively how children learn, but have never expressed and synthesized this tacit knowledge. When it is realized, it frees them from being wedded to the textbook and allows them to move beyond the textbook because they have greater confidence in their own insight.

Second, teachers have been taught as badly as the children. They are a product of the same system. Many elementary-school teachers are afraid of mathematics, yet they are obliged to devote a certain portion of class time each day to this activity. It is often a period they dread, and this fear or indifference is communicated to the children. Getting the teacher involved through manipulative material makes possible a breakthrough in understanding math concepts and illustrates that teaching math can be fun. A major theme of this book is that there is no substitute for the motor involvement of hands-on activity.

Third, even teachers who use manipulatives regularly often fail to understand how they relate to the textbook. This is because they don't understand the concepts that lie behind the manipulatives and also because they assume that children will automatically make the transition between the manipulative activity and the symbols on the page. Providing the teacher with materials and the rationale to help make that transition meaningful, such as the Chip Trading program, is a revelation to many teachers, and opens the way for children to comprehend more fully what they are being taught.

Davidson's major message is that we must make a bridge

between the why and the how, between the theoretical and the applied. You cannot learn mathematics in a vacuum and have it relate to anything meaningful. When something is demanded of us that we do not understand, our most basic psychological reaction is one of fear. Fear is overcome not by sympathy or hand-holding but by instilling competence. Defusing fear by generating competence should be the major goal of classes for "math phobics." But most important, the fear need never arise if mathematics was taught properly at the outset.

Because females prefer social stimulation to the world of objects (as discussed in chapter 8), it is possible that their sensitivity to geometric properties will be poorly developed in comparison to males. But as Davidson insists, spatial ability and spatial reasoning *must be taught,* in the same way that children are required to learn arithmetic year after year. For some children an awareness of objects and their spatial relationships becomes incorporated into their learning experience in mathematics. But for most children this integration never takes place.

As already discussed, females have far less difficulty with problems in two-dimensional space but much greater difficulty than males with three-dimensional problems. Several studies show that this effect begins early, as early as four years of age, and that it is found in a number of different cultures. The translation from a two-dimensional pattern into a three-dimensional image is a learned skill.

My research on preschool children suggests that the time to begin training on tangible forms is at the point where most children demonstrate the aptitude, which turns out to be the period where the sex difference is most noticeable. Three-dimensional problem solving was uniformly poor in most three-year-olds, but by four years of age there was a quantum leap in proficiency in both sexes, but especially in the boys. The shift in aptitude suggests that if females are not to be left behind, the time to begin training them in the manipulation and construction of three-dimensional forms is when they are four—ar at most five—years of age.[12]

Currently most of the federal funding devoted to developing spatial-visualization has been targeted for the college level. Some college mathematics programs have implemented course work with visual displays using computer graphics, based on the assumption that the images of static and moving forms represented by the mathematical formulas will aid in making the formulations more tangible, hence more meaningful. Although this is a distinct possibility and will certainly be enlightening for many students, what is more critical is whether or not this approach will help to *create* in students the capacity to generate such visual images *de novo,* or to construct them from unknown mathematical statements. We need to determine whether the intervention makes a difference in understanding and is not merely boosting motivation.

The adoption of externalized visual patterns as an aid to developing expertise in mathematics does not guarantee the internalization of the capacity in question, in exactly the same way that the Lindamoods discovered that listening to sounds did not promote a greater capacity for phonemic analysis in their nonreaders. Instead it was necessary to interpolate feedback from the muscles to help integrate sight and movement, to rectify the original failure to develop any integration between vision and the articulatory systems. Montessori combined drawing with phonemic decoding to assist children learning to write. Will passive viewing (looking at a computer screen) combine with passive viewing (looking at formulas) to produce any fundamental insight? From Davidson's work it seems more relevant to attempt to boost an impoverished capacity for imagery in three dimensions by adding *active kinesthetic manipulation.*

Learning to learn requires an integration of the various modalities of the sensorimotor system. This establishes a new mode of processing of an entirely different order, one that is truly "cognitive." Reading demands an integration of the auditory phonemic system, the visual iconic system, and the fine-motor system engaged in speech production. Writing adds the production of fine-motor manual operations. Mathematics, on the other hand, requires the integration of in-depth vision with kinesthetic motor feedback. In other words, to understand spatial relationships a child must move about in space, handling and manipulating objects. And this is precisely what the "hyperactive" child appears to be doing. Rather than assume that children only need to be told what to do and how to do it, we need to remember that children must *discover* how to do. Each child will "discover" in his or her own inimitable way.

III / Three Ounces of Prevention

Learning to Learn Without Bothering Anyone

As we have seen, there are a variety of reasons why a child exhibits "hyperactive" behavior or attention problems. Some children (males especially) are just inherently more active than others. Some children have serious learning difficulties, and their fidgetiness or inability to stick to a task is a consequence of frustration and boredom. Other children are uncomfortable in an overly structured environment, such as a formal classroom setting, where they tend to daydream or make disruptive noises. Yet in open classrooms without walls and doors, where there is more space, more freedom to move and change activities, these same children are indistinguishable from any other child. In this "open" environment, all children become more "hyperactive." There are also a small minority of children who act out in a highly aggressive fashion and exhibit what psychiatrists call "conduct disorders." Hyperactivity scales do not distinguish among these subgroups.

Hyperactivity and poor attentional control are *symptoms* of genetic and/or situational factors, just as a flushed face is a symptom of a high fever. But doctors do not treat the flushed face; they treat the fever. When dealing with hyperactive behavior or attention problems, the goal should not be to medicate the hyperactive symptoms but to deal directly with the *particular* problems that generate the inappropriate behaviors. Keeping a child drugged and passively at his desk is not the solution. While a drug regime may benefit the parents and the teacher, it has absolutely no benefit to the child, as shown in chapter 10. In fact, a drug regime can be harmful. The first consequence of being put on drugs is to attribute your bad behavior to factors beyond your control. Drugs become a substitute for learning self-discipline. This problem is compounded when children are taken off medication and problem behavior initially rebounds to fantastic proportions. Second, longitudinal studies have confirmed that children on drugs actually deteriorate in academic performance over time. And we must consider the sense of worthlessness most of these young people experience.

In reviewing the literature on hyperactivity, I was dismayed to discover how few workers direct their efforts toward remediation.

Most of the research has dealt with issues such as problems of diagnosis. An inordinate amount of time and resources have been spent on the construction of diagnostic scales, while there is no evidence that we are any closer to diagnosing "pure" hyperactivity from a rating scale. Hundreds of studies, like those reviewed in chapter 10, have been directed at discovering psychological tests that distinguish "hyperactives" from everyone else. So far this approach has had remarkably little success. Furthermore, none of the tests that hyperactive children find problematic is remotely correlated with learning to read, spell, add, or multiply, the skills they are supposedly in school to acquire.

Of the few champions of a pragmatic approach to handling problematic youngsters, Daniel and Susan O'Leary at Stony Brook are especially noteworthy.[13] They combine a refreshing down-to-earth common sense with an effective remedial technique that is steadily gaining adherents. Daniel O'Leary has been instrumental in implementing behavioral modification techniques in the classroom for nearly twenty years. With the sudden acceleration in the diagnosis of hyperactivity, he and his wife have turned more of their efforts toward dealing with hyperactivity in a balanced and constructive way. One of the major benefits of O'Leary's long experience with children in a classroom setting is that he understands children's behavior in groups, unlike many clinicians or laboratory psychologists who see children one at a time. O'Leary has discovered that "hyperactive" children look suspiciously like the children who twenty years ago were described as having "behavior problems" or as "emotionally disturbed."

Daniel O'Leary, in particular, has been insistent on rigorous methodology for both diagnosis and remediation.[14] He points out that questionnaires alone are insufficient and can be misleading. It is far more important to add observational data that are collected by someone who has no prior knowledge of the child nor of whether he or she has been labeled hyperactive. These data should be collected in the *classroom*, not in the laboratory or clinic, where there is little relationship between the tasks or the setting that the child finds troublesome. When ratings have been compared to observational data, correlations range from only moderate down to zero, depending on the setting and the particular behavior. The strongest relationship has been found between teacher ratings and the child's ability to maintain attention to tasks, the lowest between the amount of general activity or actual disruptive behavior. These discrepancies arise because "attention to task" is a much more global observation, that is, *any* type of nontask behavior is involved, whereas more precise indicators, such as the actual amount of activity, cannot be estimated. Furthermore, there is the inevitable "halo effect," in which a child who is difficult to motivate and tends to cause trouble, receives all sorts of additional negative attributions from the teacher. Teachers dislike troublemakers, and for very good reason.

If a child is being a nuisance both to himself or herself and others, especially if he or she is performing below ability, then a remedial approach can be taken. Children who consistently misbehave in classrooms have three particular needs that must be met before any effective change can occur. First, they need to be given achievable goals. Although this is true for all of us, these children need special help in structuring goals and setting up a realistic mode of achieving them. Second, the goals must be based on the reason why the children are in school in the first place. Realistic goals mean reading more stories, writing more essays, doing more math problems, and so forth. It is not enough to request merely that the child "sit still and be quiet." Children need to know why they are in school and to experience the satisfaction that competence affords. Parents should also set similar goals for the child's behavior at home: doing homework, completing chores, not annoying siblings, and the like. Finally, children need to have a consistent external reward system, even if it is only frequent praise. Generally these children seem less able to carry out a task, at least in the classroom, for its own intrinsic merit, and they certainly *will not* if they are consistently being punished or reprimanded.

For these reasons each child has to be handled on an individual basis and a regime needs to be established that can be agreed upon by the parents, the teacher, and the child. If the child has consistently failed to complete the required number of math problems, then the number should be reduced to a manageable and attainable amount. The number can be increased gradually until the child is performing at an acceptable level. In addition to frequent praise and a minimum of criticism, many children benefit from a token reward system.[15] Here children are evaluated on each activity throughout the day, and if they are meeting the set goals, they receive an award of points or a physical token, such as a paper "smile face," which has proved effective with elementary school children. These can be cashed in at school or at home for anything that the child particularly enjoys, such as a special television program, a family picnic, or a favorite food. It is important that the teacher send home daily reports or a tally of the tokens received, so that the parents are involved in the child's school performance and can offer praise when the child has had a good day.

This intervention program has two major goals: to bring the child up to the level of the class in academic skills and to reduce problematic behaviors. Thus the praise or token rewards are also given when children are conforming to the appropriate behaviors demanded by the classroom setting. This means not disturbing other children, not demanding attention from the teacher, and trying to avoid fidgety, restless, or unnecessary activities. In general, it has been found that as academic performance increases, these extraneous behaviors diminish markedly.

In several studies using these techniques carried out by the O'Learys and others, hyperactive children were found to show consistent improvement in academic performance accompanied by a diminution of disruptive behavior to within, or near, normal levels.[16] Children previously on stimulant medication are able to stop medication entirely and stabilize their behavior within the normal range. These changes are most dramatic immediately following intervention, and in most studies intervention lasts about two to four months. At follow-up several months later, academic performance continues to show strong gains over control groups. The behavior problems also diminish, but the evidence is unclear as to how much this is a result of maturation or of training.

In every study that has emphasized *academic* performance, marked improvements have occurred. Teachers and parents are so impressed with the results that they generally continue with the method. The children are equally impressed; in one study they even volunteered to continue in a weekly tutorial program during the summer. These findings are in direct contrast to the results of follow-up studies on children under medication, who have been found to be depressed and uniformly delayed in academic achievement compared to their peers and their own earlier performance.[17]

Critics have complained that the token reward methodology is similar to bribery and that these children may fail to develop their own internal reward system. In part, this is an issue of pragmatics. If a child is having trouble in school with a noticeable deterioration in academic performance, then external rewards may be the shortest route to regaining equilibrium and competence. Competence instills confidence and is generally its own reward. No child wants to endure the approbations of adults day and night, and any technique that generates behavior that meets with everyone's approval will show the child which behaviors prompt the best reactions. Without a system of praise or rewards, the child is told only which behaviors are *not* sanctioned but never provided with alternatives.

In studying how children could shift toward an internal reward system, O'Leary has discovered that children (even juveniles detained in psychiatric units for conduct disorders) can continue a token reward program through self-evaluation.[18] Observations of their behavior indicate that their evaluations are carried out honestly. It is not known to what extent children could continue this procedure, but receiving the tokens seems to be the critical factor. If the tokens are abruptly withdrawn, then performance and behavior were found to deteriorate.

Why are tokens important? There is an extensive literature on the nature of reward or reinforcement. In a summary of this literature, Karl Pribram concludes that rewards function to create markers in an ongoing stream of time.[19] That is, they demarcate sequences of behavior, but can function effectively only when the sequences of behavior are meaningful in terms of the setting and the situational demands. This is why the token reward system does not work in the absence of context-specific goals. If a child is in school, he or she is there for a reason and must behave for a reason, not merely because it pleases the teacher that he or she is quiet and well behaved. To express this in another way, tokens make it possible to see consequences of behavior. Tokens provide the markers that something has been achieved. They parse the stream of time into shorter and more meaningful segments, and for children who can barely endure a long school day, this appears essential. As Roscoe Dykman discovered, many of the boys in his "hyperactive" group estimated the time on task to be much longer than it really was.

Additional techniques could facilitate a transition from an external to an internal reward system. Virginia Douglas and her colleagues in Montreal structured an intervention program around modeling, self-verbalization, and strategy training, employing the O'Leary approach only if the child was particularly difficult.[20] Using these techniques, the child is asked to talk through the solution of a problem and is given strategies for how to search through items to reach a solution. There is also emphasis and guidance on how to plan and organize work. Performance immediately after training improved on a number of visuomotor tasks and aggressive fantasies were reduced, but minimal effects were found in reading, spelling, and math. However, at a three-month follow-up, oral reading and oral comprehension had improved in comparison to a control group.

So far, the token reward system has produced the most positive and lasting effects for both behavior and academic performance, though instructions for children in how to approach and tackle problems would be a useful addition to all such programs. Once it has been determined that the child is gaining mastery over schoolwork and behavior, the token reward system can be reduced and eventually eliminated.

Implementing this kind of intervention is time-consuming and costly, given the current problem of inadequate teacher training in behavior management. And if the child is on medication it might also involve the cooperation of the family physician, pediatrician, or psychiatrist, in addition to the parents and teacher. It comes as no surprise that drugs are a simpler and much more economic short-term solution. With drug treatment no one has to deal with the problem at all! Yet this inconvenience and expense of intervention is entirely due to our own shortsightedness.

One of the fundamental problems is how teachers are trained. This has been a consistent theme in my discussions with both Pat Lindamood and Patricia Davidson. They find themselves having to conduct workshops all over the country in order to repair what could have been accomplished if their programs had been offered in teacher training institutions. It would be far more effective if Lindamood and Davidson were able to train administrators and teachers at training colleges; then these educators would be able to pass on the techniques to large numbers of potential teachers.

Similarly, surveys have shown that teachers receive only minimal training in the management of highly problematic children, and this rarely includes an emphasis on principles of behavior therapy. Yet most research reports on behavioral techniques indicate that teachers or parents can be trained to produce very positive results in a few weeks. If this is true, then it does not seem beyond the realm of possibility to introduce courses in reward-based management at teacher training institutions. If teachers were armed with these skills initially, then few children would have to endure the harassment of a clinical referral, being labeled "hyperactive," or put on drugs. If the teacher could assist in implementing a behavioral program in cooperation with the school psychologist and parents, behavior management would become a first line of defense. This group effort would seem a far safer solution than the current practice where, in effect, teachers function as clinical diagnosticians, a role for which they are totally unqualified. It seems obvious that if reward-management techniques were introduced as a first step rather than a last, considerable suffering, time, and effort could be saved.

Meanwhile, government funding continues to pour into research projects that have little practical usefulness, while behavior management classes in teacher training colleges and special education programs could be implemented almost overnight at little additional cost. If the money currently expended on searching for a syndrome that doesn't exist was spent on workshops on behavior management, some progress might be made. They might also have the benefit of helping to demolish the myth that "hyperactivity" is a disease or due to brain damage.

As this chapter reveals, the tools are available to solve most of the problems that confront our children in classrooms. How can these very sensible solutions be brought to the attention of politicians, administrators, teachers, and clinicians? The final chapter provides a brief summary of what parents might accomplish if they speak with a united voice.

12

A Concerted Voice: A Personal Primer for Parents

Parents face two challenges when they deal with a youngster who is failing in school either scholastically or emotionally. On the one hand, they must resist being dragged into the learning disabilities mythology and all of its attendant trappings. On the other hand, they have to get the attention of educators or clinicians when their child is in trouble. Both of these paths are fraught with difficulty, and parents are placed in the position of walking a tightrope between experts who tell them "nothing is wrong, your child will just grow out of it," to experts who tell them their child has brain damage and must be put on drugs immediately. In the absence of any scientific knowledge, whom are they to believe?

This chapter provides parents with a short guide for steering through the maze of learning disability specialists. It is neither a definitive account nor a thorough "how to" exposition. It is merely my personal view based on my experience in the classroom, conversations with pediatricians, observations in the clinic, and sitting quietly (and often painfully) through case study conferences in learning disability clinics.

Avoid Labeling

First of all, parents should resist any attempt by teachers or clinicians to put their child on drugs or apply labels such as "hyperactive" or "dyslexic." They should insist that the experts and the family discuss the issue in terms of a specific problem: "James is two years behind his classmates in reading." If the child is a behavior problem in school, then the comments should be specific: "Henry is misbehaving in school. He says he doesn't like his new teacher," or "Henry doesn't sit still in class; he wanders around during lessons and annoys everyone." These behaviors can be symptoms of a number of different situational problems or they can reflect neurological or temperamental differences. The trick is to discover the root of the problem. Labels are only a convenient handle experts use to make themselves appear more scientific. But labels are dangerous because they lead to the inference that there is a real diagnosis. Labeling disguises the complexity of the situation and does considerable psychological harm to the child.

A Five-Step Plan

Whatever the problem a child exhibits, whether academic or in behavioral or attentional control, the following five questions should be asked.

1. Is the child's IQ within the normal range (85 to 90 or better)? Answering this makes it possible to rule out any difficulties that stem from an overall deficit in intelligence. Even though the IQ test is not perfect, it is the most valid and objective measure of general intellectual function. A low IQ means that parents will have to be more patient, not expect too much, and seek special remedial help. Occasionally IQ scores are depressed by very poorly

developed reading skills in contrast to normal or above-average ability in nonverbal tasks. Parents should insist on knowing both the scores from the "verbal IQ" and the "performance IQ" tests. A higher score on the performance measure than on the verbal measure may indicate the child has normal intelligence but has a specific area of weakness in verbal tasks, which is usually remediable.

2. How does the child perform on standard achievement tests? This is the next question to consider if the child's IQ score is in the normal range. It never should be assumed that school marks or teacher reports reflect actual ability. Only achievement test scores, which have national norms, can indicate where a child stands in relation to other children of the same age. If the child has very low scores in reading, spelling, or math, such as two years behind the norms, then remedial help should be sought. But remember that these test score norms are not independently standardized by sex. Boys will *normally* lag behind girls in most verbal skills, so a marginal delay of about six to twelve months is not cause for alarm. If remedial help is required, then parents must find out all they can about the remedial programs in the school or school district. They should ask remedial teachers how quickly the child can catch up with classmates or how soon a nonreader can be taught to read. If the remedial teacher replies: "They never catch up. Your child is a dyslexic!" or words to this effect, help should be sought elsewhere. There may be someone who uses the Lindamood method nearby. If not, the Lindamood materials can be obtained from Developmental Learning Materials in Allen, Texas. Other solutions are to locate a local Montessori elementary school or write to the Orton Dyslexic Society, at 724 York Road, Baltimore, Maryland 21204, for addresses of programs they recommend in your area. Above all, if there is a real problem, parents should not waste time or listen to people who say that children spontaneously grow out of reading problems.

If the child is behind in math, then the problem is considerably more difficult. Parents will have to search for local teachers who have been well trained in the use of manipulatives and who have had good results. This may not be easy. It may be possible to get a list of remedial math teachers from the local district. These people should be interviewed to discover if what they say bears any relationship to the teaching techniques described in chapter 11. Check to see that remedial teachers attend math workshops regularly.

3. Is the learning problem combined with behavior problems? While behavior problems are probably a result of learning problems, children who exhibit them should undergo a behavior management program. Parents could discuss the problem with the classroom teacher to work out what might be the best approach for the child. Even if no one has had any real training in behavior modification, applying the simple principles of reducing punishment and negative remarks, while lavishing praise for appropriate behaviors, can work wonders. This is especially true if both teacher and parents work together to structure academic goals that the child can achieve.

4. Is the child reasonably successful in school although he or she has consistent problems in self-control and self-management? This could be due to a number of factors. Only parents really know their children and can determine whether the behavior problems are part of a long history, have worsened over time, or are of sudden origin. Each one of these cases suggests a different basis for the problems.

If the child has always been fidgety or difficult to discipline, then this is probably due to an inherent temperamental trait. High activity levels and unruly behavior are considerably more common in boys. Despite this, at some point all of us must learn self-control and become aware of how we affect other people. The question is *when* should this awareness be expected to emerge. This is why questionnaire data about children's behavior will always be biased by one's expectations or "tolerance of annoying behavior." At some point parents may have to determine which behaviors must be eliminated and, if necessary, begin to use behavioral modification techniques. This means being overly positive about everything the child does that should be encouraged, even if it is just the five minutes' silence that accompanied reading a comic. Rewards can be given for major things, like completing chores on time. Most irritating behavior should be ignored, and above all parents should rarely punish and never nag or cajole. For some children it helps to shorten requests to within manageable units. Perhaps the child simply cannot deal with a string of commands. If a child frequently gets distracted halfway through such a list, then he or she has probably forgotten the instructions.

If the behavior is slowly worsening over time, grades are sliding from Bs to Cs to Ds, then the problem is probably due to some difficulty in school. Although this could be attributed to a home situation such as marital problems, research has shown that children's academic performance is fairly resilient to minor marital ups and downs. The problem is more likely to be academic, but it may be difficult to specify. Parents need to talk at length with both the child and the teacher and try to set up a regime that will work for the child. If the child is very bright, then the problem may be boredom, and special library privileges or special projects with rewards may be the answer. More often, the child may have missed some fundamental insight in learning math or may have trouble with handwriting. Here a behavior management program can be adopted, but it is important to take the pressure off the child temporarily and if necessary seek some short-term remedial help. There is nothing more prohibitive than "missing the point" of some critical new piece of information, because it may form the basis for everything that follows.

If there is a sudden deterioration in behavior, the reason is almost certain to be situational: new school, disliked teacher, illness, or some major change at home. An abrupt change in behavior should be treated as a serious symptom and should be dealt with immediately. Parents must get the child to articulate the problem. If necessary, this may mean that father or mother should take the child on a day or weekend trip, so that the child has time to express his or her feelings. It is usually unwise for both parents to be involved at this stage, because it is much easier to develop rapport on a one-to-one basis. Once the problem has been identified, then it must be solved. If the child has a genuine grievance, he or she may have to change schools or classes. Whatever the problem, parents should not punish the child.

5. Does the child's behavior require special clinical attention? Such behaviors can be classified as consistently preventing the child from leading a normal academic and social life. They are most likely to include withdrawal and depression or overt and persistent hostility and aggression. (*It is highly unlikely that a child who misbehaves in the classroom, but who is learning normally, has any serious psychiatric problem.*) Professional advice should be sought for any conditions that are unamenable to any of the

273

strategies that have been suggested above. It is very difficult to be able to draw a line between normality and psychopathology, but most parents will be sensitive to warning signals and maladaptive behavior. If the child is perfectly normal at home, with the usual number of friends and playmates, but is aggressive or antisocial at school, then this problem probably reflects some difficulty at school, or the fact that the child is acting out because of a problem at home. Generally if the parents and the teacher's perceptions of a child are radically different, the child is not coping with some aspect of his or her life. It may take some time in unraveling, but it is better to begin to tackle the problem at its source than to rush a child into the clinic.

If all attempts fail then professional advice must be sought. This is not an easy decision or an easy task; there are almost as many kinds of therapy as therapists in the Yellow Pages. The best place to start is with a pediatrician or a clinic or professional recommended by the school. As parents steer their child toward help, it is vitally important that they function as participants and not as spectators. Parents must insist that they know what diagnoses are being applied and why. They should ask for an explanation of the goals of therapy or any intervention. They should see objective test score data. They must never accept classifications or phrases that are not clarified or that are essentially meaningless jargon, such as "minimal brain damage," or "right-hemisphere involvement." At all costs, parents should continue to resist any attempt to give the child drugs, *unless* they can be shown literature that indicates the medical value of the drug. (For example, Dilantin has proved effective in the control of epileptic seizures.) *There is no drug that eliminates learning problems or trains a child in self-control.*

This brief set of precautions is not meant to be a manual on childhood disorders. Obviously I have not touched on everything that can go wrong with children neurologically, medically, or psychologically. The instructions apply to children who have throughout childhood appeared to be normal in every respect but who subsequently fall afoul of the school system or are intensively troubled by some event such as a divorce or death in the family. Similarly, I cannot speak to parents who do not have the skill to apply these safeguards because they themselves are depressed, schizophrenic, or exhibit criminal behavior. Children with these kinds of parents are indeed unfortunate, and here only relatives, close friends, or sensitive teachers can step in to help.

As a final plea, parents can exert an impetus for change if they seek knowledge and join together in an effort to improve the school system. Through the parents association, parents can be instrumental in helping to initiate teacher workshops for any of the methods that have been reviewed in chapter 11. Through political action, parents can pressure administrators and politicians to use funds to improve teacher training. The twentieth century has brought about the beginning of a scientific revolution in our understanding of how various types of learning take place, the extent to which children vary in acquiring new skills, and how to guide people toward behavioral change. It's time that these new techniques were brought into the classroom.

NOTES

Introduction

1. S. Farnham-Diggory, *Learning Disabilities* (Cambridge, Mass.: Harvard University Press, 1978).

Chapter 1

1. The information on the !Kung San comes from R. B. Lee, *The !Kung San. Men, Women and Work in a Foraging Society* (Cambridge: Cambridge University Press, 1979).

2. For details on Montessori's life and method, see E. M. Standing, *Maria Montessori Her Life and Work* (New York: New American Library, 1962); M. Montessori, *The Discovery of the Child* (New York: Ballantine Books, 1972); M. Montessori, *The Child in the Family* (New York: Avon Books, 1970).

3. Alfred Binet and Theodore Simon's classic monographs, *The Development of Intelligence in Children,* published in 1905 and 1908, are reprinted, from the translation of E. S. Kite, in *Significant Contributions to the History of Psychology, 1750–1920,* vol. 4, ed. D. N. Robinson (Washington, D.C.: University Publications of America, 1977).

4. A. Binet, *L'Etude Experimentale de L'Intelligence* (Paris: Poitiers, 1903).

5. In her detailed biography, *Alfred Binet* (Chicago: Chicago University Press, 1973), T. H. Wolf includes a discussion of how the IQ formula came into existence and was adopted in the United States by Lewis Terman at Stanford University. In *Development of Alfred Binet's Psychology* (Princeton, N.J.: Psychological Review Company, 1935), E. J. Varon mentions the sex differences in the early test results, while Wolf does not. However, Wolf does document Binet's endless search for appropriate tests, the continuous weeding and discarding of items during the ten to fifteen years of test development, plus Binet's interest in sex differences. It is highly likely that Binet's initial linguistic bias would result in a large number of test items that favored girls, especially as his early thinking was based on detailed studies of his two daughters.

6. For a review of the development of the Wechsler Intelligence scales, see D. M. Kipnis, "Intelligence, Occupational Status and Achievement Orientation," in B. Lloyd and J. Archer, eds., *Exploring Sex Differences* (London: Academic Press, 1976), pp. 95–122.

7. Much of the data on sex differences will be reviewed in the following pages. For other sources see D. McGuinness and K. H. Pribram, "Origins of Sensory Biases in Gender Differences," in M. Bortner, ed., *Cognitive Growth and Development* (New York: Brunner/ Mazel, 1979) pp. 3–56. B. Lloyd and J. Archer, eds., *Exploring Sex Differences* (London: Academic Press, 1976); M. A. Wittig and A. C. Petersen, eds., *Sex-Related Differences in Cognitive Functioning* (New York: Academic Press, 1979).

8. The most comprehensive review of the evidence for sex differences in remedial reading populations is J. M. Finucci and B. Childs, "Are There Really More Dyslexic Boys than Girls?," in A. Ansara et al., eds., *Sex Differences in Dyslexia* (Towson, Md.: The Orton Dyslexia Society, 1981), pp. 1–9.

9. See C. P. Benbow and J. C. Stanley, "Sex Differences in Mathematical Ability: Fact or Artifact?" *Science:* 210 (1980):1262–64.

10. Because most studies use only hyperactive boys, it is difficult to find an absolute

Notes

measure of sex ratios. Virginia Douglas at McGill University and head of the Montreal project told me the estimates for Montreal are six to one, or approximately 85 percent males. Other estimates put the ratios higher, but do not cite evidence.

Chapter 2

1. L. Brody and L. Fox, "An Accelerative Intervention Program for Mathematically Gifted Girls," in L. Fox, L. Brody, and D. Tobin, *Women and the Mathematical Mystique* (Baltimore: Johns Hopkins University Press, 1980), pp. 164–78.

2. Sandra Scarr's paper, "Comments on Psychology, Genetics and Social Policy from an Anti-reductionist," can be found in R. A. Kasschau and C. N. Cofer, eds., *Psychology's Second Century: Houston Symposium II* (New York: Praeger, 1981).

3. The most comprehensive discussion of the topic of environmental triggers for aggression is in K. E. Moyer's *The Psychobiology of Aggression* (New York: Harper & Row, 1976).

Chapter 3

1. The brain damage myth began as long ago as 1902. For an excellent review of the history of this myth, see D. M. Ross and S. A. Ross, *Hyperactivity: Current Issues, Research and Theory* (New York: John Wiley & Sons, 1982). An influential paper arguing for brain damage in learning disabled or hyperactive children is the paper by Laufer, Denhoff, and Solomons, "Hyperkinetic Impulse Disorder in Children's Behavior Problems," *Psychosomatic Medicine* 19 (1957):38–49. The myth has been popularized and exaggerated by the U.S. Department of Health, Education and Welfare publication by S. D. Clements, *Task Force One: Minimal Brain Dysfunction in Children*, Monograph #3 (Washington, D.C., 1966).

2. The neural correlates of peripheral physiological activity remain a mystery. Large regions of brain tissue are involved in a number of peripheral physiological indicators, but the generators of the particular portions of the activity are unknown. This problem is currently being researched. For a detailed review, see K. H. Pribram and D. McGuinness, "Arousal, Activation and Effort in the Control of Attention," *Psychological Review* 82 (1975): 116–49.

3. R. D. Hess and T. McDevitt, "Some Cognitive Consequences of Maternal Intervention Techniques: A Longitudinal Study," *Child Development*, forthcoming.

4. One of the early popularizers of the developmental lag theory was C. Hutt, *Males and Females* (Harmondsworth: Penguin Books, 1972).

5. See D. McGuinness and K. H. Pribram, "The Origins of Sensory Bias in the Development of Gender Differences in Perception and Cognition," in M. Bortner, ed., *Cognitive Growth and Development* (New York: Brunner/Mazel, 1979), pp. 3–56.

6. Dr. Stuart Mann, an optometrist specializing in children with learning problems, reported these data to me. More recently, in an unpublished research project on 1,900 school children, Dr. Eugene Helvesten, Director of Pediatric Ophthalmology, Indiana University, found no relationship between reading problems and any test of visual function using a large battery of tests. According to a March 1984 press release issued by United Press International, three major medical groups have now denounced the widely held belief that dyslexia is caused by visual problems.

7. R. C. Calfee, L. W. Fisk, and D. Piontkowski, " 'On-Off' Tests of Cognitive Skill in Reading Acquisition," in M. P. Douglas, ed., *Claremont Reading Conference, 39th Yearbook* (Claremont, Calif.: Claremont Graduate School, 1975).

8. See M. Mason, "Reading Ability and Letter Search Time: Effects of Orthographic Structure Defined by Single Letter Positional Frequency," *Journal of Experimental Psychology (General)* 104 (1975):146–66, and M. Mason, "From Print to Sound in Mature Readers as a

Notes

Function of Reader Ability and Two Forms of Orthographic Regularity," *Memory and Cognition* 6 (1978):568–81.

9. H. W. Seaton has carried out an extensive test on a perceptual training battery and found no effect on reading skill. His report is in *Dissertation Abstracts International* 3A (1973):1155.

10. Phyllis Lindamood's experiment is an unpublished senior thesis. It has been discussed in D. McGuinness, "Auditory and Motor Aspects of Language Development in Males and Females," in A. Ansara et al., eds., *Sex Differences in Dyslexia* (Towson, Md.: The Orton Dyslexia Society, 1981), pp. 55–72.

11. An excellent review of Orton's contribution is presented by N. Geschwind in "Why Orton Was Right," *Annals of Dyslexia* 32 (1982):13–30.

12. The best sources on sex differences in brain anatomy are H. Ellis *Man and Woman* (London: A. C. Black, 1930), and D. McGuinness and K. H. Pribram, "The Origins of Sensory Bias in the Development of Gender Differences in Perception and Cognition," in M. Bortner, ed., *Cognitive Growth and Development* (New York: Brunner/Mazel, 1979), pp. 3–56.

13. See J. A. Wada, R. Clark, and A. Hamm, "Cerebral Hemispheric Asymmetry in Humans," *A.M.A. Archives of Neurology* 32 (1975):239–46.

14. R. L. Holloway, "The Indonesian Homo Erectus Brain Endocasts Revisited," *American Journal of Physical Anthropology* 55 (1981):503–21.

15. Reviews of the impact of hormones on brain function are provided in McGuinness and Pribram, "The Origins of Sensory Bias," and in R. W. Goy and B. S. McEwen, *Sexual Differentiation of the Brain* (Cambridge, Mass.: MIT Press, 1980).

16. For an extensive review of the literature on laterality and sex differences, see J. McGlone, "Sex Differences in Human Brain Asymmetry: A Critical Review," *The Behavioral and Brain Sciences* 3 (1980):215–64.

17. Kimura has evidence to support a different brain organization in males and females. See D. Kimura, "Sex Differences in Cerebral Organization for Speech and Praxic Functions, *Canadian Journal of Psychology* 37 (1983):19–35.

18. Differential brain organization is also supported by evidence from C. A. Mateer, S. B. Polen, and G. A. Ojemann, "Sexual Variation in Cortical Localization of Naming as Determined by Stimulation Mapping," *The Behavioral and Brain Sciences* 5 (1982):310–11.

19. D. Waber, "Cognitive Abilities and Sex-related Variations in the Maturation of Cerebral Cortical Functions, in M. A. Wittig and A. C. Petersen, eds., *Sex-Related Differences in Cognitive Functioning* (New York: Academic Press, 1979), pp. 161–86.

20. A survey of Jean Piaget's work can be found in J. H. Flavell, *The Developmental Psychology of Jean Piaget* (Princeton, N.J.: D. Van Nostrand, 1963).

21. The anatomical and physiological distinctions between fine-motor and gross-motor systems can be found in S. Grossman, *A Textbook of Physiological Psychology* (New York: John Wiley & Sons, 1967).

22. Sex differences in brain weight and cranial capacity are described in R. D. Martin, "Ontogenetic and Phylogenetic Aspects of Human Brain Size," in M. Sakka, ed., *Table Ronde du C. N. R. S.* (Paris: Masson et Cie, 1983).

23. Descriptions of male rough-and-tumble play can be found in a number of sources. For nonhuman primates, see G. Mitchell *Behavioral Sex Differences in NonHuman Primates* (New York: Van Nostrand Reinhold, 1979); for nonhuman and human primates, see D. McGuinness, ed., *Dominance, Aggression, and War* (New York: Paragon House Press, in press). For the impact of sex hormones, see A. A. Ehrhardt and S. W. Baker, "Fetal Androgens, Human Central Nervous System Differentiation, and Behavior Sex Differences," in R. C. Friedman, R. M. Richart, and R. L. Vande Wiele, eds., *Sex Differences in Behavior* (New York: John Wiley & Sons, 1974).

24. The theory of firsthand versus secondhand acquisition of knowledge is explored in D. McGuinness and K. H. Pribram, "The Origins of Sensory Bias."

25. See K. H. Pribram and F. T. Melges, "Psychophysiological Basis of Emotion," in P. J. Vinken and G. W. Bruyn, eds., *Handbook of Clinical Neurology* (Amsterdam: North Holland Publishing Co, 1969), pp. 316–42; K. H. Pribram, *Languages of the Brain* (New York: Brandon House, 1971).

Notes

Chapter 4

1. For descriptions of these teachers' techniques, see S. B. Childs, ed., *Education and Specific Language Disability: The Papers of Anna Gillingham* (Pomfret, Conn.: The Orton Society, 1968); A. Gillingham and B. Stillman, *Remedial Training for Children with Specific Disability in Reading, Spelling and Penmanship* (Educators Publishing Service, 1960); M. B. Rawson, *Developmental Language Disability: Adult Accomplishments of Dyslexic Boys* (Baltimore: Johns Hopkins University Press, 1968). P. Lindamood discussed in chapter 11.

2. The most thorough discussion of the topic of rules in English orthography is presented by R. L. Venezky, *The Structure of English Orthography* (The Hague: Mouton, 1970).

3. R. C. Calfee, P. C. Lindamood, and C. H. Lindamood, "Acoustic-phonetic Skills and Reading. Kindergarten Through Twelfth Grade," *Journal of Educational Psychology* 64 (1973): 293–298.

4. C. H. Lindamood and P. C. Lindamood, *Lindamood Auditory Conceptualization Test* (Boston: Teaching Resources Corporation, 1971). The copyright for these materials has been transferred to Developmental Learning Materials, Allen, Texas.

5. For a review of syllable and phonemic segmenting studies, see I. Y. Liberman and V. Mann, "Should Reading Instruction and Remediation Vary with the Sex of the Child?" in A. Ansara et al., eds., *Sex Differences in Dyslexia* (Towson, Md.: Orton Dyslexic Society, 1981), pp. 151–67. This reference provides a review of the syllable and phonemic segmenting studies.

6. P. Tallal, "Auditory Temporal Perception, Phonics and Reading Disabilities in Children," *Brain and Language* 9 (1980):182–98. P. Tallal and M. Piercy, "Developmental Aphasia: Rate of Auditory Processing and Selective Impairment of Consonant Perception, *Neuropsychologia* 12 (1974):83–93; P. Tallal and M. Piercy, "Developmental Aphasia: The Perception of Brief Vowels and Extended Stop Consonants, *Neuropsychologia* 13 (1975):69–74.

7. P. Tallal and R. Stark, "Perceptual/Motor Profiles of Reading Impaired Children With or Without Concomitant Oral Language Deficits," *Annals of Dyslexia* 32 (1982):163–76.

8. R. Conrad and A. J. Hull, "Information, Acoustic Confusion, and Memory Span," *British Journal of Psychology* 55 (1964):429–37.

9. D. Shankweiler et al., "The Speech Code and Learning to Read," *Journal of Experimental Psychology: Human Learning and Memory* 5 (1979):531–45; V. Mann, I. Y. Liberman, and D. Shankweiler, "Children's Memory for Sentences and Word Strings in Relation to Reading Ability," *Memory and Cognition* 8 (1980):329–35.

10. A. D. Baddeley, N. Thomson, and M. Buchanan, "Word Length and the Structure of Short-term Memory," *Journal of Verbal Learning and Verbal Behavior* 14 (1975):575–89.

11. L. Bradley and P. E. Bryant, "Categorizing Sounds and Learning to Read—A Causal Connection," *Nature* 301 (1983):419–21.

12. M. B. Denckla and R. G. Rudel, "Rapid Automatized Naming (RAN): Dyslexia Differentiated from Other Disorders," *Neuropsychologia* 14 (1976):471–79.

13. C. Spring and C. Capps, "Encoding Speed, Rehearsal and Probed Recall of Dyslexic Boys," *Journal of Educational Psychology* 66 (1974):780–86.

14. Tallal and Stark, "Perceptual-Motor Profiles of Reading Impaired Children with or without Concomitant Oral Language Deficits," *Annals of Dyslexia* 32 (1982):163–76.

15. S. Farnham-Diggory and L. W. Gregg, "Short-term Memory Function in Young Readers," *Journal of Experimental Child Psychology* 19 (1975):279–98.

16. N. A. Badian, "The Prediction of Good and Poor Reading Before Kindergarten Entry: A 4-year Follow-up," *Journal of Special Education* 16 (1982):309–18.

17. Shelley Smith, "The Search for a Dominantly Inherited Form of Dyslexia." Paper presented at the 33rd annual conference of the Orton Dyslexia Society, Baltimore, Maryland, 1982. Less detailed reports of behavioral indices are S. D. Smith et al., "Specific Reading Disability: Identification of an Inherited Form Through Linkage Analysis, *Science* 219 (1983): 1345–47, and "A genetic analysis of specific reading disability" in C. L. Ludlow and J. A. Cooper, eds., *Genetic Aspects of Speech and Language Disorders* (New York: Academic Press, 1983), pp. 169–78.

Notes

18. E. O. Jarvis, "Auditory Abilities of Primary School Children," *Dissertation Abstracts International* 35A (1974):890–91.

19. M. D. Jackson and J. L. McClelland, "Processing Determinants of Reading Speed," *Journal of Experimental Psychology (General)* 108 (1979):151–81.

20. B. A. Blachman, "Are We Assessing the Linguistic Factors Critical in Early Reading?" *Annals of Dyslexia* 33 (1983):91–109.

21. Smith presented these data at the 1982 Orton Dyslexia Society annual conference.

22. N. A. Badian, "The Prediction of Good and Poor Reading before Kindergarten Entry: A 4-Year Follow-up, *Journal of Special Education* 16 (1982):309–18.

Chapter 5

1. Chimpanzee termite fishing was first reported by Jane van Lawick-Goodall, *In the Shadow of Man* (New York: Dell, 1972).

2. J. M. Ross and H. R. Simpson, "The National Survey of Health and Development: 1. Educational Attainment," *British Journal of Psychology* 41 (1971):49–61.

3. J. F. Corso, "Age and Sex Differences in Thresholds," *Journal of the Acoustic Society of America* 31 (1959):498–507. D. McGuinness, "Hearing: Individual Differences in Perceiving," *Perception* 1 (1972):465–73.

4. McGuinness, "Hearing: Individual Differences in Perceiving," *Perception* 1 (1972):465–73.

5. C. D. Elliott, "Noise Tolerance and Extraversion in Children," *British Journal of Psychology* 62 (1971):375–80.

6. D. G. Hays and J. A. Lienau, "Listening to Rock Music: Loudness Preferences and Differences in Style." Unpublished manuscript, University of Alabama, Huntsville.

7. A. R. Zaner, R. F. Levee, and R. R. Giunta, "The Development of Auditory Perceptual Skills as a Function of Maturation," *Journal of Auditory Research* 8 (1968):313–22.

8. V. Pishkin and R. Blanchard, "Auditory Concept Identification as a Function of Subject Sex and Stimulus Dimensions," *Psychonomic Science* 1 (1964):177–78.

9. V. Pishkin and J. T. Shurley, "Auditory Dimensions and Irrelevant Information in Concept Identification of Males and Females," *Perceptual and Motor Skills* 20 (1965):673–83.

10. R. Shuter reports this experiment in her book *The Psychology of Music* (London: Methuen, 1968).

11. P. Mittler and J. Ward, "The Use of the Illinois Test of Psycholinguistic Abilities on British Four-year-old Children: A Normative and Factorial Study," *British Journal of Educational Psychology* 40 (1970):43–54.

12. P. J. Mirabile et al., "Dichotic Lag Effect in Children 7–15," *Developmental Psychology* 14 (1978):277–85.

13. C. McCoy, "Experimental Study of Hearing in the Aged as Measured by Pure Tones, Word Discrimination and the SSW," *Dissertation Abstracts International* 38 (1978):4719.

14. C. Knox and D. Kimura, "Cerebral Processing of Nonverbal Sounds in Boys and Girls," *Neuropsychologia* 8 (1970):227–37.

15. The sex differences in strength and speed are reviewed in D. Monagan, "The Failure of Coed Sports," *Psychology Today* (March 1983):58–63.

16. The distinctions between the gross-motor (extrapyramidal system) and fine-motor (pyramidal) systems are covered in S. Grossman, *A Textbook of Physiological Psychology* (New York: John Wiley & Sons, 1967).

17. M. Annett, "The Growth of Manual Preference and Speech," *British Journal of Psychology* 61 (1970):545–58.

18. See M. B. Denckla, "Development of Speeds in Repetitive and Successive Finger-movements in Normal Children," *Developmental Medicine and Child Neurology* 15 (1973): 635–45, and a follow-up article, "Development of Motor Co-ordination in Normal Children, *Developmental Medicine and Child Neurology* 16 (1974):729–41.

Notes

19. The study on men and women novice dancers was carried out by my students at the University of California at Santa Cruz.

20. D. W. Gaffney, "Assessing Receptive Language Skills of Five- to Seven-year-old Deaf Children," *Dissertation Abstracts International* 38 (1977):1665–66.

21. For a most entertaining account of an ape learning sign language, see F. Patterson and E. Linden, *The Education of Koko* (New York: Holt, Rinehart and Winston, 1981).

22. The four-year research project on Genie is presented by S. Curtiss, et al., "The Linguistic Development of Genie," *Language* 50 (1974):544.

23. See T. Moore, "Language and Intelligence: A Longitudinal Study of the First 8 Years," *Human Development* 10 (1967):88–106, for information on the British sample. A longitudinal study on American children was carried out by J. Cameron, N. Livson, and N. Bayley and reported in "Infant Vocalizations and Their Relationship to Mature Intelligence, *Science* 157 (1967):331–32.

24. E. T. Paynter and N. A. Petty, "Articulatory Sound Acquisition of Two-year-old Children," *Perceptual and Motor Skills* 39 (1974):1079–85.

25. Several large surveys on speech development in children have been carried out, showing females consistently accelerated and exhibiting far less speech pathology than males over all ages. These data can be found in E. L. Eagles et al., *Hearing Sensitivity and Related Factors in Children* (Pittsburgh: University of Pennsylvania Press, 1963); F. M. Hull et al., "The National Speech and Hearing Survey: Preliminary Results," *ASHA* 3 (1971): 501–9; T. T. S. Ingram, "Speech Disorders in Childhood," in E. H. Lenneberg and E. Lenneberg, eds., *Foundations of Language Development* (New York: Academic Press, 1975).

26. M. Potasova found that five-year-old girls were well ahead of boys on three of four language measures—articulation, mean length of utterance, grammar, and word types. See "Speech Development in Collectively Reared Preschool Children," *Psychologia a Patopsychologia Dietata* 10 (1975):43–60. In "Sex Differences in Elicited Color Lexicon Size," *Perceptual and Motor Skills* 47 (1978):77–78, L. L. Thomas, A. T. Curtis, and R. Bolton found Nepalese women more verbally fluent than the men in a test of color naming.

27. For a description of the types of language anomalies exhibited by men in various countries of the world, see B. W. Eakins and R. G. Eakins, *Sex Differences in Human Communication* (Boston: Houghton Mifflin, 1978).

28. C. Fraser and N. Roberts, "Mother's Speech to Children of Four Different Ages," *Journal of Psycholinguistic Research* 4 (1975):9–16; and J. R. Phillips, "Syntax and Vocabulary of Mother's Speech to Young Children: Age and Sex Comparisons," *Child Development* 44 (1973):182–85.

29. Potasova's "Speech Development in Collectively Reared Preschool Children," *Psychologia a Patopsychologia Dietata* 10 (1975):43–60.

30. M. Lewis, "State as an Infant-environment Interaction: An Analysis of Mother-infant Interaction as a Function of Sex," *Merrill-Palmer Quarterly* 18 (1972):95–121.

31. J. H. Hittelman and R. Dickes, "Sex Differences in Neonatal Eye Contact Time," *Merrill Palmer Quarterly* 25 (1979):171–84. This finding was replicated by J. H. Hittelman et al., "Sex Differences in Neonatal Eye Contact Time. A Relication," Paper presented at the American Psychological Association Meeting, Montreal, 1980. J. Hittelman and associates observed the same sex difference at six weeks and no difference in how mothers responded to male or female infants in "Sex Differences in Eye-contact and Mother-infant Interaction," Paper presented to the American Psychological Association Meeting, Washington, D.C., 1982.

32. A. Bentley, *Monotones* (London: Novello, 1968); and E. Roberts, "Poor Pitch Singing," Unpublished doctoral thesis (Liverpool: University of Liverpool, 1972).

33. P. K. Smith and K. Connolly, "Patterns of Play and Social Interaction in Preschool Children," in N. Blurton-Jones, ed., *Ethological Studies of Child Behaviour* (Cambridge: Cambridge University Press, 1972).

34. R. L. Majeres, "Sex Differences in Clerical Speed. Perceptual Encoding Versus Verbal Encoding," *Memory and Cognition* 5 (1977):468–76.

35. S. N. Decker and J. C. DeFries, "Cognitive Abilities in Families with Reading Disabled Children," *Journal of Learning Disabilities* 13 (1980):517–22.

36. D. McGuinness and A. Olson, "Sex Differences in Incidental Recall and Reminiscence for Verbal and Visual Material," manuscript in preparation.

37. D. Kimura, "Acquisition of a Motor Skill After Left-hemisphere Damage," *Brain* 100 (1977):527–42. Kimura borrows from a theory of neurologist Hugo Liepmann to help explain her data on left-hemisphere–lesioned patients and their inability to execute fluent sequential movement.

38. P. K. Kuhl and A. N. Meltzoff, "The Bimodal Perception of Speech in Infancy," *Science* 218 (1982):1138–40.

39. K. A. Gurucharri, "Haptic Performance and First-grade Reading Achievement," *Dissertation Abstracts International* 35A (1974):887–88.

40. G. Rae, "Auditory-visual Integration, Sex and Reading Ability," *Perceptual and Motor Skills* 45 (1977):826.

41. Angela Bateson's study was carried out as a senior thesis project for honors in a Bachelor of Science degree at Hatfield Polytechnic, Hatfield, England.

42. D. McGuinness and A. Courtney, "Sex Differences in Visual and Phonetic Search," *Journal of Mental Imagery* 7 (1983):95–104.

Chapter 6

1. For a description of the psychological deficits in frontal lobe patients, see A. R. Luria, *Higher Cortical Functions in Man* (New York: Basic Books, 1966), chapter 5, pp. 218–92.

2. The mechanism by which memories become distributed in the brain is explored in K. H. Pribram, *Languages of the Brain* (New York: Brandon House, 1971), pp. 140–66.

3. R. Netsell, "The Acquisition of Speech Motor Control: A Perspective with Directions for Research," in R. Stark, ed., *Language Behavior and Early Childhood* (Amsterdam: Elsevier, 1981).

4. Personal communication.

5. D. Kimura, "Acquisition of a Motor Skill After Left-hemisphere Brain Damage," *Brain* 100 (1977):527–42.

6. The complete account of Gordon's research on aphasia can be found in W. P. Gordon, "Memory Disorders in Aphasia. 1. Auditory Immediate Recall," *Neuropsychologia* 21 (1983): 325–39, and "Neuropsychological Assessment of Aphasia," in J. Darby, ed., *Speech and Language Evaluation in Neurology: Adult Disorders* (in press).

7. D. Kimura, "Sex Differences in Cerebral Organization of Speech and Praxic Functions," *Canadian Journal of Psychology* 37 (1983):19–35.

8. D. Kimura and R. A. Harshman, "Sex Differences in Brain Organization for Verbal and Nonverbal Functions," in G. J. De Vries et al., eds., *Progress in Brain Research* 61 (Amsterdam: Elsevier Science Publishers, 1984), pp. 423–41.

9. G. A. Ojemann, "Brain Organization for Language from the Perspective of Electrical Stimulation," *Behavioral and Brain Sciences* 6 (1983):189–230.

10. C. A. Mateer, S. B. Polen, and G. A. Ojemann, "Sexual Variation in Cortical Localization of Naming as Determined by Stimulation Mapping," *Behavioral and Brain Sciences* 5 (1982):310–11.

11. The most extensive published review of this material is A. Galaburda, "Developmental Dyslexia: Current Anatomical Research," *Annals of Dyslexia* 33 (1983):41–54. In a personal communication to me, the late N. Geschwind, Professor of Neurology at Harvard University, stated that four dyslexic brains investigated by Galaburda have developmental anomalies in regions of the left hemisphere that involve abnormal migrations of cells. However, there is no report on the degree of speech pathology of these individuals, nor whether they suffered from reading-related disorders, such as phonemic discrimination deficits. In a personal communication S. Witelson of the Department of Anatomy at McMaster University reports that in an investigation of a dyslexic brain in her laboratory, these anomalies were not found, although the splenium of the corpus callosum was abnormally small.

12. C. de Lacoste-Utamsing and R. Holloway, "Sexual Dimorphism in the Corpus Callosum," *Science* 216 (1982):1431–32.

Notes

13. S. Witelson studied forty-three brains and found no evidence to support sex differences in the anatomy of the corpus callosum (personal communication). A similarly negative finding on thirty brains was reported to me by J. Levy of the University of Chicago.

14. J. R. Kershner, "Lateralization in Normal 6-year-olds as Related to Later Reading Disability," *Developmental Psychobiology* 11 (1978):309–18.

15. M. Annett, "The Right Shift Theory of Handedness and Developmental Language Problems," *Bulletin of the Orton Society* 31 (1981):103–21.

16. S. N. Decker and J. C. DeFries, "Cognitive Abilities in Families with Reading Disabled Children," *Journal of Learning Disabilities* 13 (1980):517–22.

17. J. C. DeFries and S. N. Decker, "Genetic Aspects of Reading Disability: A Family Study," in R. N. Malatesha and P. G. Aaron, eds., *Reading Disorders: Varieties and Treatments* (New York: Academic Press, 1982).

18. S. Smith, "The Search for a Dominantly Inherited Form of Dyslexia." Paper presented at the 33rd annual conference of the Orton Dyslexia Society, Baltimore, Maryland, 1982. See also S. D. Smith et al., "Specific Reading Disability: Identification of an Inherited Form Through Linkage Analysis," *Science* 219 (1983):1345–47.

19. The sex ratios in special schools and clinical populations are higher than in the remedial reading classes. Evidence on these ratios is provided by J. M. Finucci and B. Childs, "Are There Really More Dyslexic Boys Than Girls?" in A. Ansara et al., eds., *Sex Differences in Dyslexia* (Towson, Md.: Orton Dyslexia Society, 1981), pp. 1–9. See also W. Yule and M. Rutter, "Educational Aspects of Childhood Maladjustment: Some Epidemiological Findings," *British Journal of Psychology* 38 (1968):7–13. Pat Lindamood (personal communication) finds the sex ratio in her clinic to be the same as in the population at large, three to one.

20. S. R. Asher and R. A. Markell, "Sex Differences in Comprehension of High and Low Interest Reading Material," *Journal of Educational Psychology* 66 (1974):680–87.

21. E. H. Rowell, "Do Elementary Students Read Better Orally or Silently?" *Reading Teacher* 29 (1976):367–70.

22. F. J. Gies et al., "Effects of Organizational Climate and Sex on the Language Arts Achievement of Disadvantaged Sixth Graders," *Journal of Education Research* 67 (1973): 177–81.

23. S. Hesselholdt and G. Aggerholm-Madsen, "Process and Product in the Marbleboard Test. The Biosocial Interaction and Reading Ability," *Skolepsykologi* 11 (1974):277–303.

24. W. Yule and M. Rutter, "Educational Aspects of Childhood Maladjustment: Some Epidemiological Findings," *British Journal of Psychology* 38 (1968):7–13.

25. I. J. Lanthier and T. E. Deiker, "Achievement Scores of Emotionally Disturbed Adolescents and Parents' Educational Level," *Child Study Journal* 4 (1974):163–68.

26. S. Cotler and R. J. Palmer, "Social Reinforcement, Individual Difference Factors, and the Reading Performance of Elementary School Children," *Journal of Personality and Social Psychology* 18 (1971):97–104.

27. V. G. Cicirelli, "Sibling Constellation, Creativity, I.Q. and Academic Achievement," *Child Development* 38 (1967):481–90.

Chapter 7

1. J. Steeves, "Multi-sensory Math," Paper presented at the 33rd annual conference of The Orton Dyslexia Society, Baltimore, Maryland, 1982.

2. R. R. Skemp, *The Psychology of Learning Mathematics* (Harmondsworth: Penguin Books, 1971).

3. P. S. Davidson, "Neuropsychological Perspective of Mathematics Learning." Paper presented at the 33rd annual conference of The Orton Dyslexic Society, Baltimore, Maryland, 1982.

Notes

4. Davidson and Marolda have not published their data except as a progress report to the National Institute of Education (grant #NIE-G-79-0089).

5. J. M. Ross and H. R. Simpson, "The National Survey of Health and Development: 1. Educational Attainment," *British Journal of Psychology* 41 (1971):49–61.

6. T. L. Hilton and G. W. Berglund, "Sex Differences in Mathematics Achievement—A Longitudinal Study," *Journal of Education Research* 67 (1974):231–37.

7. C. P. Benbow and J. C. Stanley, "Sex Differences in Mathematical Reasoning Ability: More Facts," *Science* 22 (1983):1029–31. More extensive reports of their fourteen-year project are found in C. P. Benbow and J. S. Stanley, "Consequences in High School and College of Sex Differences in Mathematical Reasoning Ability: A Longitudinal Perspective," *American Educational Research Journal* 19 (1982):598–622; C. P. Benbow and R. M. Benbow, "Biological Correlates of High Mathematical Reasoning Ability," in G. J. De Vries et al., eds., *Progress in Brain Research* 61 (Amsterdam: Elsevier, 1984). An extensive review of the earlier 1972–1974 project is provided in J. C. Stanley, D. P. Keating, and L. N. Fox, eds., *Mathematical Talent* (Baltimore: Johns Hopkins University Press, 1974).

8. C. P. Benbow and J. C. Stanley, "Sex Differences in Mathematical Ability: Fact or Artifact?" *Science* 210 (1980):1262–64.

9. E. Fennema and J. Sherman, "Sex-related Differences in Mathematics Achievement, Spatial Visualization and Affective Factors," *American Educational Research Journal* 14 (1977):51–71.

10. Ibid., pp. 66, 67.

11. J. Sherman and E. Fennema, "The Study of Mathematics by High School Girls and Boys: Related Variables," *American Educational Research Journal* 14 (1977):159–68.

12. J. Sherman, "Mathematics, Spatial Visualization and Related Factors: Changes in Girls and Boys, Grades 8–11," *Journal of Educational Psychology* 72 (1980):476–82.

13. J. Sherman, "Mathematics, the Critical Filter: A Look at Some Residues," *Psychology of Women Quarterly* 6 (1982):428–49. Also presented at the American Psychological Association in New York, 1979.

14. J. A. Stallings, "Comparison of Men's and Women's Behaviors in High School Math Classes," Paper presented to the American Psychological Association, New York, 1979. Also published as a research report from the Stanford Research Institute.

15. A. Lantz, "Synthesis of Evidence and Theoretical Explanations of the Underrepresentation of Women in Science," National Science Foundation Project #SED 80-20854, 1981.

16. L. H. Fox and S. J. Cohn, "Sex Differences in the Development of Precocious Mathematical Talent," in L. H. Fox, L. Brody, and D. Tobin, eds., *Women and the Mathematical Mystique* (Baltimore: Johns Hopkins University Press, 1980), pp. 94–111.

Chapter 8

1. E. Fennema and J. Sherman, "Sex-related Differences in Mathematics Achievement, Spatial Visualization and Affective Factors," *American Educational Research Journal* 14 (1977):51–71.

2. J. A. Stallings, "Comparison of Men's and Women's Behaviors in High School Math Classes," Paper presented at the American Psychological Association, New York, 1979. (Also reprinted as a bulletin of the Stanford Research Institute, 1979.)

3. M. K. Barakat, "A Factorial Study of Mathematical Abilities," *British Journal of Psychology* (Statistical Section) 4 (1951):137–56.

4. Differential Aptitude Test norms are published in G. K. Bennett, H. G. Seashore, and A. G. Wesman, *Differential Aptitude Tests* (New York: The Psychological Corporation, 1959).

5. Ibid.

6. D. McGuinness and T. E. Bartell, "Lateral Asymmetry: Hard or Simple Minded?" *Neuropsychologia* 20 (1982):629–39; D. McGuinness and L. A. Brabyn, "In Pursuit of Visuo-spatial Ability," Part 1: Visual Systems *Journal of Mental Imagery* 8 (1984):1–12.

7. A comprehensive description of Piaget's research and model of child development can

Notes

be found in J. H. Flavell, *The Developmental Psychology of Jean Piaget* (Princeton, N.J.: D. Van Nostrand, 1963).

8. Young infants are found to process information about objects that are three-dimensional but not two-dimensional as shown by T. G. R. Bower, "The Object in the World of the Infant," *Scientific American* 225 (1971):30–38. Infants begin to distinguish between three-dimensional rubber faces at around four to six months, before they can tell the difference between two-dimensional drawings or photographs of faces. Females are advanced relative to males by about two months. J. F. Fagan III, "Infant's Recognition Memory for Faces," *Journal of Experimental Child Psychology* 14 (1972):453–76.

9. D. McGuinness and C. Morley, "Sex Differences in 2-dimensional and 3-dimensional Problem Solving in Pre-school Children," in preparation.

10. G. Jahoda, "On the Nature of Difficulties in Spatial-perceptual Tasks: Ethnic and Sex Differences," *British Journal of Psychology* 70 (1979):351–63. G. Jahoda, "Sex and Ethnic Differences on a Spatial-Perceptual Task: Some Hypotheses Tested," *British Journal of Psychology* 71 (1980):425–31.

11. I. R. Brooks, "Cognitive Ability Assessment with Two New Zealand Ethnic Groups," *Journal of Cross Cultural Psychology* 7 (1976):347–56.

12. J. D. C. Shea and G. Yerua, "Conservation in Community School Children in Papua New Guinea," *International Journal of Psychology* 15 (1980):11–25.

13. L. J. Harris, "Sex Differences in Spatial Ability: Possible Environmental, Genetic and Neurological Factors," in M. Kinsbourne, ed., *Hemisphere Asymmetries of Function* (Cambridge: Cambridge University Press, 1978).

14. E. R. Geiringer and J. S. Hyde, "Sex Differences on Piaget's Water-level Task: Spatial Ability Incognito," *Perceptual and Motor Skills* 42 (1976):1323–28. The authors found that Piaget's task was highly correlated to the spatial subtest of the Primary Mental Abilities test, accounting for 69 percent of the variance in men's scores and 94 percent in women's.

15. L. S. Liben and S. L. Golbeck, "Performance on Piagetian Horizontality and Verticality Tasks: Sex-related Differences in Knowledge of Relevant Physical Phenomena," *Developmental Psychology* 30 (1984):595–606.

16. S. Heywood and K. Chessell, "Expanding angles?" *Perception* 6 (1977):571–82.

17. C. Porac, S. Coren, J. S. Girgus, and M. Verde, "Visual-geometric Illusions: Unisexed Phenomena," *Perception* 8 (1979):401–12.

18. E. S. Barratt, "The Space-visualization Factors Related to Temperamental Traits," *Journal of Psychology* 39 (1955):279–87.

19. M. A. Just and P. A. Carpenter, "Cognitive Coordinate Systems: Accounts of Mental Rotation and Individual Differences in Spatial Ability," *Psychological Review* 92 (1985):137–72.

20. L. L. Thurstone, "Some Primary Abilities in Visual Thinking," *Psychometric Laboratory Report* 5 (Chicago: Chicago University Press, 1950).

21. Harris, "Sex Differences in Spatial Ability."

22. D. McGuinness and J. Sparks, "Cognitive Style and Cognitive Maps: Sex Differences in Representations of a Familiar Terrain," *Journal of Mental Imagery* 7 (1983):91–100.

23. T. W. Cook and A. H. Shephard, "Performance on Several Control-display Relationships as a Function of Age and Sex," *Perceptual and Motor Skills* 8 (1958):339–45; A. H. Shephard, D. S. Abbey, and M. Humphries, "Age and Sex in Relation to Perceptual-motor Performance on Several Control Display Relations on the TCC," *Perceptual and Motor Skills* 14 (1962): 103–18.

24. C. E. Noble, B. L. Baker, and T. A. Jones, "Age and Sex Parameters in Psychomotor Learning," *Perceptual and Motor Skills* 19 (1964):934–45; H. Fairweather and S. J. Hutt, "Sex Differences in a Perceptual Motor Skill in Children," in C. Ounsted and D. C. Taylor, eds., *Gender Differences: Their Ontogeny and Significance* (Edinburgh: Churchill Livingstone, 1972).

25. L. J. Harris, "Sex Differences in Spatial Ability: Possible Environmental, Genetic, and Neurological Factors," in M. Kinsbourne, ed., *Hemisphere Asymmetries of Function* (Cambridge: Cambridge University Press, 1978).

26. C. S. Rebert, D. W. Low, and F. Larsen, "Differential Hemisphere Activation During

Complex Visuomotor Performance: Alpha Trends and Theta," *Biological Psychology* (in press).

27. A. Burg, "Visual Acuity as Measured by Dynamic and Static Tests: A Comparative Evaluation," *Journal of Applied Psychology* 50 (1966):460–66.

28. S. G. Vandenberg and A. R. Kuse, "Spatial Ability: A Critical Review of the Sex-linked Major Gene Hypothesis," in M. A. Wittig and A. C. Petersen, *Sex-Related Differences In Cognitive Functioning* (New York: Academic Press, 1979), pp. 67–95.

29. S. D. Smith et al., "Specific Reading Disability: Identification of an Inherited Form Through Linkage Analysis," *Science* 219 (1983):1345–47. See also S. D. Smith et al., "A Genetic Analysis of Specific Reading Disability," in C. L. Ludlow and J. A. Cooper, eds., *Genetic Aspects of Speech and Language Disorders* (New York: Academic Press, 1983), pp. 169–78.

30. K. J. Steeves, "Memory as a Factor in the Computational Efficiency of Dyslexic Children with High Abstract Reasoning Ability," *Annals of Dyslexia* 33 (1983):141–52.

31. M. C. Diamond, G. A. Dowling, and R. E. Johnson, "Morphological Cerebral Cortical Asymmetry in Male and Female Rats," *Experimental Neurology* 71 (1981):261–68.

32. Left-hemisphere electroencephalogram activation has been observed for complex three-dimensional problem solving, as reported by R. Ornstein et al., "Differential Right Hemisphere Engagement in Visuospatial Tasks," *Neuropsychologia* 18 (1980):49–64. See also McGuinness and Bartell, "Lateral Asymmetry." We found an overwhelming accuracy in *left*-hemisphere processing for the capacity to rotate both two- and three-dimensional shapes.

33. M. Moskovitch presents a thorough review of the problems of attribution of function to the left or right hemispheres in "Information Processing and the Cerebral Hemispheres," in M. S. Gazzaniga, ed., *Handbook of Behavioral Neurology*, vol. 2 (New York: Plenum Press, 1979), pp. 379–446. Indications of right-hemisphere superiority in rapid two-dimensional pattern analysis has been found in a number of studies, such as G. Cohen, "Hemispheric Differences in a Letter Classification Task," *Perception and Psychophysics* 108 (1972):337–45. Some of this evidence is reviewed in M. I. Posner, "Chronometric Analysis of Classification," *Psychological Review* 74 (1967): 392–409.

34. J. E. LeDoux, "Neuroevolutionary Mechanisms of Cerebral Asymmetry in Man," *Brain, Behavior and Evolution* 20 (1982):197–213.

35. See B. Milner, "Hemispheric Specialization: Scope and Limits," in F. O. Schmitt and F. G. Worden, eds., *The Neurosciences: Third Study Program* (Cambridge, Mass.: MIT Press, 1974), pp. 75–89. Data on frontal involvement in spatial ability are reviewed in D. McGuinness and K. H. Pribram, "The Origins of Sensory Bias in the Development of Gender Differences in Perception and Cognition," in M. Bortner, ed., *Cognitive Growth and Development* (New York: Brunner/Mazel, 1978), pp. 3–56.

36. The most comprehensive summary of sex differences in brain/behavior relationships can be found in table 7 of McGuinness and Pribram, "Origins of Sensory Bias." An extensive review of sex differences in right- and left-hemisphere activation of the electroencephalogram shows no sex difference on a number of verbal and spatial tasks for the side of activation. D. Galin et al., "Sex and Handedness Differences in EEG Measures of Hemispheric Specialization," *Brain and Language* 16 (1982):19–55.

37. D. Kimura also has evidence for frontal involvement in spatial ability for both men and women, especially the fact that women with lesions to the left frontal region have enormous deficits in solving "block design" problems. Males are considerably more handicapped by right-hemisphere lesions in spatial tasks than females, but are also handicapped by posterior *left*-hemisphere lesions in these same tasks. D. Kimura, "Sex Differences in Cerebral Organization for Speech and Praxic Functions," *Canadian Journal of Psychology* 37 (1983):19–35; D. Kimura and R. A. Harshman, "Sex Differences in Brain Organization for Verbal and Nonverbal Functions," in G. J. De Vries et al., eds., *Progress in Brain Research* 61 (Amsterdam: Elsevier, 1984). pp. 423–41.

38. D. McGuinness, "Away from Unisex Psychology: Individual Differences in Visual Perception," *Perception* 5 (1976):279–94; L. B. Brabyn and D. McGuinness, "Gender Differences in Response to Spatial Frequency and Stimulus Orientation," *Perception and*

Notes

Psychophysics 26 (1979):319–24. For a more extensive review see McGuinness and Pribram, "Origins of Sensory Bias."

39. D. McGuinness and L. A. Brabyn, "In Search of Visuo-spatial Ability, Part 1: Visual Systems," *Journal of Mental Imagery,* 8 (1984):1–12.

40. D. McGuinness and L. McLaughlin, "An Investigation of Sex Differences in Visual Recognition and Recall," *Journal of Mental Imagery* 6 (1982): 203–12.

41. D. McGuinness and A. Olson, "Sex Differences in Incidental Recall and Reminiscence for Verbal and Visual Material," in preparation.

42. The impact of sex hormones on the enhancement of rough and tumble play has been demonstrated in studies of children exposed to sex hormones in utero. A. A. Ehrhardt and S. W. Baker, "Fetal Androgens, Human Central Nervous Systems Differentiation, and Behavior Sex Differences," and S. W. Baker and A. A. Ehrhardt, "Prenatal Androgen, Intelligence and Cognitive Sex Differences," in R. C. Friedman, R. M. Richart, and R. L. Vande Wiele, eds., *Sex Differences in Behavior* (New York: John Wiley & Sons, 1974), pp. 33–51 and pp. 53–76.

43. C. Hutt, "Curiosity in Young Children," *Science Journal* 6 (1970):68–72.

44. E. Greenberger, J. O'Connor, and A. Sorensen, "Personality, Cognitive and Academic Correlates of Problem-solving Ability," *Developmental Psychology* 4 (1971):416–24; S. Kreitler, H. Kreitler, and E. Zigler, "Cognitive Orientation and Curiosity," *British Journal of Psychology* 65 (1974):43–52.

45. J. Sherman, "Problem of Sex Differences in Space Perception and Aspects of Intellectual Functioning," *Psychological Review* 74 (1967):290–99.

46. E. W. Goodenough, "Interest in Persons as an Aspect of Sex Differences in the Early Years," *Genetic Psychological Monographs* 55 (1957):287–323.

47. N. D. Feshbach and M. A. Hoffman, "Sex Differences in Children's Reports of Emotion Arousing Situations," Paper presented at the Western Psychological Association, San Francisco, 1978.

48. D. McGuinness and J. Symonds, "Sex Differences in Choice Behavior: The Object-person Dimension," *Perception* 6 (1977):691–94. This experiment has been replicated on an Australian population by S. Jobson and J. S. Watson, "Sex and Age Differences in Choice Behavior: The Object-person Dimension," *Perception* (in press). They found that the sex difference diminished with age. Men above thirty-five years were less likely to prefer objects to people.

Chapter 9

1. K. D. O'Leary, D. Vivian, and C. Cornoldi, "Assessment and Treatment of 'hyperactivity' in Italy and the United States," *Journal of Clinical Child Psychology* 13 (1984):56–60.

2. E. Taylor and S. Sandberg, "Hyperactive Behavior in English Schoolchildren: A Questionnaire Survey," *Journal of Abnormal Child Psychology* 12 (1984): 143–55.

3. A review of the proportion of learning disabilities in hyperactive populations is provided by D. Safer and R. Allen, *Hyperactive Children: Diagnosis and Management* (Baltimore: University Park Press, 1976). See also N. Lambert and J. Sandoval, "The Prevalence of Learning Disabilities in a Sample of Children Considered Hyperactive," *Journal of Abnormal Child Psychology* 8 (1980):33–50.

4. For a review of epidemiological research, see K. D. O'Leary, "Pills or Skills for Hyperactive Children," *Journal of Applied Behavioral Analysis* 13 (1980):191–204. Also interesting is the finding for parent/teacher ratings on the Conners Hyperactivity Scale, given to 605 children (seven to fifteen years) in Israel. One hundred sixty-nine children (28 percent) were found to be "hyperactive." M. Malka, "Diagnostic Application of the Conners Abbreviated Symptom Questionnaire," *Journal of Clinical Child Psychology* 12 (1983):3555–57. It might be noted that as 85 percent of these "hyperactive" children are likely to be boys, 48 percent of all schoolboys in Israel are diagnosed as hyperactive.

5. Department of Health, Education and Welfare, Office of Child Development, *Report at the Conference on the Use of Stimulant Drugs in the Treatment of Behaviorally Disturbed*

Young School Children (Washington, D.C.: U.S. Government Printing Office, January 1971).

6. P. Schrag and D. Divoky, *The Myth of the Hyperactive Child* (New York: Dell Publishing Co., 1975).

7. D. G. Renshaw, *The Hyperactive Child* (Boston: Little, Brown and Company, 1974); D. P. Cantwell, ed., *The Hyperactive Child* (New York: Spectrum, 1975); D. M. Ross and S. A. Ross, *Hyperactivity: Current Issues, Research, and Theory* (New York: John Wiley & Sons, 1982); C. K. Whalen and B. Henker, "Psychostimulants and Children: A Review and Analysis," *Psychological Review* 83 (1976):1113–30.

8. K. D. O'Leary, "Pills or Skills for Hyperactive Children," *Journal of Applied Behavioral Analysis* 13 (1980):191–204.

9. S. Chess, "Diagnosis and Treatment of The Hyperactive Child," *New York State Journal of Medicine* 60 (1960):2379–85; P. Conrad, *Identifying Hyperactive Children* (Lexington, Mass.: D.C. Heath and Co., 1976); Ross and Ross, *Hyperactivity*.

10. See *Developmental Psychology* 20 #4 (1984) for the following articles: J. L. Jacobson et al., "Prenatal Exposure to an Environmental Toxin: A Test of the Multiple Effects Model," pp. 522–32; A. P. Streissguth et al., "Intrauterine Alcohol and Nicotine Exposure: Attention and Reaction Time in 4-year-old Children," pp. 533–541; S. J. Shaheen, "Neuromaturation and Behavior Development: The Case of Childhood Lead Poisoning," pp. 542–550.

11. J. P. Harley reviews these studies in "Dietary Treatment in Behavioral Disorders," in B. W. Camp, ed., *Advances in Behavioral Pediatrics* (Greenwich, Conn.: JAI Press, 1980).

12. C. Bradley, "The Behavior of Children Receiving Benzedrine," *American Journal of Psychiatry* 94 (1937):579–85.

13. M. W. Laufer, E. Denhoff, and G. Solomons, "Hyperkinetic Impulse Disorder in Children's Behavior Problems," *Psychosomatic Medicine* 19 (1957):38–49.

14. P. Conrad, *Identifying Hyperactive Children*, (Lexington, Mass.: D.C. Heath and Co., 1976).

15. S. D. Clements, "Task Force One: Minimal Brain Dysfunction in Children," *National Institute of Neurological Diseases and Blindness*, Monograph 3 (Washington, D.C.: U.S. Department of Health, Education and Welfare, 1966).

16. D. G. Renshaw, *The Hyperactive Child*, (Boston: Little, Brown and Company, 1974).

17. M. A. Stewart, "The Hyperactive Child Syndrome," *American Journal of Orthopsychiatry* 36 (1966):861–67.

18. J. S. Werry published the Werry-Weiss-Peters Scale in "Developmental Hyperactivity," *Pediatric Clinics of North America* 15 (1968):581–99.

19. D. M. Ross and S. A. Ross, *Hyperactivity: Current Issues, Research, and Theory* (New York: Wiley, 1982).

20. M. A. Stewart, B. T. Thach, and M. R. Freidin, "Accidental Poisoning and the Hyperactive Child Syndrome," *Diseases of the Nervous System* 31 (1970):403–07.

21. C. H. Goyette, C. K. Conners, and R. F. Ulrich, "Normative Data on Revised Conners' Parent and Teacher Rating Scales," *Journal of Abnormal Child Psychology* 6 (1978):221–36.

22. *Diagnostic and Statistical Manual of Mental Disorders*, 3rd ed. [DSM-III] (Washington, D.C.: American Psychiatric Association, 1980).

23. R. A. Rubenstein and R. T. Brown, "An Evaluation of the Validity of the Diagnostic Category of Attention Deficit Disorder," *American Journal of Orthopsychiatry* 54 (1984):398–414.

24. D. McGuinness and C. Morley, "Spontaneous Play Behavior in Preschool Boys and Girls" (in preparation).

25. J. E. Goggin reports findings very similar to my own on sex differences in the number of changes from one activity to another. Furthermore, he found an extremely high correlation between these shifts and eleven measures of attention seeking and dependency behavior for boys *only*. By contrast, there were no significant correlations for girls. J. E. Goggin, "Sex Differences in the Activity Level of Preschool Children as a Possible Precursor of Hyperactivity," *Journal of Genetic Psychology* 127 (1975):75–81.

26. R. A. Barkley and C. E. Cunningham, "Do Stimulant Drugs Improve the Academic Performance of Hyperkinetic Children?" *Clinical Pediatrics* 17 (1978):85–92.

Notes

Chapter 10

1. There has been an extended controversy concerning whether hyperactive children are indeed more active than other children. In an early review of studies edited by D. Cantwell (*The Hyperactive Child*, New York: Spectrum, 1975), he concludes that the results are equivocal. The extreme importance of situational factors is emphasized by C. K. Whalen and B. Henker, "Psychostimulants and Children: A Review and Analysis," *Psychological Review* 83 (1976):1113–30. Recently M. Solanto argued that there have been few objective measurements of activity levels. Comparing six studies using stabilimeters or actometers, hyperactive children were found to be more active. M. V. Solanto, "Neuropharmacological Basis of Stimulant Drug Action in Attention Deficit Disorder with Hyperactivity: A Review and Synthesis," *Psychological Bulletin* 95 (1984):387–409.

2. R. G. Jacob, K. D. O'Leary, and C. Rosenblad, "Formal and Informal Classroom Settings: Effects on Hyperactivity," *Journal of Abnormal Child Psychology* 6 (1978):47–59.

3. D. M. Ross and S. A. Ross, *Hyperactivity: Current Issues, Research, and Theory* (New York: John Wiley & Sons, 1982).

4. J. L. Rapoport, "Dextroamphetamine: Cognitive and Behavioral Effects in Normal Prepubertal Boys," *Science* 199 (1978):560–63.

5. J. Schulman, J. Kasper, and F. Throne, *Brain Damage and Behavior: A Clinical-Experimental Study* (Springfield, Ill.: Charles C Thomas, 1965).

6. See M. Schleifer et al., "Hyperactivity in Pre-schoolers and the Effect of Methylphenidate," *American Journal of Orthopsychiatry* 45 (1975):38–50; J. L. Rapoport and M. Benoit, "The Relation of Direct Home Observation to the Clinical Evaluation of Hyperactive School-age Boys," *Journal of Child Psychology and Psychiatry* 16 (1975):141–47.

7. D. P. Cantwell, ed., *The Hyperactive Child* (New York: Spectrum, 1975); D. M. Ross and S. A. Ross, *Hyperactivity: Current Issues, Research, and Theory* (New York: John Wiley & Sons, 1982).

8. S. J. Hutt and C. Hutt, "Hyperactivity in a Group of Epileptic (and Some Non-epileptic) Brain-damaged Children," *Epilepsia* 5 (1964):334–51.

9. P. Reynolds, personal communication.

10. I. H. Pearse and L. H. Crocker, *The Peckham Experiment* (London: Allen and Unwin, 1943).

11. S. B. Campbell, V. I. Douglas, and G. Morgenstern, "Cognitive Styles in Hyperactive Children and the Effect of Methylphenidate," *Journal of Child Psychology and Psychiatry* 12 (1971):55–67; N. J. Cohen, V. I. Douglas, and G. Morgenstern, "The Effect of Methylphenidate on Attentive Behavior and Autonomic Activity in Hyperactive Children," *Psychopharmacologia* 22 (1971):282–94.

12. S. Kroener, "Concept Attainment in Normal and Hyperactive Boys as a Function of Stimulus Complexity and Type of Instruction," *Dissertation Abstract International* 36 (1975): 1913.

13. S. B. Campbell, "Mother-child Interaction in Reflective, Impulsive and Hyperactive Children," *Developmental Psychology* 8 (1973):341–49.

14. D. H. Sykes, V. I. Douglas, and G. Morgenstern, "Sustained Attention in Hyperactive Children," *Journal of Child Psychology and Psychiatry* 14 (1973):213–21.

15. For reaction time results see N. J. Cohen and V. I. Douglas, "Characteristics of the Orienting Response in Hyperactive and Normal Children," *Psychophysiology* 9 (1972):238–45; R. A. Dykman, et al., "Specific Learning Disabilities: An Attentional Deficit Syndrome," in H. R. Mykelbust, ed., *Progress in Learning Disabilities*, vol. 2 (New York: Grune & Stratton, 1971); E. Grünewald-Zuberbier, G. Grünewald, and A. Rasche, "Hyperactive Behavior and EEG Arousal Reactions in Children," *Electroencephalography and Clinical Neurophysiology* 38 (1975):149–59; L. A. Sroufe et al., "Anticipatory Heart Rate Deceleration and Reaction Time in Children With and Without Referral for Learning Disability," *Child Development* 44 (1973):267–73; A. J. Zambelli et al., "Auditory Evoked Potentials and Selective Attention in Formerly Hyperactive Adolescents," *American Journal of Psychiatry* 134 (1977):742–47.

16. N. J. Cohen, V. I. Douglas, and G. Morgenstern, "The Effect of Methylphenidate on Attentive Behavior and Autonomic Activity in Hyperactive Children," *Psychopharmacologia*

22 (1971):282–94. S. W. Porges, G. F. Walter, R. J. Korb and R. L. Sprague, "The Influences of Methylphenidate on Heart Rate and Behavioral Measures of Attention in Hyperactive Children," *Child Development* 46 (1975):727–33.

17. A. C. Bower and D. L. Tate, "Cardiovascular and Skin Conductance Correlates of a Fixed Foreperiod Reaction Time Task in Retarded and Non-retarded Youth," *Psychophysiology* 13 (1976):1–9; G. Czudner and B. P. Rourke, "Age Differences in Visual Reaction Time of 'Brain Damaged' and Normal Children Under Regular and Irregular Preparatory Interval Conditions," *Journal of Experimental Child Psychology* 13 (1972):516–26; B. P. Rourke and G. Czudner, "Age Differences in Auditory Reaction Time of 'Brain Damaged' and Normal Children Under Regular and Irregular Preparatory Conditions," *Journal of Experimental Child Psychology* 14 (1972):372–78.

18. N. J. Cohen, "Physiological Concomitants of Attention in Hyperactive Children," Unpublished Ph.D. dissertation, McGill University, 1970.

19. Sykes, Douglas, and Morgenstern, "Sustained Attention in Hyperactive Children," *Journal of Child Psychology and Psychiatry* 14 (1973):213–20.

20. S. B. Campbell, V. I. Douglas, and G. Morgenstern, "Cognitive Styles in Hyperactive Children and the Effect of Methylphenidate," *Journal of Child Psychology and Psychiatry* 12 (1971):55–67; N. J. Cohen, V. I. Douglas, and G. Morgenstern, "The Effect of Methylphenidate on Attentive Behavior and Autonomic Activity in Hyperactive Children," *Pharmacologia* 22 (1971):282–94.

21. Campbell, Douglas, and Morgenstern, "Cognitive Styles in Hyperactive Children."

22. D. H. Sykes, V. I. Douglas, G. Weiss, and K. Minde, "Attention in the Hyperactive Child and the Effect of Methylphenidate (Ritalin)," *Journal of Child Psychology and Psychiatry* 12 (1971):129–39.

23. D. A. Bremer and J. A. Stern, "Attention and Distractibility During Reading in Hyperactive Boys," *Journal of Abnormal Child Psychology* 4 (1976):381–87.

24. V. Freiberg and V. I. Douglas, "Concept Learning in Hyperactive and Normal Children," *Journal of Abnormal Psychology* 74 (1969):388–95.

25. R. A. Dykman, P. T. Ackerman, and M. Oglesby, "Selective and Sustained Attention in Hyperactive, Learning-disabled and Normal Boys," *Journal of Nervous and Mental Diseases* 167 (1979):288–97.

26. R. A. Dykman, P. T. Ackerman, and D. S. McCray, "Effects of Methylphenidate on Sustained Attention in Hyperactive, Reading-disabled and Presumably Attention-disordered Boys," *Journal of Nervous and Mental Diseases* 168 (1980):745–52.

27. Two sets of studies have found enhanced memory effects with methylphenidate: H. E. Rie et al., "Effects of Methylphenidate on Underachieving Children," *Journal of Consulting and Clinical Psychology* 44 (1976):250–60; H. E. Rie et al., "Effect of Ritalin on Underachieving Children: A Replication," *American Journal of Orthopsychiatry* 46 (1976): 313–22. See also H. Weingartner et al., "Cognitive Processes in Normal and Hyperactive Children and Their Response to Amphetamine Treatment," *Journal of Abnormal Psychology* 89 (1980):25–37.

28. R. A. Barkley and C. E. Cunningham, "Do Stimulant Drugs Improve the Academic Performance of Hyperkinetic Children?," *Clinical Pediatrics* 17 (1978):85–92.

29. P. O. Quinn and J. L. Rapoport, "One-year Follow-up of Hyperactive Boys Treated with Imipramine and Methylphenidate," *American Journal of Psychiatry* 132 (1975):241–45; D. Riddle and J. L. Rapoport, "A 2-year Follow-up of 72 Hyperactive Boys," *Journal of Nervous and Mental Diseases* 126 (1976):126–34.

30. G. Weiss et al., "Studies on the Hyperactive Child," *Archives of General Psychiatry* 24 (1971):409–14. K. Minde et al., "The Hyperactive Child in Elementary School: A 5 Year, Controlled, Follow-up," *Exceptional Children* (November 1971):215–21: L. Charles and R. Schain, "A Four-year Follow-up Study of the Effects of Methylphenidate on the Behavior and Academic Achievement of Hyperactive Children," *Journal of Abnormal Child Psychology* 9 (1981):495–505.

31. R. A. Barkley and C. E. Cunningham, "Do Stimulant Drugs Improve the Academic Performance of Hyperkinetic Children?," *Clinical Pediatrics* 17 (1978):85–92.

32. R. A. Barkley, "Predicting the Response of Hyperactive Children to Stimulant Drugs: A Review," *Journal of Abnormal Child Psychology* 4 (1976):327–48.

Notes

33. For a comprehensive review of the relationship between the physiological responses and attentional factors, see D. McGuinness and K. H. Pribram, "The Neuropsychology of Attention: Emotional and Motivational Controls," in M. C. Wittrock, ed., *The Brain and Psychology* (New York: Academic Press, 1980), pp. 95–139.

34. J. H. Satterfield and M. E. Dawson, "Electrical Correlates of Hyperactivity in Children," *Psychophysiology* 8 (1971):191–97.

35. J. H. Satterfield et al., "Physiological Studies of the Hyperkinetic Child: I," *American Journal of Psychiatry* 128 (1972):1418–24.

36. J. E. Hastings and R. A. Barkley, "A Review of Psychophysiological Research with Hyperkinetic Children," *Journal of Abnormal Child Psychology* 6 (1978):413–47.

37. N. J. Cohen and V. I. Douglas, "Characteristics of the Orienting Response in Hyperactive and Normal Children," *Psychophysiology* 9 (1972):238–45.

38. N. J. Cohen, V. I. Douglas, and G. Morgenstern, "The Effect of Methylphenidate on Attentive Behavior and Autonomic Activity in Hyperactive Children, *Psychopharmacologia* 22 (1971):282–94.

39. P. Firestone and V. I. Douglas, "The Effects of Reward and Punishment on Reaction Times and Automatic Activity in Hyperactive and Normal Children," *Journal of Abnormal and Child Psychology* 3 (1975):201–16.

40. R. A. Dykman et al., "Specific Learning Disabilities: An Attentional Deficit Syndrome," in H. R. Mykelbust, ed., *Progress in Learning Disabilities* (New York: Grune and Stratton, 1971).

41. T. P. Zahn et al., "Minimal Brain Dysfunction, Stimulant Drugs and Autonomic Nervous System Activity," *Archives of General Psychiatry* 32 (1975):381–87.

42. C. Spring et al., "Electrodermal Activity in Hyperactive Boys Who Are Methylphenidate Responders," *Psychophysiology* 11 (1974):436–42.

43. A full account of the relationship between heart rate changes and attention can be found in J. I. Lacey and B. C. Lacey, "Some Autonomic Central Nervous System Interrelationships," in P. Black, ed., *Physiological Correlates of Emotion* (New York: Academic Press, 1970), pp. 205–27. See also McGuinness and Pribram, "Neurophysiology of Attention."

44. These early studies are reviewed in Hastings and Barkley, "A Review of Psychophysiological Research with Hyperkinetic Children." Specific studies include J. A. Boydstun et al., "Physiologic and Motor Conditioning and Generalization in Children with Minimal Brain Dysfunction," *Conditioned Reflex* 3 (1968):81–104; Dykman et al., "Specific Learning Disabilities."

45. Sroufe et al., "Anticipatory Heart Rate Deceleration and Reaction Time in Children with and without Referral for Learning Disability," *Child Development* 44 (1973):267–73.

46. Hastings and Barkley, "A Review of Psychophysiological Research with Hyperkinetic Children," *Journal of Abnormal Child Psychology* 128 (1972):1418–24.

47. Porges et al., "The Influences of Methylphenidate on Heart Rate and Behavioral Measures of Attention in Hyperactive Children," *Child Development* 46 (1975):727–33.

48. Cohen, Douglas, and Morgenstern, "The Effect of Methylphenidate on Attentive Behavior and Autonomic Activity in Hyperactive Children," *Psychopharmacologia* 22 (1971): 282–94.

49. Zahn et al., "Minimal Brain Dysfunction, Stimulant Drugs and Autonomic Nervous System Activity," *Archives of General Psychiatry* 32 (1975):381–87.

50. J. R. Hughes, "Electroencephalography and Learning Disabilities," in H. R. Mykelbust, ed., *Progress in Learning Disabilities*, vol. 2 (New York: Grune & Stratton, 1971).

51. Satterfield et al., "Physiological Studies of the Hyperkinetic Child: I," *American Journal of Psychiatry* 128 (1972):1418–24.

52. J. H. Satterfield et al., "Response to Stimulant Drug Treatment in Hyperactive Children: Prediction from EEG and Neurological Findings," *Journal of Autism and Childhood Schizophrenia* 3 (1973):36–48.

53. J. H. Satterfield et al., "Intelligence, Academic Achievement and EEG Abnormalities in Hyperactive Children," *American Journal of Psychiatry* 131 (1974):391–95.

54. E. Grünewald-Zuberbier, G. Grünewald, and A. Rasche, "Hyperactive Behavior and

EEG Arousal Reactions in Children," *Electroencephalography and Clinical Neurophysiology* 38 (1975):149–59.

55. M. Buchsbaum and P. Wender, "Average Evoked Responses in Normal and Minimally Brain Dysfunctioned Children Treated with Amphetamine," *Archives of General Psychiatry* 29 (1973):764–70.

56. Buchsbaum's own data show sex differences in averaged evoked responses. See M. Buchsbaum and A. Pfefferbaum, "Individual Differences in Stimulus Intensity Response," *Psychophysiology* 8 (1971):600–11.

57. R. A. Hall et al., "Evoked Potential, Stimulus Intensity and Drug Treatment in Hyperkinesis," *Psychophysiology* 13 (1976):405–18.

58. R. Halliday et al., "Averaged Evoked Potential Predictors of Clinical Improvement in Hyperactive Children Treated with Methylphenidate: An Initial Study and Replication," *Psychophysiology* 13 (1976):429–40.

59. L. S. Prichep, S. Sutton, and G. Hakerem, "Evoked Potentials in Hyperkinetic and Normal Children Under Certainty and Uncertainty: A Placebo and Methylphenidate Study," *Psychophysiology* 13 (1976):419–28.

60. A. J. Zambelli et al., "Auditory Evoked Potentials and Selective Attention in Formerly Hyperactive Adolescents," *American Journal of Psychiatry* 134 (1977):742–47.

61. D. L. Loiselles, A. J. Zambelli, and J. S. Stamm, "Auditory Evoked Potentials as Measures of Selective Attention in Older MBD Children," Paper presented at the International Neuropsychological Society, New Mexico, 1977.

62. M. S. Buchsbaum and J. L. Rapoport, "Dextroamphetamine Effects on Evoked Potentials in Normal and Hyperactive Children," Paper presented at the American Psychological Association, New York, 1979.

63. J. H. Satterfield's comments during the discussion of Buchsbaum's paper at the same meeting.

64. The National Institute of Mental Health studies include J. L. Rapoport et al., "Dextroamphetamine: Cognitive and Behavioral Effects in Normal Prepubertal Boys," *Science* 199 (1978):560–63; J. L. Buchsbaum et al., "Dextroamphetamine. Its Cognitive and Behavioral Effects in Normal and Hyperactive Boys and Normal Men," *Archives of General Psychiatry* 37 (1980):933–43; A. J. Sostek, M. S. Buchsbaum, and J. L. Rapoport, "Effects of Amphetamine on Vigilance Performance in Normal and Hyperactive Children," *Journal of Abnormal Child Psychology* 8 (1980):491–500; H. Weingartner et al., "Cognitive Processes in Normal and Hyperactive Children and Their Response to Amphetamine Treatment," *Journal of Abnormal Psychology* 89 (1980):25–37.

65. J. L. Buchsbaum et al., "Dextroamphetamine: Its Cognitive and Behavioral Effects in Normal and Hyperactive Boys and Normal Men," *Archives of General Psychiatry* 37 (1980): 933–43.

66. D. Riddle and J. L. Rapoport, "A 2-Year Follow-up of 72 Hyperactive Boys," *Journal of Nervous and Mental Diseases* 162 (1976):126–34.

67. G. Thorley, "Review of Follow-up and Follow-back Studies of Childhood Hyperactivity," *Psychological Bulletin* 96 (1984):116–32.

68. L. Charles and R. Schain, "A Four-year Follow-up Study of the Effects of Methylphenidate on the Behavior and Academic Achievement of Hyperactive Children," *Journal of Abnormal Child Psychology* 9 (1981):495–505.

69. K. Minde et al., "The Hyperactive Child in Elementary School: A 5 Year, Controlled, Follow-up," *Exceptional Children* (November 1971):215–21.

70. E. Hoy et al., "The Hyperactive Child at Adolescence: Cognitive, Emotional and Social Functioning," *Journal of Abnormal Child Psychology* 6 (1978):311–24; G. Weiss et al., "Hyperactives as Young Adults: A Controlled Prospective Ten-year Follow-up of 75 Children," *Archives of General Psychiatry* 6 (1979):675–81.

71. Whalen and Henker, "Psychostimulants and Children: A Review and Analysis," *Psychological Bulletin* 83 (1976):1113–30.

72. G. Weiss, L. Hechtman, and T. Perlman, "Hyperactives as Young Adults: School, Employer and Self-rating Scales Obtained During Ten-year Follow-up Evaluation," *American Journal of Orthopsychiatry* 48 (1978):438–45.

Notes

73. See O'Leary, "Pills or Skills for Hyperactive Children," *Journal of Applied Behavioral Analysis* 13 (1980):191–204.

74. P. Conrad, *Identifying Hyperactive Children* (Lexington, Mass.: D. C. Heath and Company, 1976).

Chapter 11

1. This translation is found in a number of sources; perhaps the best and most complete is in S. N. Kramer, *History Begins at Sumer* (Philadelphia: University of Pennsylvania Press, 1981).

2. The debate between pupil and master is found in S. N. Kramer, *The Sumerians* (Chicago: University of Chicago Press, 1963). The story ends with a threat from the school principal to the ungrateful and argumentative pupil: "I would beat you with a mace, and having put copper chains on your feet, would lock you in the house for two months and not let you out of the school building." This may be in jest, or it could be a warning to all schoolboys who do not take school authorities seriously.

3. M. Montessori, *The Discovery of the Child* (New York: Ballantine Books, 1972).

4. For an exposition of the Gillingham/Slingerland methodology, see A. Gillingham and B. Stillman *Remedial Training for Children with Specific Disability in Reading, Spelling and Penmanship* (Cambridge, Mass.: Educators Publishing Service, 1956); B. H. Slingerland, *A Multisensory Approach to Language Arts For Specific Language Disability Children: A Guide for Primary Teachers* (Cambridge, Mass.: Educators Publishing Service, 1971).

5. C. H. Lindamood and P. C. Lindamood, *Lindamood Auditory Conceptualization Test* (Boston: Teaching Resources Corporation, 1971). The complete kit of training materials is called "Auditory Discrimination in Depth," published originally by Teaching Resources Corporation in 1979. The copyrights for both of these programs are now the property of Developmental Learning Materials, Allen, Texas.

6. The results from the Santa Barbara study and the Santa Maria study are unpublished. A full report of the Butte County project is in M. Howard, "Utilizing Oral-motor Feedback in Auditory Conceptualization," *Journal of Education and Neuropsychology* 2 (1982):24–35.

7. The information on Patricia Davidson is largely based on the author's extensive interview with her.

8. P. S. Davidson, "An Annotated Bibliography of Manipulative Devices," *The Arithmetic Teacher* (October 1968).

9. J. Piaget, "How Children Form Mathematical Concepts," *Scientific American* 189 (1953): 74–79. An extensive bibliography and exposition of Piaget's methods for teaching mathematics and logic are provided in J. L. Phillips, Jr., *The Origins of Intellect. Piaget's Theory* (San Francisco, W. H. Freeman and Co., 1969). The most complete work on Bruner's approach is in J. S. Bruner, *Beyond the Information Given* (New York: W. W. Norton, 1973).

10. Almost all of Davidson's published works are techniques for using mathematical manipulatives. These include: P. Davidson, G. K. Galton, and A. W. Fair, *Chip Trading Activities* (Scott Resources, 1975); P. Davidson and A. B. Bennett, *Fraction Bars Program* (Scott Resources, 1973). A number of books and problem sets have been published by Cuisenaire Company of America, such as: P. Davidson, *Idea Book for the Use of Cuisenaire Rods at the Primary Level* 1977); Cuisenaire Co. of America, P. Davidson and R. E. Wilcutt, *From Here to There with Cuisenaire Rods, Area, Perimeter, and Volume:* (Cuisenaire Co. of America, 1981); and P. Davidson and R. E. Wilcutt, *Spatial Problem Solving with Cuisenaire Rods:* (Cuisenaire Co. of America, 1983). See also P. Davidson, "Neurobiological Research and Its Implications for Mathematics Education," *The Virginia Mathematics Teacher* (May 1979), and "Rods Can Help Children Learn at All Grade Levels," *Learning Magazine* (Nov. 1977).

11. P. S. Davidson and M. R. Marolda, *The Neuropsychology of Mathematics Learning* (Menlo Park, Calif.: Addison-Wesley, forthcoming).

12. D. McGuinness and C. Morley, "Sex Differences in 2-Dimensional and 3-Dimensional Problem Solving in Preschool Children," in preparation.

13. The O'Learys have recently published a book summarizing their work: K. D. O'Leary and S. G. O'Leary, *Classroom Management: The Successful Use of Behavior Modification* (Elmsford, N.Y.: Pergamon Press, 1977).

14. K. D. O'Leary, "Assessment of Hyperactivity: Observational and Rating Methodologies," in S. A. Miller, ed., *Nutrition and Behavior* (Philadelphia: Fauklin Institute Press, 1981).

15. For a description of the token reward system, see O'Leary and O'Leary, *Classroom Management.*

16. Reports from the O'Learys' studies are to be found in A. Rosenbaum, K. D. O'Leary, and R. G. Jacob, "Behavioral Intervention with Hyperactive Children: Group Consequences as a Supplement to Individual Contingencies," *Behavior Therapy* 6 (1975):315–23; K. D. O'Leary et al., "Behavioral Treatment of Hyperkinetic Children," *Clinical Pediatrics* 15 (1976):510–13; R. N. Kent and K. D. O'Leary, "A Controlled Evaluation of Behavior Modification with Conduct Problem Children," *Journal of Consulting and Clinical Psychology* 44 (1976):586–96; S. G. O'Leary and W. E. Pelham, "Behavioral Therapy and Withdrawal of Stimulant Medication with Hyperactive Children," *Pediatrics* 61 (1978):211–17; C. Friedling and S. G. O'Leary, "Teaching Self-instruction to Hyperactive Children: A Replication," *Journal of Applied Behavioral Analysis* 12 (1979):211–19. Other reports confirming similar effects of behavior modification are T. Allyon, D. Layman, and H. J. Kandel, "A Behavioral Educational Alternative to Drug Control of Hyperactive Children," *Journal of Applied Behavioral Analysis* 8 (1975):137–46; M. Wolraich et al., "Effects of Methylphenidate Alone and in Combination with Behavior Modification Procedures on the Behavior and Academic Performance of Hyperactive Children," *Journal of Abnormal Child Psychology* 6 (1978):149–61.

17. In contrast to the studies that emphasize academic performance are those that only attempt to alter behavior. For example, Gittelman-Klein and associates could find no difference between methylphenidate alone and in combination with behavior therapy in general behavioral improvement. No attempt was made to emphasize or measure academic performance. See R. Gittelman-Klein et al., "Relative Efficacy of Methylphenidate and Behavior Modification in Hyperkinetic Children: An Interim Report," *Journal of Abnormal Child Psychology* 4 (1976):361–79.

18. K. F. Kaufman and K. D. O'Leary, "Reward, Cost and Self-evaluation Procedures for Disruptive Adolescents in a Psychiatric Hospital School," *Journal of Applied Behavioral Analysis* 5 (1972):293–309; J. J. Felixbrod and K. D. O'Leary, "Effects of Reinforcement on Children's Academic Behavior as a Function of Self-determined and Externally Imposed Contingencies," *Journal of Applied Behavioral Analysis* 6 (1973):241–50; R. S. Drabman, R. Spitalnik, and K. D. O'Leary, "Teaching Self-control to Disruptive Children," *Journal of Abnormal Psychology* 82 (1973):10–16; J. J. Felixbrod and K. D. O'Leary, "Self-determination of Academic Standards by Children: Toward Freedom from External Control," *Journal of Educational Psychology* 66 (1974):845–50.

19. K. H. Pribram, "Cognition and Performance: The Relation to Neural Mechanisms of Consequence, Confidence and Competence," in A. Routtenberg and A. Rolles, eds., *Biology of Reinforcement* (New York: Academic Press, 1980), pp. 11–36.

20. V. I. Douglas et al., "Assessment of a Cognitive Training Program for Hyperactive Children," *Journal of Abnormal Child Psychology* 4 (1976):389–411.

NAME INDEX

297

SUBJECT INDEX